Y- Y- L
H-Y

ADVANCED TURBO C®
Second Edition

ADVANCED TURBO C ®

Second Edition

Herbert Schildt

BORLAND·OSBORNE/McGRAW·HILL

PROGRAMMING SERIES

Berkeley   New York   St. Louis   San Francisco
Auckland   Bogotá   Hamburg   London   Madrid
Mexico City   Milan   Montreal   New Delhi   Panama City
Paris   São Paulo   Singapore   Sydney
Tokyo   Toronto

Osborne **McGraw-Hill**
2600 Tenth Street
Berkeley, California 94710
U.S.A.

For information on translations and book distributors outside of the U.S.A., please write to Osborne **McGraw-Hill** at the above address.

A complete list of trademarks appears on page 433.
Screens produced with InSet, from InSet Systems, Inc.

ADVANCED TURBO C®, Second Edition

1234567890 DOCDOC 898

ISBN 0-07-881479-0

CONTENTS

FOREWORD

The C language is firmly established as the favorite programming language of serious developers. The freedom, unmatched portability, and remarkable access of this language have made it the choice of computer professionals around the world.

It makes sense that Borland, a software company dedicated to serving programmers and known for its exceptional programming tools, should create Turbo C. Turbo C's power, versatility, and simplicity of design allow programmers to create better tools, utilities, and applications more quickly and more easily than they could in any other language development environment. Users will appreciate Turbo C's incredible compilation speed and the quality of the code it generates.

Now veteran C programmer and author Herb Schildt has revised the best-selling *Advanced Turbo C* to include integrated debugging and other new functions in the latest release of Turbo C. In these pages he leads readers through a thorough discussion of C's components and their uses. In addition, he covers the conversion of Turbo Pascal to Turbo C.

This readable instruction guide and reference is the programmer's key to that most powerful of programming language environments—Turbo C.

Philippe Kahn
President
Borland International, Inc.

PREFACE

In its design the C language presents an irresistible combination of elegance and power. And Turbo C, with its speed and efficiency, makes programming in C even more exciting. Now that Turbo C includes a built-in source-level debugger, it is hard to justify programming in any other language.

This book helps you unlock the power of Turbo C through an applications-oriented approach. Each chapter examines a specific programming topic and develops programs that address that topic. Through this process you will see many of the advanced features of Turbo C applied to some common programming tasks, while, at the same time, you will sharpen your programming skills.

ADDITIONS AND CHANGES IN THE SECOND EDITION

This is the second edition of *Advanced Turbo C*. The main changes from the first concern Turbo C's graphics subsystem. The original version of Turbo C did not include any graphics support. Therefore, the first edition of this book developed a small but useful graphics subsystem. However, beginning with version 1.5, Turbo C has included graphics, and the code in this book now uses it.

Since the original version, the proposed ANSI standard has become very stable, and the code in this book conforms closely with the modern form recommended by the standard. Also, all programs contain full function prototyping. Although prototyping is not strictly necessary, it is recommended by ANSI and is a good practice to follow.

ACKNOWLEDGMENTS

I want to thank Borland's excellent technical support staff for the help and suggestions that they have contributed to this book. In particular, I want to thank Robert Goosey and James L. Turley for their tireless effort in reading the original manuscript for accuracy and running every line of code in the book to ensure that it worked. Keep up the good work.

I also want to thank all the people at Osborne/McGraw-Hill for the long hours and hard work that they put into this project.

—H.S.

DISKETTE OFFER

There are many useful and interesting functions and programs contained in this book. If you're like me, you probably would like to use them but hate typing them into the computer. For this reason, I am offering the source code on diskette for all the functions and programs contained in this book for $24.95. Just fill in the order blank on the next page and mail it, along with your payment, to the address shown. Or, if you are in a hurry, just call (217) 586-4021 and place your order by telephone. (VISA and MasterCard accepted.)

—Herbert Schildt

Advanced Turbo C Disk Order Form

Please send me _____ copies, at $24.95 each, of the programs in *Advanced Turbo C, 2nd Edition*. For foreign orders, please add $5 shipping and handling.

_____
Name

_____
Address

_____
City   *State*   *ZIP*

_____
Telephone

Diskette size (check one):   5 1/4" _____   3 1/2" _____

Method of payment: Check _____   VISA _____   MC _____

Credit card number: _____

Expiration date: _____

Signature: _____

Send to: Herbert Schildt
             RR 1, Box 130
             Mahomet, IL 61853
             or phone: (217)586-4021

1

SORTING AND SEARCHING

In the world of computer science, perhaps no tasks are more fundamental than, or as extensively analyzed as, sorting and searching. Sorting and searching routines are used in virtually all database programs and in compilers, interpreters, and operating systems. This chapter introduces the basics of sorting and searching. Generally the point of sorting data is to make searching for that data easier and faster. For this reason sorting will be discussed first.

SORTING

Sorting is the process of arranging a set of similar information into an increasing or decreasing order. Specifically, given a sorted list i of n elements,

$$i_1 <= i_2 <= \ldots <= i\ n$$

Even though Turbo C supplies the standard **qsort( )** function as part of the standard library, the study and understanding of sorting is important for four main reasons:

1. A generalized function like **qsort( )** cannot be applied to all situations.

2. Because **qsort( )** is parameterized to operate on a wide variety of data, it runs more slowly than a similar sort that operates on only one type of data. (The generalization process inherently increases run time because of the extra processing time needed to handle various data types.)

3. The quicksort algorithm (used by **qsort( )**), although very good for the general case, may not be the best sort for specialized situations.

4. The study of sorting provides an excellent method of illustrating some interesting Turbo C programming techniques.

There are two general categories of sorting algorithms: (1) the sorting of arrays, both in memory and in random access disk files, and (2) the sorting of sequential disk or tape files. This chapter is concerned only with the first category because it is of the most interest to the average programmer.

Generally, when information such as a mailing list is sorted, only a portion of that information is used as the *sort key*. This key is used in comparisons, but when an exchange is made, the entire data structure is swapped. For example, in a mailing list the ZIP code field might be used as the key, but the entire address is sorted. For simplicity while developing the various sorting methods, you will be sorting character arrays. Later you will learn how to adapt these methods to any type of data structure.

Classes of Sorting Algorithms

There are three general methods that can be used to sort arrays:

1. Exchange

2. Selection

3. Insertion

To understand these three methods, imagine a deck of cards. To sort the cards by *exchange*, you would spread out the cards face up and then proceed to exchange out-of-order cards until the deck is ordered. To sort by *selection*, you would spread the cards on the table, select the lowest value card, take it out of the deck, and hold it in your hand. You would then select the lowest of the remaining cards and place it behind the one already in your hand. This process would continue until all the cards were in your hand. Because you always select the lowest of the remaining cards to place at the end of the cards in your hand, when you have finished the process, the cards in your hand will be sorted. To sort the cards by *insertion*, you would hold the cards in your hand, and place them one at a time into a new deck on the table, always inserting them in the correct position. The deck will be sorted when you have no more cards in your hand.

Judging Sorting Algorithms

There are many different algorithms for each classification of sorting method. They all have some merits, but the general criteria for judging a sorting algorithm are

- How fast can it sort information in an average case?
- How fast is its best and worst case?
- Does it exhibit *natural* or *unnatural* behavior?
- Does it rearrange elements with equal keys?

Let's look closely at the purpose behind each of these questions.

How fast a particular algorithm sorts is clearly of great concern. It can be shown that the speed with which an array can be sorted is directly related to the number of comparisons and the number of exchanges, with exchanges taking more time. A *comparison* occurs when one array element is compared to another; an exchange happens when two elements are swapped in the array. As you will see later in this chapter, some sorts require an exponential amount of time per element to sort and some require logarithmic time.

The best and worst case run times are important if you expect to encounter one of these situations frequently. Often a sort will have a good average case but a really terrible worst case.

A sort is said to exhibit natural behavior if it works least when the list is already in order, works harder as the list becomes less ordered, and hardest when a list is in inverse order. How hard a sort works is based on the number of comparisons and exchanges that are executed.

To understand why rearranging elements with equal keys may be important, imagine a mailing list database that is sorted on a main key and a subkey, with the main key being the ZIP code and the last name being the subkey. When a new address is added to the list and the list is re-sorted, you do not want the subkeys (that is, last names within ZIP codes) rearranged. To guarantee this, a sort must not exchange main keys of equal value.

The next three sections examine representative sorts from each category, analyzing the efficiency of each.

The Bubble Sort

The best-known (and most infamous) sort is the *bubble sort*. Its popularity is derived from its catchy name and its simplicity. For reasons that will become evident, however, it is one of the worst sorts ever conceived.

The bubble sort is an exchange sort. The general concept behind the bubble sort is repeated comparison and, if necessary, exchange of adjacent elements. It is a little like bubbles in a tank of water, each bubble seeking its own level. The simplest form of the bubble sort is shown here:

```
/* The Bubble Sort. */
void bubble(char *item, int count)
{
  register int a, b;
  register char t;
```

```
for(a=1; a<count; ++a)
  for(b=count-1; b>=a; --b) {
    if(item[b-1] > item[b]) {
      /* exchange elements */
      t = item[b-1];
      item[b-1] = item[b];
      item[b] = t;
    }
  }
}
```

Here **item** is a pointer to the character array to be sorted and *count* is the number of elements in the array. The bubble sort is driven by two loops. Given *count* elements in the array, the outer loop causes the array to be scanned **count−1** times. This is necessary to ensure that every element is in its proper position when the function terminates. The inner loop actually performs the comparisons and exchanges. (A slightly optimized version of the bubble sort terminates if no exchanges occur, but this adds another comparison to each pass through the inner loop.)

This version of the bubble sort can be used to arrange a character array in ascending order. For example, the following short program will sort a string typed in from the keyboard:

```
/* Sort Driver */

#include <string.h>
#include <stdio.h>
#include <stdlib.h>

void bubble(char *item, int count);

main()
{
  char s[80];

  printf("enter a string:");
  gets(s);
  bubble(s, strlen(s));
  printf("the sorted string is: %s\n", s);
  return 0;
}
```

To see how the bubble sort works assume that the array to be sorted is *dcab*. Each pass is shown here:

Initial:	d	c	a	b
Pass 1:	a	d	c	b
Pass 2:	a	b	d	c
Pass 3:	a	b	c	d

In analyzing any sort it is important to determine how many comparisons and exchanges will be performed for the best, average, and worst case. The number of comparisons is always the same in a bubble sort because the two **for** loops repeat the specified number of times whether the list is initially ordered or not. This means that the bubble sort always performs

$$1/2(n^2-n)$$

comparisons, where n is the number of elements to be sorted. This formula is derived from the fact that the outer loop executes $n-1$ times and the inner loop $n/2$ times. Multiplying these two produces the formula.

The number of exchanges is zero for the best case—an already sorted list. The numbers for the average and worst case exchanges are

Average:	$3/4(n^2-n)$
Worst:	$3/2(n^2-n)$

It is beyond the scope of this book to explain the derivation of these formulas, but as the list becomes less ordered, the number of elements out of order approaches the number of comparisons. (Remember, there are three exchanges in a bubble sort for every element out of order). The bubble sort is said to be an n-squared algorithm because its execution time is a multiple of the square of the number of elements. This is very bad for a large number of elements because execution time is directly related to the number of comparisons and exchanges. For example, ignoring the time it takes to exchange any out-of-position element, if each comparison takes 0.001 second, sorting 10 elements will take about 0.05 second, sorting 100 elements will take about 5 seconds, and sorting 1000 elements will take about 500 seconds. A 100,000 element sort (the size of a small phone book) would take about 5,000,000 seconds, or about 1400 hours (about two months of continuous sorting). Figure 1-1 shows how execution time increases relative to the size of the array.

You can make some slight improvements that speed up the bubble sort. For example, the bubble sort has one peculiarity: An out-of-order element at the large end, such as the a in the above

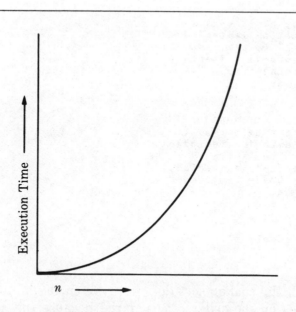

Figure 1-1.   Execution time of an n^2 sort in relation to array size

example, will go to its proper position in one pass, but a misplaced element in the small end, such as the *d*, will rise very slowly to its proper place. This suggests an improvement to the bubble sort.

Instead of always reading the array in the same direction, subsequent passes could reverse direction. In this way, greatly out-of-place elements will travel quickly to their correct position. This version of the bubble sort is called the *shaker sort*, after its shaking motion over the array:

```
/* The Shaker Sort. */
void shaker(char *item, int count)
{
  register int a, b, c, d;
  char t;

  c = 1;
  b = count-1; d = count-1;

  do {
    for(a=d; a>=c; --a) {
      if(item[a-1]>item[a]) {
        t = item[a-1];
        item[a-1] = item[a];
        item[a] = t;
        b = a;
      }
    }
    c = b+1;
    for(a=c; a<d+1; ++a) {
      if(item[a-1]>item[a]) {
        t = item[a-1];
        item[a-1] = item[a];
        item[a] = t;
        b = a;
      }
    }
    d = b-1;
  } while (c<=d);
}
```

Although the shaker sort does improve on the bubble sort, it still executes on the order of *n*-squared because the number of comparisons has not changed and the number of exchanges has been reduced by only a relatively small constant. Although the shaker sort is better than the bubble sort, there are still better sorts.

Sorting by Selection

A selection sort selects the element with the lowest value and exchanges it with the first element. From the remaining $n-1$ elements it finds the element with the least key, exchanges it with the with second element, and so forth, up to the last two elements. For example, if the selection method were used on the array *bdac*, each pass would look like this:

Initial:	b	d	a	c
Pass 1:	a	d	b	c
Pass 2:	a	b	d	c
Pass 3:	a	b	c	d

The basic selection sort program for this array is

```
/* The Selection Sort. */
void select(char *item, int count)
{
  register int a, b, c;
  char t;

  for(a=0; a<count-1; ++a) {
    c = a;
    t = item[a];
    for(b=a+1; b<count; ++b) {
      if(item[b]<t) {
        c = b;
        t = item[b];
      }
    }
    item[c] = item[a];
    item[a] = t;

  }
}
```

Unfortunately the outer loop executes $n-1$ times and the inner loop $1/2(n)$ times, so the selection sort, like the bubble sort, requires

$$1/2(n^2-n)$$

comparisons—too slow for a large number of items. The number of exchanges for the best and worst cases are as follows:

Best: $3(n-1)$
Worst: $n^2/4 +3(n-1)$

For the best case—if the list is ordered—only $n-1$ elements need to be moved, and each move requires three exchanges. The worst case approximates the number of comparisons. The average case is

$$n(\ln\ n+y)$$

where y is Euler's constant, about 0.577216.

This means that although the number of comparisons are the same for the bubble sort and the selection sort, the number of exchanges in the average case are far less for the selection sort. However, still better sorts exist.

Sorting by Insertion

The insertion sort is the third and last of the simple sorting algorithms. The insertion sort initially sorts the first two members of the array. Then it inserts the third member into its sorted position in relation to the first two members. Next it inserts the fourth element into the list of three elements and so on, until all elements have been sorted. Given the array *dcab*, each pass of the insertion sort is as follows:

Initial: d   c   a   b

Pass 1:   c   d   a   b

Pass 2:   a   c   d   b

Pass 3:   a   b   c   d

This version of the insertion sort is

```
/* The Insertion Sort. */
void insert(char *item, int count)
{

  register int a, b;
  char t;

  for(a=1; a<count; ++a) {
    t = item[a];
    b = a-1;
    while(b>=0 && t<item[b] ) {
      item[b+1] = item[b];
      b--;
    }
    item[b+1] = t;
  }
}
```

Unlike the bubble sort and the selection sort, the number of comparisons needed for an insertion sort depends on how the list is initially ordered. If the list is in order, the number of comparisons is $n-1$. If the list is out of order, the number of comparisons is

$$1/2(n^2+n)-1$$

and the average number is

$$1/4(n^2+n-2)$$

The numbers of exchanges are

Best: $2(n-1)$

Average: $1/4(n^2+9n-10)$

Worst: $1/2(n^2+3n-4)$

Therefore, for worst cases the insertion sort is as bad as the bubble and selection sorts, and for average cases it is only slightly better. It does have two advantages, however:

1. It behaves naturally. That is, it works the least when the array is already sorted and the hardest when the array is sorted in inverse order. This makes the insertion sort excellent for lists that are already mostly in order.

2. It leaves the order of equal keys the same. This means that if a list is sorted with two keys, it remains sorted for both keys after an insertion sort.

Even though the comparisons may be fairly good for certain sets of data, the fact that the array must always be shifted over each time an element is placed in its proper location means that the number of moves can be very significant. However, it still behaves naturally, with the least exchanges occurring for a mostly sorted list and the most for an inversely ordered array.

However, still better sorts exist, and they are discussed in the next three sections.

IMPROVED SORTS

All the algorithms in the preceding section had the fatal flaw of executing in n-squared time. This means that for large amounts of data, the sorts would be very slow; in fact at some point they would be too slow to use. Every computer programmer has heard or told the horror story of the "sort that took three days."

Unfortunately these stories are often real. When a sort takes too long, it is usually the fault of the underlying algorithm, but a sad commentary is that often the first response is "let's write it in assembly code." Although this will sometimes speed up a routine by a constant factor, if the underlying algorithm is bad the sort will be slow no matter how "optimal" the coding. Remember that when a routine is running relative to n-squared, increasing the efficiency of the coding or the speed of the computer will produce only a slight improvement. (In essence the graph in Figure 1-1 is shifted to the right slightly, but the curve is unchanged.) The rule of thumb is that if it is not fast enough written in Turbo C, it won't be fast enough written in assembler. The solution is to use a better sorting algorithm.

There are two excellent sorts discussed in the next sections. The first is the Shell sort and the second, generally considered the best sorting routine, is the quicksort. These sorts run so fast that if you blink you will miss them!

The Shell Sort

The *Shell sort* is named after its inventor D.L. Shell, but the name probably stuck because its method of operation actually resembles sea shells piled on one another.

The general method, which is derived from the insertion sort, is based on diminishing increments. Consider the diagram in Figure 1-2.

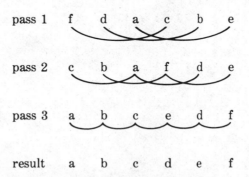

Figure 1-2.   The Shell sort

First, all elements that are three positions apart are sorted. Then all elements that are two positions apart are sorted. Finally, all items adjacent to each other are sorted.

It is not at all intuitive that this method yields good results or that it will even sort the array. But it does. Each sorting pass involves relatively few elements, or elements that are already in reasonable order, so the method is efficient and each pass increases order.

The exact sequence for the increments can be changed. The only rule is that the last increment must be 1. For example, the sequence

9, 5, 3, 2, 1

works well and is used in the Shell sort shown here. Sequences with elements that are powers of 2 should be avoided because, for mathematically complex reasons, they reduce the efficiency of the sorting algorithm (although the sort still works).

```c
/* The Shell Sort. */
void shell(char *item, int count)
{

  register int i, j, k, s, w;
  char x, a[5];

  a[0]=9; a[1]=5; a[2]=3; a[3]=2; a[4]=1;

  for(w=0; w<5; w++) {
    k = a[w]; s = -k;
    for(i=k; i<count; ++i) {
      x = item[i];
      j = i-k;
      if(s==0) {
        s = -k;
        s++;
        item[s] = x;
      }
      while(x<item[j] && j>=0 && j<=count) {
        item[j+k] = item[j];
        j = j-k;
      }
      item[j+k] = x;
    }
  }
}
```

You may have noticed that the inner **while** loop has three test conditions. The comparison $x<$**item[j]** is obviously necessary for the sorting process. The tests $j>=0$ and $j<=$**count** are used to keep the sort from overrunning the boundary of the array item. These extra checks will degrade the performance of a Shell sort to some extent. Slightly different versions of the Shell sort employ special array elements called *sentinels*, which are not actually part of the array to be sorted but hold special termination values that indicate the least and greatest possible elements. This makes the bounds checks unnecessary. However, using sentinels requires specific knowledge of the data, which limits the generality of the sort function.

Analysis of the Shell sort presents some very difficult mathematical problems that are far beyond the scope of this discussion. However, it has been shown that execution time is proportional to $\mathbf{n^{1.2}}$ for sorting n elements. This is a significant improvement over the n-squared sorts previously discussed. To understand how great an improvement it is, see Figure 1-3, which shows both an n-squared and an $n^{1.2}$ graph together. Before getting too excited about the Shell sort, however, you should be aware that the quicksort is even better.

The Quicksort

The *quicksort*, invented and named by C.A.R. Hoare, is the last sort discussed in this book. Its performance is superior to all the others discussed here, and it is generally considered the best sorting algorithm currently available.

The quicksort is built on the idea of partitions. The general procedure is to select a partition value, called the *comparand*, and then partition the array into two sections, with all elements greater than or equal to the comparand on one side and those less than the comparand on the other. This process is repeated for each remaining half until the array is sorted. For example, given the array *fedacb* and using the value *d* as the comparand, the first

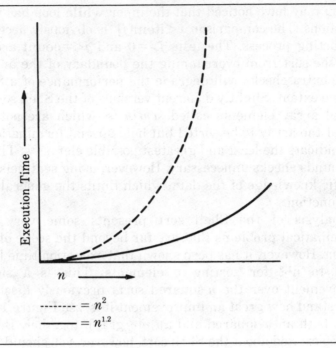

Figure 1-3.   The n^2 and $n^{1.2}$ curves

pass of the quicksort would rearrange the array thus:

Initial: f   e   d   a   c   b
Pass 1:   b   c   a   d   e   f

This process is then repeated for each half, that is, *bca* and *def*. The process is essentially recursive; indeed, the cleanest implementations of quicksort are recursive algorithms.

The selection of the comparand value can be accomplished in two ways. It can be chosen either at random or by averaging a small set of values taken from the array. For optimal sorting, it is desirable to select a value that is precisely in the middle of the range of values. However, this is not easy to do for most sets of data. In the worst case the value chosen is at one extremity. Even in this case, quicksort performs well. The version of quicksort shown here selects the middle element of the array.

```
/* Quicksort setup function. */
void quick(char *item, int count)
{
  qs(item, 0, count-1);
}

/* The Quicksort. */
void qs(char *item, int left, int right)
{

  register int i, j;
  char x, y;

  i = left; j = right;
  x = item[(left+right)/2];

  do {
    while(item[i]<x && i<right) i++;
    while(x<item[j] && j>left) j--;

    if(i<=j) {
      y = item[i];
      item[i] = item[j];
      item[j] = y;
      i++; j--;
    }
  } while(i<=j);

  if(left<j) qs(item, left, j);
  if(i<right) qs(item, i, right);
}
```

In this version, the function **quick( )** is used to set up a call to the main sorting function called **qs( )**. This enables the same common interface of **item** and *count* to be maintained, but it is not essential because **qs( )** could have been called directly by using three arguments.

The derivation of the number of comparisons and exchanges that quicksort performs requires advanced mathematics. However, it has been shown that the number of comparisons is

$$n \log n$$

and the number of exchanges is about

$$n/6 \log n$$

These are significantly better than any of the previous sorts we have seen.

In case you have forgotten,

$$N = a^x$$

can be rewritten as

$$x = \log_x N$$

For example, to sort 100 elements quicksort would require 200 comparisons (2 * 100, because log 100 is 2). Compared with the bubble sort's 990 comparisons, this is good indeed.

You should be aware of one nasty aspect of quicksort. If the comparand value for each partition happens to be the largest value, quicksort degenerates into *slowsort* with an *n*-squared run time. Generally, however, this does not happen.

You must choose a method of determining the value of the comparand carefully. Often this is determined by the actual data that you are sorting. In very large mailing lists, where the sorting is often by ZIP code, the selection is simple because the ZIP codes are fairly evenly distributed and a simple algebraic function can determine a suitable comparand. In the case of certain other databases, however, the keys may be so close in value, with many being the same, that a random selection is often best. A common and fairly effective method is to sample three elements from a partition and take the middle value.

CHOOSING A SORT

Before making a decision about which sort to use, run the following program. It measures the amount of time it takes each of the sorting methods to sort a 2000-element character array that has been initialized to contain a random string of letters. The program uses the standard library function **time( )** to time the sorts. It returns the system time in seconds elapsed since 00:00:00 GMT.

```c
#include <stdlib.h>
#include <stdio.h>
#include <string.h>
#include <time.h>

/* This program shows how long it takes each of the six
   sort algorithms to sort 2000 elements.
*/
void bubble(char *item, int count);
void shaker(char *item, int count);
void select(char *item, int count);
void insert(char *item, int count);
void shell(char *item, int count);
void qs(char *item, int left, int right);
void quick(char *item, int count);

main()
{
  char s[2001], temp[2001];
  register int i;
  time_t start, end;

  /* generate a random string of characters */
  for(i=0; i<2000; i++) temp[i] = (char) (rand()%26) + 'A';
  temp[2000] = '\0';

  strcpy(s, temp);
  start = time('\0');
  bubble(s, strlen(s));
  end = time('\0');
  printf("Bubble sort took %ld seconds.\n", end-start);
```

```
    strcpy(s, temp);
    start = time('\0');
    shaker(s, strlen(s));
    end = time('\0');
    printf("Shaker sort took %ld seconds.\n", end-start);

    strcpy(s, temp);
    start = time('\0');
    select(s, strlen(s));
    end = time('\0');
    printf("Selection sort took %ld seconds.\n", end-start);

    strcpy(s, temp);
    start = time('\0');
    insert(s, strlen(s));
    end = time('\0');
    printf("Insertion sort took %ld seconds.\n", end-start);

    strcpy(s, temp);
    start = time('\0');
    shell(s, strlen(s));
    end = time('\0');
    printf("Shell sort took %ld seconds.\n", end-start);

    strcpy(s, temp);
    start = time('\0');
    quick(s,strlen(s));
    end = time('\0');
    printf("Quicksort took %ld seconds.\n", end-start);
    return 0;
}

/* The Bubble Sort. */
void bubble(char *item, int count)
{
  register int a, b;
  register char t;

  for(a=1; a<count; ++a)
    for(b=count-1; b>=a; --b) {
      if(item[b-1] > item[b]) {
        /* exchange elements */
        t = item[b-1];
        item[b-1] = item[b];
        item[b] = t;
      }
    }
}


/* The Shaker Sort. */
void shaker(char *item, int count)
{

  register int a, b, c, d;
  char t;
```

```
      c = 1;
      b = count-1; d = count-1;

      do {
        for(a=d; a>=c; --a) {
          if(item[a-1]>item[a]) {
            t = item[a-1];
            item[a-1] = item[a];
            item[a] = t;
            b = a;
          }
        }
        c = b+1;
        for(a=c; a<d+1; ++a) {
          if(item[a-1]>item[a]) {
            t = item[a-1];
            item[a-1] = item[a];
            item[a] = t;
            b = a;
          }
        }
        d = b-1;
      } while (c<=d);
    }


    /* The Selection Sort. */
    void select(char *item, int count)
    {
      register int a, b, c;
      char t;

      for(a=0; a<count-1; ++a) {
        c = a;
        t = item[a];
        for(b=a+1; b<count; ++b) {
          if(item[b]<t) {
            c = b;
            t = item[b];
          }
        }
        item[c] = item[a];
        item[a] = t;
      }
    }


    /* The Insertion Sort. */
    void insert(char *item, int count)
    {

      register int a, b;
      char t;

      for(a=1; a<count; ++a) {
```

```
      t = item[a];
      b = a-1;
      while(b>=0 && t<item[b] ) {
        item[b+1] = item[b];
        b--;
      }
      item[b+1] = t;
  }
}


/* The Shell Sort. */
void shell(char *item, int count)
{

  register int i, j, k, s, w;
  char x, a[5];

  a[0]=9; a[1]=5; a[2]=3; a[3]=2; a[4]=1;
  for(w=0; w<5; w++) {
    k = a[w]; s = -k;
    for(i=k; i<count; ++i) {
      x = item[i];
      j = i-k;
      if(s==0) {
        s = -k;
        s++;
        item[s] = x;
      }
      while(x<item[j] && j>=0 && j<=count) {
        item[j+k] = item[j];
        j = j-k;
      }
      item[j+k] = x;
    }
  }
}


/* Quicksort setup function. */
void quick(char *item, int count)
{
  qs(item, 0, count-1);
}

/* The Quicksort. */
void qs(char *item, int left, int right)
{
```

```
register int i, j;
char x, y;

i = left; j = right;
x = item[(left+right)/2];

do {
  while(item[i]<x && i<right) i++;
  while(x<item[j] && j>left) j--;

  if(i<=j) {
    y = item[i];
    item[i] = item[j];
    item[j] = y;
    i++; j--;
  }
} while(i<=j);
if(left<j)  qs(item, left, j);
if(i<right) qs(item, i, right);
}
```

When run on a 10mhz IBM model 60, the output obtained is shown here. As you can see, the results are as the mathematical models predict:

Bubble sort took 21 seconds.
Shaker sort took 17 seconds.
Selection sort took 12 seconds.
Insertion sort took 8 seconds.
Shell sort took 1 second.
Quicksort took 0 seconds.

Quicksort obviously took more than 0 seconds to execute! It is just that it executed in less than 1 second.

Generally quicksort is the sort of choice because it is so fast. However, when only very small lists of data are to be sorted (less than 100), the overhead created by quicksort's recursive calls may offset the benefits of its superior algorithm. In rare cases like this, one of the simpler sorts, perhaps even the bubble sort, will be quicker. There is another reason that you might not want to use quicksort. In situations where available RAM is very limited, or unknown, you might need to avoid the somewhat heavy recursion of quicksort. As you probably know, recursive functions have a tendency to eat up large quantities of RAM, and, if the supply of RAM is exhausted before quicksort finishes, it will fail and your program will probably crash.

Generic Sorts Versus Specific Sorts

As mentioned earlier in this chapter, Turbo C's library contains the standard, generic quicksort **qsort( )**, which has this prototype:

    void qsort(void *start, int count, int size, int (*cmp( ));

Here, *start* is a pointer to the beginning of the list of items to be sorted. The *count* parameter specifies the number of elements in the list. The *size* parameter specifies the length of each item in the list in bytes. Finally, **cmp** is a pointer to a comparison function that has the prototype

    int cmp(*type* *a, *type* *b);

where *type* is the type of elements being sorted. It must return a negative value if *a<*b; Zero if *a == *b; and a positive value if *a > *b. This function is called by **qsort( )** when it compares elements.

While **qsort( )** is well implemented in Turbo C, because of its generic nature it cannot achieve the performance levels attained by a version coded specifically for a particular type of data. This loss of performance is due mostly to the added overhead of the call to the comparison function. To demonstrate this, the following program uses **qsort( )** and a specific verson of quicksort to sort a 5000-element character array. On a 10mhz model 60, the specific version of quicksort sorts the array in 1 second; **qsort( )** does it in 10 seconds. If you need the fastest possible sort, it pays to write your own.

```c
#include <stdio.h>
#include <string.h>
#include <conio.h>
#include <stdlib.h>
#include <time.h>

/* This program compares a specific version of Quicksort
   to the generic qsort found in Turbo C's library.
*/


void qs(char *item, int left, int right);
void quick(char * item, int count);
int cmp(char *, char *);

main()
{
   char s[5001], temp[5001];
   register int i;
   time_t start, end;

   /* generate a random string of characters */
   for(i=0; i<5000; i++) temp[i] = (char) (rand()%26) + 'A';
   temp[5001] = '\0';

   strcpy(s, temp);
   start = time('\0');
   quick(s, strlen(s));
   end = time('\0');
   printf("Quicksort took %ld seconds. Press a key\n", end-start);
   getch();
   printf("%s\n", s);

   strcpy(s, temp);
   start = time('\0');
   qsort(s, strlen(s), 1, cmp);
   end = time('\0');
   printf("qsort took %ld seconds. Press a key\n", end-start);
   getch();
   printf("%s\n", s);
   return 0;
}
```

```
/* Quicksort setup function. */
void quick(char *item, int count)
{
   qs(item, 0, count-1);
}

/* The Quicksort. */
void qs(char *item, int left, int right)
{

   register int i, j;
   char x, y;

   i = left; j = right;
   x = item[(left+right)/2];

   do {
     while(item[i]<x && i<right) i++;
     while(x<item[j] && j>left) j--;

     if(i<=j) {
       y = item[i];
       item[i] = item[j];
       item[j] = y;
       i++; j--;
     }
   } while(i<=j);

   if(left<j)  qs(item, left, j);
   if(i<right) qs(item, i, right);
}

cmp(char *a, char *b)
{
   return *a - *b;
}
```

SORTING OTHER DATA STRUCTURES

Until now you have only been sorting arrays of characters. This has made it easy to present each of the sorting routines. Obviously, arrays of any of the built-in data types can be sorted simply by changing the data types of the parameters and variables to the sort function. Generally, however, it is complex data types like strings, or groupings of information like structures, that need to be sorted. Most sorting involves a key and information linked to that key. To change the algorithms to accommodate this you need to alter the comparison section, the exchange section, or both. The algorithm itself remains unchanged.

Quicksort is used in the following examples because it is one of the best general-purpose routines available at this time, but the same techniques apply to any of the sorts described earlier.

Sorting Strings

It is easy to modify the quicksort developed earlier so that it can sort strings. The following program shows how this can be done:

```
#include <stdio.h>
#include <string.h>
#include <stdlib.h>

void qs_string(char item[3][10], int left, int right);
void quick_string(char item[3][10], int count);

main()
{
   int i;
   char p[3][10] = {
           "one",
           "two",
           "three"};

   quick_string(p, 3);

   for(i=0; i<3; i++) printf("%s ", p[i]);
   return 0;
}


/* A Quicksort for strings. */
void quick_string(char item[][10], int count)
{
   qs_string(item, 0, count-1);
}

void qs_string(char item[][10], int left, int right)
{
   register int i, j;
   char *x;
   char temp[10];
```

```
  i = left; j = right;
  x = item[(left+right)/2];

  do {
    while(strcmp(item[i],x)<0 && i<right) i++;
    while(strcmp(item[j],x)>0 && j>left) j--;
    if(i<=j) {
      strcpy(temp, item[i]);
      strcpy(item[i], item[j]);
      strcpy(item[j], temp);
      i++; j--;
    }
  } while(i<=j);

  if(left<j)  qs_string(item, left, j);
  if(i<right) qs_string(item, i, right);
}
```

Notice that the comparison step has been changed to use the function **strcmp( )**, which returns a negative number if the first string is lexicographically less than the second, 0 if the strings are equal, and a positive number if the first string is lexicographically greater than the second. Also note that the exchange part of the routine has been modified to swap strings using **strcpy( )**.

The use of **strcmp( )** will slow down the sort for two reasons: (1) It involves a function call, which always takes time; and (2) the **strcmp( )** function performs several comparisons to determine the relationship of the two strings. In the first case, if speed is absolutely critical the code for **strcmp( )** should be placed inside the routine by duplicating the **strcmp( )** code. In the second case, there is no way to avoid comparing the strings, since by definition this is what the task involves.

Sorting Structures

Most application programs that require a sort will probably want to have a grouping of data sorted. A mailing list, which links a name, street, city, state, and ZIP code, is an excellent example. When this conglomerate unit of data is sorted, a sort key is used but the entire structure is exchanged. To see how this is done, first you need to create a structure. Following the mailing list example, a convenient structure is

```
struct address {
        char name[40];
        char street[40];
        char city[20];
        char state[3];
        char zip[10];
};
```

The reason *state* is three characters long and *zip* is ten characters long is that a string array always needs one more character than the maximum length of any string in order to store the null terminator.

Since it is reasonable to arrange a mailing list as an array of structures, assume for this example that the sort routine will be sorting an array of structures of type **address** using the ZIP code field. Such a routine is shown here, along with a simple **main( )** which verifies its operation:

```
#include <stdio.h>
#include <string.h>
#include <stdlib.h>

struct address {
        char name[40];
        char street[40];
        char city[20];
        char state[3];
        char zip[10];
} sample[3];

void qs_struct(struct address item[], int left, int right);
void quick_struct(struct address item[], int count);

main()
{
  int i;

  strcpy(sample[0].zip, "99999");
  strcpy(sample[1].zip, "55555");
  strcpy(sample[2].zip, "11111");
```

```
  quick_struct(sample, 3);

  for(i=0; i<3; i++) printf("%s ", sample[i].zip);
  return 0;
}


/* A Quicksort for structures of type address. */
void quick_struct(struct address item[], int count)
{
  qs_struct(item,0,count-1);
}

void qs_struct(struct address item[], int left, int right)
{

  register int i, j;
  char *x;
  struct address temp;

  i = left; j = right;
  x = item[(left+right)/2].zip;

  do {
    while(strcmp(item[i].zip,x)<0 && i<right) i++;
    while(strcmp(item[j].zip,x)>0 && j>left) j--;
    if(i<=j) {
      temp = item[i];
      item[i] = item[j];
      item[j] = temp;
      i++; j--;
    }
  } while(i<=j);

  if(left<j)  qs_struct(item, left, j);
  if(i<right) qs_struct(item, i, right);
}
```

SORTING RANDOM
ACCESS DISK FILES

There are two types of disk files: sequential and random access. If
either type of disk file is small enough, it can be read into memory
and the array sorting routines presented earlier will be able to
sort it. Disk files that are too large to be sorted easily in memory
require special techniques. Most microcomputer database applications use random access files. This section looks at how to sort
them.

Sorting Random Access Disk Files as Arrays

Random access disk files have two major advantages over sequential disk files:

1. They are easy to maintain. Information can be updated without having to copy the entire list over.

2. They can be treated as an array on disk, that is, any of the array sorting routines can be applied to them with small modification.

Applying this method means that you can use the basic quicksort with modifications to seek different records on the disk instead of indexing an array. Also, unlike sorting a sequential disk file, sorting a random file in place means that a very full disk does not have to have room for both the sorted and unsorted file.

In reality, each sorting situation differs in relation to the exact data structure sorted and the key used. However, the general idea of sorting random access disk files can be understood by developing a program to sort the mailing list structure defined earlier and called **address**. This sample program assumes that the number of elements is fixed at 100. However, a record count would have to be maintained dynamically in reality. The mailing list sorting program is given here:

```
/* Disk sort for structures of type address */
#include <stdio.h>
#include <stdlib.h>
#include <string.h>

#define NUM_ELEMENTS 100   /* this is an arbitrary number
                              that should be determined
                              dynamically for each list */

struct address {
  char name[30];
  char street[40];
  char city[20];
  char state[3];
```

```
  char zip[10];
}ainfo;

void quick_disk(FILE *fp, int count);
void qs_disk(FILE *fp, int left, int right);
void swap_all_fields(FILE *fp, long i, long j);
char *get_zip(FILE *fp, long rec);

main()
{
  FILE *fp;

  if((fp=fopen("mlist","rb+"))==NULL) {
    printf("cannot open file for read/write\n");
    exit(1);
  }

  quick_disk(fp, NUM_ELEMENTS);
  fclose(fp);
  printf("List sorted.\n");
  return 0;
}

/* A Quicksort for files. */
void quick_disk(FILE *fp, int count)
{
  qs_disk(fp, 0, count-1);
}

void qs_disk(FILE *fp, int left, int right)
{

  long int i, j;
  char x[100], *y;

  i = left; j = right;

  strcpy(x, get_zip(fp,(long)(i+j)/2)); /* get the middle zip */

  do {
    while(strcmp(get_zip(fp,i),x)<0 && i<right) i++;
    while(strcmp(get_zip(fp,j),x)>0 && j>left) j--;

    if(i<=j) {
      swap_all_fields(fp, i, j);
      i++; j--;
    }
  } while(i<=j);

  if(left<j)  qs_disk(fp, left, (int) j);
  if(i<right) qs_disk(fp, (int) i, right);
}
```

```
void swap_all_fields(FILE *fp, long i, long j)
{
    char a[sizeof(ainfo)], b[sizeof(ainfo)];

    /* first read in record i and j */
    fseek(fp, sizeof(ainfo)*i, 0);
    fread(a, sizeof(ainfo), 1, fp);

    fseek(fp, sizeof(ainfo)*j, 0);
    fread(b, sizeof(ainfo), 1, fp);

    /* then write them back in opposite slots */
    fseek(fp, sizeof(ainfo)*j, 0);
    fwrite(a, sizeof(ainfo), 1, fp);

    fseek(fp, sizeof(ainfo)*i, 0);
    fwrite(b, sizeof(ainfo), 1, fp);
}

/* Return a pointer to the zip code */
char *get_zip(FILE *fp, long rec)
{
    struct address *p;
    register int t;

    p = &ainfo;

    fseek(fp, rec*sizeof(ainfo), 0);
    fread(p, sizeof(ainfo), 1, fp);

    return ainfo.zip;
}
```

Several support functions had to be written to accomplish the sorting of the address records. For the comparison section of the sort, the function **get—zip( )** was used to return a pointer to the ZIP code of the comparand and the record being checked. The function **swap—all—fields( )** performs the actual exchange of data. It is important to note that the order of the reads and writes has a great impact on the speed of this sort. That is, the code forces a seek to record i, and then to record j. While the head of the disk drive is still positioned at j, i's data is written. This means that it is not necessary for the head to move a great distance. Had the code been written with i's data to be written first, an extra seek would have been necessary.

Sorting Random Access Files Using Index Files

Depending on the application, it is sometimes possible to not physically sort the information in a disk data file but rather to sort another file that contains the keys and the data file record numbers of the information associated with each key. In this case the much smaller index file is sorted in memory. This approach, shown in Figure 1–4, greatly reduces the time it takes to sort the data. Of course, to access the actual data requires that you read the index file first to find the location of each entry. No example of this method is shown, but the general procedure should be clear.

SEARCHING

In reality, databases of information exist so that a user can locate a record by knowing its key. There is only one method of finding information in an unsorted file or array and another for a sorted file or array. Turbo C supplies search functions as part of the standard library. These functions are called **bsearch( ), lsearch ( ),** and **lfind( )**. However, as with sortings, general-purpose search routines are sometimes too inefficient to use in demanding situations because of the extra overhead created by their generalization. Therefore, the end of this chapter concentrates on specific search algorithms. (You will take a quick look at **bsearch( )** at the end of the chapter.)

Searching Methods

Finding information in an unsorted array requires a sequential search starting at the first element and stopping either when a match is found or at the end of the array. This method must be used on unsorted data, but it can be applied to sorted data as well. If the data has been sorted, a binary search can be used, which will greatly speed up the process.

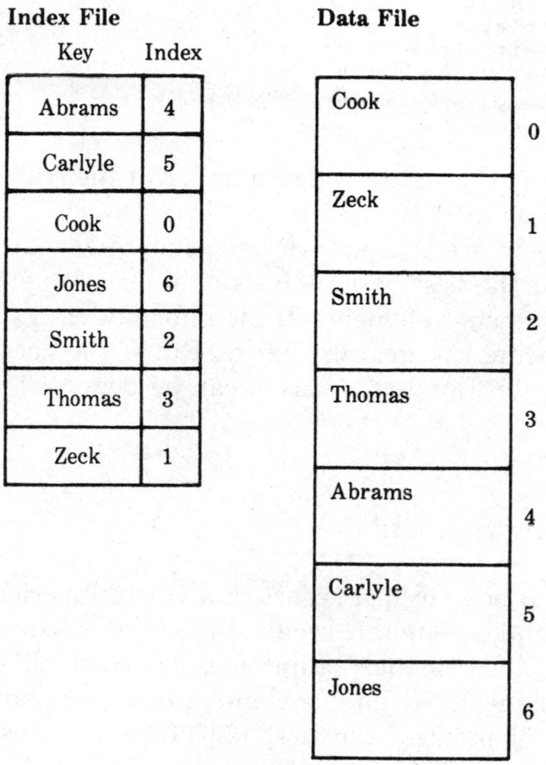

Index File			Data File	
Key	**Index**		Cook	0
Abrams	4			
Carlyle	5		Zeck	1
Cook	0			
Jones	6		Smith	2
Smith	2			
Thomas	3		Thomas	3
Zeck	1			
			Abrams	4
			Carlyle	5
			Jones	6

Figure 1-4.   Using an index file with a data file

The Sequential Search

The *sequential search* is very simple to code. The following function searches a character array of known length until a match is
found with the specified key:

```
sequential_search(char *item, int count, char key)
{
  register int t;
  for(t=0; t<count; ++t)
    if(key==item[t]) return t;
  return -1;  /* no match */
}
```

This function returns the index number of the matching entry if there is one or a -1 if there is not.

It is easy to see that an average sequential search tests $1/2n$ elements. In the best case, it tests only one element, and in the worst case it tests n elements. If the information is stored on disk, the search time can get very large. But if the data is unsorted, this is the only way that a search can be done.

The Binary Search

If the data to be searched is sorted, a vastly superior method can be used to find a match. It is called the *binary search*, and it uses the "divide and conquer" approach. The method is to test the middle element. If the middle element is larger than the key, test the middle element of the first half; otherwise test the middle element of the second half. Repeat this until either a match is found, or there are no more elements to test.

For example, given the array

1 2 3 4 5 6 7 8 9

to find the number 4, the binary search would first test the middle, which is 5. Since this is greater than 4, the search would continue with the first half, or

1 2 3 4 5

Here the middle element is 3. This is less than 4, so the first half is discarded and the search continues with

4 5

This time the match is found.

In the binary search the number of comparisons in the worst case is

$$\log_2 n$$

with average cases being somewhat better and the best case being one comparison.

A binary search function for character arrays is shown here. You can make this function search any arbitrary data structure by changing the comparison portion of the routine.

```
/* The Binary search. */
binary(char *item, int count, char key)
{
  int low,high, mid;

  low = 0; high = count-1;
  while(low<=high) {
    mid = (low+high)/2;
    if(key<item[mid]) high = mid-1;
    else if(key>item[mid]) low = mid+1;
    else return mid;  /* found */
  }
  return -1;
}
```

The following program demonstrates the operation of both sequential and binary searches:

```
#include <stdio.h>
#include <stdlib.h>

sequential_search(char *item, int count, char key);
binary(char *item, int count, char key);
```

```
main()
{
  char s[10] = "abcdefghij";

  if(sequential_search(s, 10, 'd')!=-1)
    printf("found\n");

  if(binary(s, 10, 'd')!=-1)
    printf("found\n");
  return 0;
}
sequential_search(char *item, int count, char key)
{
  register int t;
  for(t=0; t<count; ++t)
    if(key==item[t]) return t;
  return -1;  /* no match */
}


/* The Binary search. */
binary(char *item, int count, char key)
{
  int low,high, mid;

  low = 0; high = count-1;
  while(low<=high) {
    mid = (low+high)/2;
    if(key<item[mid]) high = mid-1;
    else if(key>item[mid]) low = mid+1;
    else return mid;  /* found */
  }
  return -1;
}
```

Using bsearch and lsearch

You will conclude this discussion of searching by examining two of Turbo C's standard library search functions: **bsearch( )** and **lsearch( )**. The **bsearch( )** function performs a binary search on sorted data. It has this prototype:

> void *bsearch(const void *key, const void *start,
>   size_t num, size_t width,
>   int (*cmp) (const void *, const void *));

Here, *key* is a pointer to the key you are looking for. The *start* parameter is a pointer to the start of the sorted array of size *num*. The number of bytes used by each element is specified by *width*. Each element must be the same size. The **cmp( )** function is used to compare the key with an element in the array. It is similar to the one we used with the **qsort( )** function. It must be declared like this:

    int cmp (*type *a, type *b*)

The parameter *type* is the proper type for the data being sorted. The **cmp( )** function must return a negative value if *a*<*b*; 0 if *a* == *b*; and a positive value if *a*>*b*. This function is called by **bsearch( )** when it compares elements.

If you have only unsorted data to work with, you must use the **lsearch( )** function. It has this prototype:

    void *lsearch(const void *key, const void *start,
            size_t *num, size_t width,
            int (*cmp) (const void *, const void *));

Here, *key* is a pointer to the key you are looking for. The *start* parameter is a pointer to the start of the array. The size of the array must be pointed to by *num*. The number of bytes used by each element is specified by *width*. Each element must be the same size. The **cmp( )** function can be the same as that used for **bsearch( )**. However, technically, it need only return two values: 0 if the key and an element are the same, non-zero otherwise.

To see these two searches in action, the demonstration program from the preceding section is reworked here, using **bsearch( )** and **lsearch( )**:

```
#include <stdio.h>
#include <stdlib.h>

int cmp(char *, char *);

main()
{
```

```
char s[10] = "abcdefghij";
int num;

num = 10;

if(lsearch("d", s, &num, 1, cmp))
  printf("lsearch found it\n");

if(bsearch("d", s, num, 1, cmp))
  printf("bsearch found it\n");

return 0;
}

cmp(char *a, char *b)
{
  return *a-*b;
}
```

2

QUEUES, STACKS, LINKED LISTS, AND TREES

A good program is a blend of two things: algorithms and data structures. The choice and implementation of a data structure are as important as the routines that manipulate it. The nature of the programming problem usually determines how information is organized and accessed. Therefore, as a programmer, it is important for you to have in your "bag of tricks" the right storage and retrieval methods for many different situations.

How closely the logical concept of an item of data is bound with its physical machine representation is in inverse correlation to its abstraction. That is, as data types become more complex, the way the programmer thinks of them bears an ever-decreasing resemblance to the way they are actually represented in memory. For example, a simple type, such as **int**, is tightly bound to its machine representation; that is, the value that an integer has in its machine representation closely approximates the value that the programmer conceives of it having. Simple arrays, which are organized collections of the simple data types, are not quite as tightly bound as the simple types themselves because an array may not appear in memory the way the programmer thinks of it.

Less tightly bound yet are **float**s because the actual representation inside the machine is little like the average programmer's conception of a floating point number. The structure is even more abstracted from the machine representation. The final level of abstraction transcends the mere physical aspects of the data and concentrates instead on the sequence in which the data will be accessed, that is, *stored* and *retrieved*. In essence the physical data is linked with a "data engine" that controls the way information can be accessed by your program. There are four archetypal engines:

- A queue
- A stack
- A linked list
- A binary tree

Each of these methods provides a solution to a class of problems. These methods are essentially devices that perform a specific storage and retrieval operation on the information that they are given and the requests they receive. They share two operations: (1) store an item and (2) retrieve an item, where an item is one informational unit. The rest of this chapter will show you how to implement these data engines in your own Turbo C programs.

QUEUES

A *queue* is simply a linear list of information that is accessed in *first-in, first-out* order, sometimes called FIFO. That is, the first item placed on the queue is the first item retrieved, the second item put in is the second item retrieved, and so on. This is the only means of storage and retrieval; random access of any specific item is not possible.

Queues are very common in real life. For example, lines at a bank or a fast food restaurant are queues. To visualize how a queue works, consider two functions: **qstore( )** and **qretrieve( )**.

Action	Contents of Queue
qstore(A)	A
qstore(B)	A B
qstore(C)	A B C
qretrieve( ) returns **A**	B C
qstore(D)	B C D
qretrieve( ) returns **B**	C D
qretrieve( ) returns **C**	D

Figure 2-1.   A queue in action

qstore( ) places an item on the end of the queue and **qretrieve( )** removes the first item from the queue and returns its value. Figure 2-1 shows the effect of a series of these operations.

Remember that a retrieve operation removes an item from the queue and, if it is not then stored elsewhere, destroys it. Therefore, even though the program using a queue is still active, the queue itself may be empty because all of its items have been removed.

Queues are used in many types of programming situations. One of the most common is the simulation, which will be covered later in Chapter 9. Two other main uses are for event scheduling, such as a PERT or Gantt chart, and for I/O buffering.

For example, you might use a queue to organize a day's appointments. The simple appointment scheduler program that follows allows you to enter a number of appointments and then takes each appointment off the list as it occurs. For the sake of simplicity there is an array of pointers to the event strings and each appointment description is limited to 256 characters. The number of entries is arbitrarily limited to 100 and is represented by the macro **MAX**. First, you need the functions **qstore( )** and **qretrieve( )**:

```
/* Store an appointment. */
void qstore(char *q)
{
  if(spos==MAX) {
    printf("List full\n");
    return;
  }
  p[spos] = q;
  spos++;
}

/* Retrieve an appointment. */
char *qretrieve()
{
  if(rpos==spos) {
    printf("No (more) appointments.\n");
    return NULL;
  }
  rpos++;
  return p[rpos-1];
}
```

Notice that these functions require two global variables: *spos*, which holds the index of the next free storage location, and *rpos*, which holds the index of the next item to retrieve. It is possible to use these functions to maintain a queue of other data types by simply changing the base type of the array they operate on.

The function **qstore( )** places pointers to new appointments on the end of the list and checks to see if the list is full. **qretrieve( )** takes appointments off the queue as they occur. With each new appointment scheduled, *spos* is incremented, and with each appointment removed *rpos* is incremented. In essence *rpos* chases *spos* through the queue. Figure 2-2 shows how this may appear in memory as the program executes. When *rpos* and *spos* are equal, there are no appointments left in the schedule.

The entire program for this simple appointment scheduler is

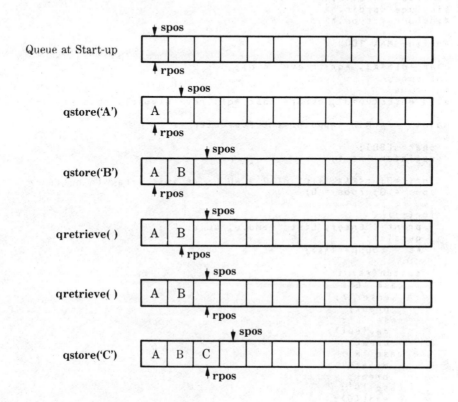

Figure 2-2.   The retrieve index chasing the store index

listed here. You might enjoy enhancing this program for your own specific use.

```
#include <string.h>
#include <stdlib.h>
#include <stdio.h>
#include <ctype.h>

#define MAX 100

char *p[MAX], *qretrieve(void);
int spos;
int rpos;
void enter(void), qstore(char *q), review(void), delete(void);

main()  /* Mini Appointment-Scheduler */
{
  char s[80];
  register int t;

  for(t=0; t<MAX; ++t) p[t] = NULL; /* init array to nulls */
  spos = 0; rpos = 0;

  for(;;) {
    printf("Enter, List, Remove, Quit: ");
    gets(s);
    *s = toupper(*s);

    switch(*s) {
      case 'E':
        enter();
        break;
      case 'L':
        review();
        break;
      case 'R':
        delete();
        break;
      case 'Q':
        exit(0);
    }
  }
}

/* Enter appointments in queue. */
void enter(void)
{
  char s[256], *p;

  do {
    printf("enter appointment %d: ", spos+1);
    gets(s);
    if(*s==0) break;  /* no entry */
    p = malloc(strlen(s));
    if(!p) {
      printf("out of memory.\n");
      return;
    }
```

```
    strcpy(p, s);
    if(*s) qstore(p);
  }while(*s);
}

/* See what's in the queue. */
void review(void)
{
  register int t;

  for(t=rpos; t<spos; ++t)
    printf("%d. %s\n", t+1, p[t]);
}

/* Delete an appointment from the queue. */
void delete(void)
{
  char *p;

  if((p=qretrieve())==NULL) return;
  printf("%s\n", p);
}

/* Store an appointment. */
void qstore(char *q)
{
  if(spos==MAX) {
    printf("List full\n");
    return;
  }
  p[spos] = q;
  spos++;
}

/* Retrieve an appointment. */
char *qretrieve(void)
{
  if(rpos==spos) {
    printf("No (more) appointments.\n");
    return NULL;
  }
  rpos++;
  return p[rpos-1];
}
```

Here is a sample run of the appointment scheduler:

```
Enter, List, Remove, Quit: E
enter appointment 1: Jon at 9 about the phone system
enter appointment 2: Ted at 10:30 - wants that raise...humm.
enter appointment 3: lunch with Mary and Tom at Harry's
```

```
enter appointment 4: <cr>
Enter, List, Remove, Quit: L
1. Jon at 9 about the phone system
2. Ted at 10:30 - wants that raise...humm.
3. lunch with Mary and Tom at Harry's
Enter, List, Remove, Quit: R
Jon at 9 about the phone system
Enter, List, Remove, Quit: L
2. Ted at 10:30 - wants that raise...humm.
3. lunch with Mary and Tom at Harry's
Enter, List, Remove, Quit: Q
```

The Circular Queue

In studying the appointment scheduler program in the previous
section, you may have thought of an improvement. Instead of having the program stop when it reached the limit of the array used
to store the queue, you could have both the store index, *spos*, and
the retrieve index, *rpos*, loop back to the start of the array. In this
way, any number of items could be placed on the queue as long as
items were also being taken off. This method of implementing a
queue is called a *circular queue* because it uses its storage array
as if the end were attached to the beginning.

To create a circular queue for use in the appointment scheduler program, you need to change the functions **qstore( )** and **qre-
trieve** as shown here:

```
void qstore(char *q)
{
  /* The queue is full if either spos is one less than rpos
     or if spos is at the end of the queue array and rpos
     is at the beginning.
  */
  if(spos+1==rpos || (spos+1==MAX && !rpos)) {
    printf("list full\n");
    return;
  }
  p[spos] = q;
  spos++;
  if(spos==MAX) spos = 0; /* loop back */
}

char *qretrieve(void)
{
```

```
if(rpos==MAX) rpos = 0; /* loop back */
if(rpos==spos) {
  printf("No events to perform.\n");
  return NULL;
}
rpos++;
return p[rpos-1];
}
```

The queue is full only when the store index has caught up to the retrieve index; otherwise there is room in the queue for another event. Conceptually, the array used for the circular version of the appointment scheduler program looks like Figure 2-3.

Perhaps the most common use of a circular queue is to hold the information in operating systems that is read from and written to disk files or the console. Another very common use of the circular queue is in real-time application programs, which must continue to process information while buffering I/O requests. Many word processors do this when they reformat a paragraph or justify a line. There is a brief period of time during which what is being typed is not displayed until after some other process, such as for-

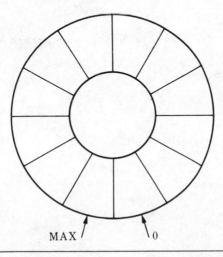

MAX   0

Figure 2-3.   The circular array for the scheduler program

matting a paragraph, is completed. To accomplish this, the application program needs to continue to check for keyboard entry during the other process's execution. If a key has been typed, it is quickly placed in the queue, and the process continues. Once the process is complete, the characters are retrieved from the queue.

The simple program that follows contains two processes to show how the circular queue works. The first process in the program will print the numbers 1 to 32,000 on the screen. The second process will place characters in a circular queue as they are typed, without displaying them on the screen, until you type a semicolon. The characters you type will not be displayed because the first process is given priority on the screen at this time. When you type a semicolon, the characters in the queue are retrieved and displayed. Pressing CTRL-Z terminates the program. The proposed ANSI standard does not define library functions that check keyboard status or read keyboard characters without displaying them because these functions are highly operating-system dependent. However, Turbo C does supply routines to do these things. The short program shown here will work with the IBM PC and uses the Turbo C **kbhit( )** and **getch( )** functions to determine the keyboard status and read a character without displaying it on the screen.

```
/* A circular queue example using a keyboard buffer. */
#include <stdio.h>
#include <conio.h>
#include <stdlib.h>

#define MAX 80

char buf[MAX+1];
int spos=0;
int rpos=0;

void qstore(char q);
char qretrieve(void);

main()
{
  register char ch;
  int t;

  buf[80] = NULL;
```

```
  /* input characters until a control-z is typed */
  for(ch=' ',t=0; t<32000 && ch!=26; ++t) {
    if(kbhit()) {
      ch = getch();
      qstore(ch);
    }
    printf("%d ", t);
    if(ch==';') /* display and empty the key buffer */
      while((ch=qretrieve())!=NULL) putchar(ch);
  }
  return 0;
}
/* Store characters in the queue. */
void qstore(char q)
{
  if(spos+1==rpos || (spos+1==MAX && !rpos)) {
    printf("list full\n");
    return;
  }
  buf[spos] = q;
  spos++;
  if(spos==MAX) spos = 0; /* loop back */
}

/* Retrieve a character. */
char qretrieve(void)
{
  if(rpos==MAX) rpos = 0; /* loop back */
  if(rpos==spos) {
    return NULL;
  }
  rpos++;
  return buf[rpos-1];
}
```

STACKS

A *stack* is the opposite of a queue because it uses *last-in, first-out* accessing, sometimes called LIFO. To visualize a stack you need only imagine a stack of plates. The first plate on the table is the last to be used and the last plate on the stack is the first to be used. Stacks are used a great deal in system software, including compilers and interpreters. In fact Turbo C uses the computer's stack when passing arguments to functions.

The two basic operations, *store* and *retrieve* are, for historical reasons, usually called *push* and *pop* respectively. To implement a

stack you need two functions: **push( )**, which places a value on the
stack, and **pop( )**, which retrieves a value from the stack. You also
need a region of memory to use for the stack. You could either use
an array or allocate a region of memory with Turbo C's dynamic
memory allocation functions. Like the queue, the retrieval function takes a value off the list and, if it is not stored elsewhere,
destroys it. The general form of **push( )** and **pop( )** using an
integer array are shown here. You can maintain stacks of other
data types by changing the base type of the array that the **push( )**
and **pop( )** functions operate on.

```
int stack[MAX];
int tos=0;   /* top of stack */

/* Put an element on the stack. */
void push(int i)
{
  if(tos>=MAX) {
    printf("stack full\n");
    return;
  }
  stack[tos] = i;
  tos++;
}

/* Retrieve the top element from the stack. */
pop(void)
{
  tos--;
  if(tos<0) {
    printf("stack underflow\n");
    return HUGE_VAL;
  }
  return stack[tos];
}
```

The size of the stack is determined by the value you choose for
MAX. In the calculator example that follows, the value 100 is
used. The variable *tos* is the index of the next open stack location.
When implementing these functions, you must always remember
to prevent overflow and underflow. In these routines *tos* is 0 when
the stack is empty, and it is greater than the last storage location
when the stack is full. To see how a stack works, see Figure 2-4.

Action	Contents of Stack
push(A)	A
push(B)	B A
push(C)	C B A
pop( ) retrieves **C**	B A
push(F)	F B A
pop( ) retrieves **F**	B A
pop( ) retrieves **B**	A
pop( ) retrieves **A**	*empty*

Figure 2-4.   A stack in action

An excellent example of stack use is a four-function calculator. Most calculators today accept a standard form of expression evaluation called *infix* notation, which takes the general form operand-operator-operand. For example, to add 100 to 200, you enter **100**, type +, enter **200**, and press =. However, in an effort to save memory (which used to be expensive), many early calculators used a form of expression evaluation called *postfix* notation in which both operands are entered first and then the operator is entered. For example, using postfix to add 100 to 200, you enter **100**, enter **200**, and then press +. As you enter the operands, they are placed on a stack. Each time you enter an operator, two operands are removed from the stack and the result is pushed back on the stack. The advantage of the postfix form is that very complex expressions can be evaluated easily by the calculator.

Before developing the full four-function calculator for postfix expressions, you need to modify the basic **push( )** and **pop( )** functions. The program will use Turbo C's dynamic memory allocation **malloc( )** to provide memory for the stack. (Dynamic allocation is discussed in detail in Chapter 3.) The stack functions are shown next as they will be used in the calculator example.

```
int *p;   /* will point to a region of free memory */
int *tos; /* points to top of stack */
int *bos; /* points to bottom of stack */

/* Store an element on the stack. */
void push(int i)
{
  if(p>bos) {
    printf("stack full\n");
    return;
  }
  *p = i;
  p++;
}

/* Retrieve the top element from the stack. */
pop(void)
{
  p--;
  if(p<tos) {
    printf("stack underflow\n");
    return 0;
  }
  return *p;
}
```

Before these functions can be used, you must allocate a region of free memory by using **malloc( )**, the address of the beginning of that region assigned to *tos*, and the address of the end assigned to *bos*.

The entire calculator program is shown here. In addition to the operators $+$, $-$, $\times$, and $/$, you may also enter a period, which causes the current value on the top of the stack to be displayed.

```
/* A simple four-function calculator. */

#include <stdio.h>
#include <alloc.h>
#include <stdlib.h>
#define MAX 100

int *p;   /* will point to a region of free memory */
int *tos; /* points to top of stack */
int *bos; /* points to bottom of stack */
void push(int i);
int pop(void);
```

```
main()
{
  int a, b;
  char s[80];   .

  p = (int *) malloc(MAX*sizeof(int)); /* get stack memory */
  if(!p) {
    printf("allocation failure\n");
    exit(1);
  }
  tos = p;
  bos = p+MAX-1;

  printf("Four Function Calculator\n");

  do {
      printf(": ");
      gets(s);
      switch(*s) {
        case '+':
          a = pop();
          b = pop();
          printf("%d\n", a+b);
          push(a+b);
          break;
        case '-':
          a = pop();
          b = pop();
          printf("%d\n", b-a);
          push(b-a);
          break;
        case '*':
          a = pop();
          b = pop();
          printf("%d\n", b*a);
          push(b*a);
          break;
        case '/':
          a = pop();
          b = pop();
          if(a==0) {
            printf("divide by 0\n");
            break;
          }
          printf("%d\n", b/a);
          push(b/a);
          break;
        case '.': /* show  contents of top of stack */
          a = pop();
          push(a);
          printf("Current value on top of stack: %d\n", a);
```

```
          break;
        default:
          push(atoi(s));
      }
  } while(*s!='q');
  return 0;
}

/* Put an element on the stack. */
void push(int i)
{
  if(p>bos) {
    printf("stack full\n");
    return;
  }
  *p = i;
  p++;
}

/* Retrieve the top element from the stack. */
pop(void)
{
  p--;
  if(p<tos) {
    printf("stack underflow\n");
    return 0;
  }
  return *p;
}
```

A sample session at the calculator is shown here:

```
Four Function Calculator
: 10<cr>
: 10<cr>
: +<cr>
20
: 5<cr>
: /<cr>
4
: .<cr>
Current value on top of stack: 4
: q<cr>
```

LINKED LISTS

Queues and stacks share two traits:

1. They have strict rules for referencing the data stored in them.
2. Their retrieval operations are by nature consumptive. That is, accessing an item in a stack or queue requires its removal and, unless stored elsewhere, its destruction.

Both stacks and queues also use, at least conceptually, a contiguous region of memory to operate. Unlike a stack or a queue, a *linked list* can access its storage in a random fashion because each piece of information carries with it a *link* to the next data item in the chain. Moreover, a linked list retrieval operation does not remove and destroy an item from the list. In fact, you have to add a specific *deletion* operation to do this.

Linked lists are used for two main purposes:

1. To create arrays of unknown size in memory. If you know the amount of storage in advance, you could use an array, but if you do not know the actual size of a list, you must use a linked list.
2. For disk file storage of databases. The linked list allows you to insert and delete items quickly and easily in a disk file without rearranging the entire file.

For these reasons, linked lists are used extensively in database managers.

Linked lists can be either singly linked or doubly linked. A singly linked list contains a link to the next data item. A doubly linked list contains links to both the next and the previous elements in the list. You will use one or the other depending on your application.

Singly Linked Lists

A singly linked list requires that each item of information contains a link to the next element in the list. Each data item generally consists of a structure that contains both information fields and a link pointer. Conceptually, a singly linked list looks like the one in Figure 2-5.

There are two basic ways to build a singly linked list. The first is simply to put each new item on the end of the list. The second is to add items at specific places in the list; for example, in ascending sorted order. How you build the list determines the way the store function will be coded. First let's look at the simpler case of creating a linked list by adding items to the end.

Before beginning you need to define a data structure to hold the information and the links. Because mailing lists are common let's use one here. The data structure for each element in the mailing list is defined as follows:

```
struct address {
  char name[40];
  char street[40];
  char city[20];
  char state[3];
  char zip[10];
  struct address *next;
} info;
```

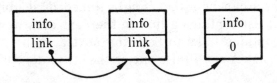

Figure 2-5.   Singly linked list in memory

The function **slstore( )** will build a singly linked list by placing each new element on the end. It must be passed a pointer to a structure of type **address** that contains the address information and a pointer to a pointer that holds the memory address of the last entry in the list. The function is

```
void slstore(struct address *i,
             struct address **last)
{
  if(!*last) *last = i; /* first item in list */
  else (*last)->next = i;
  i->next = NULL;
  *last = i;
}
```

The first time this function is called, the value pointed to by **last** must be **NULL**. It is also your program's responsibility to keep a pointer to the start of the list, which will be a pointer to the first structure passed to **slstore( )**.

Although it is possible to sort the list created with the function **slstore( )** as a separate operation, it would be easier simply to sort the list while building it by inserting each new item in the proper sequence of the chain. If the list is already sorted, it would also be advantageous to keep it sorted by inserting new items in their proper location. This is done by scanning the list sequentially until you find the proper location, inserting the new address at that point, and rearranging the links as necessary.

Three possible situations can occur when inserting an item in a singly linked list: (1) it can become the new first item; (2) it could go in the middle between two other items; and (3) it could become the last element. Figure 2-6 shows diagrammatically how the links are changed for each case.

Keep in mind that if you change the first item in the list, you must update the entry point to the list elsewhere in your program. To avoid this overhead, it is possible to use a *sentinel* as a first item instead. In this case a special value is chosen that will always be first in the list so the entry point to the list will not change. One disadvantage of this method is that one extra storage location is needed to hold the sentinel. A more important problem, however,

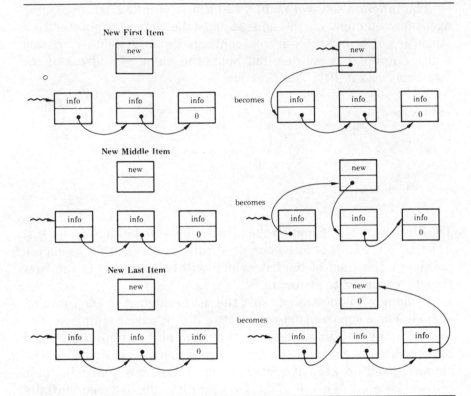

Figure 2-6.   Inserting an item into a singly linked list

is that it requires a value that can never constitute valid data—a difficult thing to guarantee in certain situations. This chapter will not use the sentinel.

The function **sls_store( )** will insert addresses into the mail list in ascending order based on the **name** field. It must be passed a pointer to the pointer to the first element and last element in the list along with a pointer to the information to be stored. Since it is possible for either the first or last element in the list to change, **sls_store( )** automatically updates these pointers when a change occurs. The first time your program calls the function, both **start** and **last** must be **NULL**.

```
/* Store in sorted order. */
void sls_store(struct address *i, /* new element to store */
               struct address **start, /* start of list */
               struct address **last) /* end of list */

{
  struct address *old, *p;

  p = *start;

  if(!*last) {  /* first element in list */
    i->next = NULL;
    *last = i;
    *start = i;
    return;
  }

  old = NULL;
  while(p) {
    if(strcmp(p->name, i->name)<0) {
      old = p;
      p = p->next;
    }
    else {
      if(old) {  /* goes in middle */
        old->next = i;
        i->next = p;
        return;
      }
      i->next = p; /* new first element */
      *start = i;
      return;
    }
  }
  (*last)->next = i; /* put on end */
  i->next = NULL;
  *last = i;
}
```

The following code fragment shows the proper way to call this function:

```
struct address *top, *bottom;
struct address *info;

/* assume info points to some address information */

sls_store(info, &top, &bottom);
```

It is uncommon to find a specific function in a linked list dedicated to the retrieve process, that is, returning item after item in list order. Usually this code is so short that it is simply placed inside another routine such as a search, delete, or display function. For example, the routine shown here will display all the names in a mailing list:

```
void display(struct address *start)
{
  while(start) {
    printf(start->name);
    start = start->next;
  }
}
```

Here **start** is a pointer to the first structure in the list. Retrieving items from the list is as simple as following a chain. A search routine based on the **name** field could be written like this:

```
struct address *search(struct address *start, char *n)
{
  while(start) {
    if(!strcmp(n, start->name)) return start;
    start = start->next;
  }
  return NULL;  /* no match */
}
```

Because **search( )** is returning a pointer to the list item that matches the search name, it must be declared to be returning a structure pointer of type **address**. If there is no match, a **NULL** is returned.

The process of deleting an item from a singly linked list is straightforward. As with insertion, there are three situations: (1) deleting the first item, (2) deleting an item in the middle, and (3) deleting the last item. Figure 2-7 shows each of these operations diagrammatically.

The function shown here will delete a given item from a list of structures of type **address**:

```
void sldelete(
        struct address *p, /* previous item */
        struct address *i, /* item to delete */
        struct address **start, /* start of list */
```

```
            struct address **last);  /* end of list */
{
  if(p)  p->next = i->next;
  else   *start = i->next;

  if(i==*last & p) *last = p;

}
```

The **sldelete( )** function must be sent pointers to the deleted item, the item before it in the chain, and the pointers that hold the addresses of the start and end items on the list. If the first item is to be removed, the pointer to the previous list entry must be **NULL**. The function automatically updates the **start** and **last** pointers, in cases where the first or last item is deleted.

Singly linked lists have one major drawback: The list cannot be followed in reverse order. For this reason doubly linked lists are generally used.

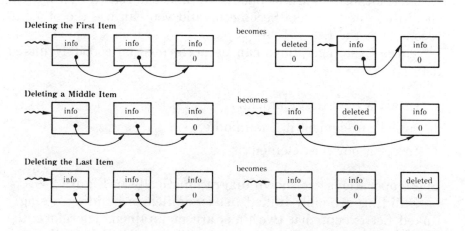

Figure 2-7.   Deleting an item from a singly linked list

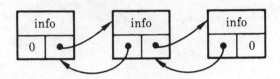

Figure 2-8. Arrangement of a doubly linked list

Doubly Linked Lists

Doubly linked lists consist of data plus links to both the next item and the preceding item. Figure 2-8 shows how these links are arranged.

Having two links instead of just one has two major advantages. The first is that the list can be read in either direction. This not only simplifies sorting the list but also, in the case of a database, allows a user to scan the list in either direction. The second advantage is meaningful only in the case of equipment failure. Because either forward or backward links can read the entire list, should one of the links become invalid you can use the other to reconstruct the list.

Three basic operations can be performed on a doubly linked list:

1. Insert a new first element.

2. Insert an element in the middle.

3. Insert a new last element.

These operations are shown diagrammatically in Figure 2-9.

Building a doubly linked list is similar to building a singly linked list except that two links are maintained. Therefore, the structure will need room for both links. Using the mailing list

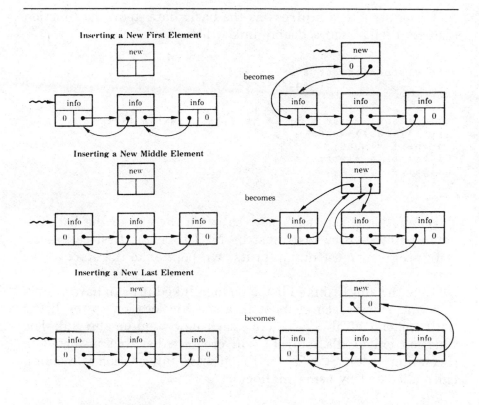

Figure 2-9.   Inserting an item into a doubly linked list

example again, you can modify structure **address** as shown here to accommodate both links:

```
struct address {
  char name[40];
  char street[40];
  char city[20];
  char state[3];
  char zip[10];
  struct address *next;
  struct address *prior;
} info;
```

Using structure **address** as the basic data item, the function **dlstore( )** will build a doubly linked list:

```
void dlstore(struct address *i,
             struct address **last)
{
  if(!*last) *last = i; /* is first item in list */
  else (*last)->next = i;
  i->next = NULL;
  i->prior = *last;
  *last = i;
}
```

This function places each new entry on the end of the list. The value pointed to by **last** must be **NULL** on the first call. Also, your program must maintain its own pointer to the start of the list.

Like the singly linked list, a doubly linked list can have a function that stores each element in a specific location as the list is built instead of always placing each new item on the end. The function called **dls_store( )** will create a list that is sorted in ascending order. Storage for the address information is dynamically allocated by using **malloc( )**.

```
/* Create a doubly linked list in sorted order.
*/
void dls_store(
  struct address *i,   /* new element */
  struct address **start, /* first element in list */
  struct address **last /* last element in list */
)
{
  struct address *old, *p;

  if(*last==NULL) {  /* first element in list */
    i->next = NULL;
    i->prior = NULL;
    *last = i;
    *start = i;
    return;
  }

  p = *start; /* start at top of list */
```

```
old = NULL;
while(p) {
  if(strcmp(p->name, i->name)<0){
    old = p;
    p = p->next;
  }
  else {
    if(p->prior) {
      p->prior->next = i;
      i->next = p;
      i->prior = p->prior;
      p->prior = i;
      return;
    }
    i->next = p; /* new first element */
    i->prior = NULL;
    p->prior = i;
    *start = i;
    return;
  }
}
old->next = i; /* put on end */
i->next = NULL;
i->prior = old;
*last = i;
}
```

The **dls—store( )** automatically updates pointers to the beginning
and ending elements of the list by using the *start* and *last*
parameters. When sorting the incoming data remember that it is
possible for either the first or last element in the list to change.

As with the singly linked list, retrieving a specific data item
simply involves following the links until the proper element is
found.

There are three situations to consider when deleting an element from a doubly linked list: (1) deleting the first item, (2)
deleting an item from the middle, and (3) deleting the last item.
Figure 2-10 shows how the links are rearranged.

The following function will delete an item of type **address**
from a doubly linked list:

```
void dldelete(
  struct address *i, /* item to delete */
  struct address **start,  /* first item */
  struct address **last)  /* last item */
```

```
{
  if(i->prior) i->prior->next = i->next;
  else { /* new first item */
    *start = i->next;
    if(start) start->prior = '\0';
  }
  if(i->next) i->next->prior = i->prior;
  else   /* deleting last element */
    *last = i->prior;
}
```

This function requires one fewer pointer to be passed to it than the singly linked list version because the data item being deleted already carries a link to the previous and next elements. Again, because the first element in the list could change, the pointer to the top element is passed back to the calling routine.

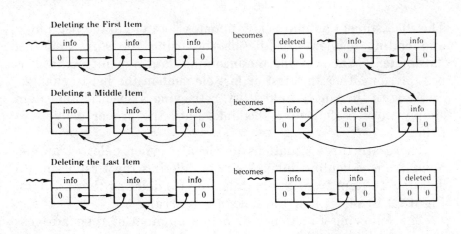

Figure 2-10.   Deleting an item from a doubly linked list

A Mailing List Example

A simple but complete mailing list program closes this section on doubly linked lists. The entire list is kept in memory while in use, but it can be stored in a disk file and loaded for later use.

```c
/* A simple mailing list program that illustrates the
   use and maintenance of doubly linked lists.
*/
#include <stdio.h>
#include <stdlib.h>
#include <alloc.h>
#include <string.h>

struct address {
  char name[30];
  char street[40];
  char city[20];
  char state[3];
  char zip[10]; /* hold US and Canadian zips */
  struct address *next;  /* pointer to next entry */
  struct address *prior;  /* pointer to previous record */
} list_entry;

struct address *start;  /* pointer to first entry in list */
struct address *last;  /* pointer to last entry */
struct address *find(char *);

void enter(void), search(void), save(void);
void load(void), list(void);
void delete(struct address **, struct address **);
void dls_store(struct address *i, struct address **start,
                         struct address **last);
void inputs(char *, char *, int), display(struct address *);

int menu_select(void);


main()
{

  start = last = NULL; /* initialize top and bottom pointers */
  for(;;) {
    switch(menu_select()) {
      case 1: enter();
        break;
      case 2: delete(&start, &last);
        break;
```

```
      case 3: list();
        break;
      case 4: search(); /* find a street */
        break;
      case 5: save();  /* save list to disk */
        break;
      case 6: load();  /* read from disk */
        break;
      case 7: return 0;
    }
  }
}

/* Select an operation. */
menu_select(void)
{
  char s[80];
  int c;

  printf("1. Enter a name\n");
  printf("2. Delete a name\n");
  printf("3. List the file\n");
  printf("4. Search\n");
  printf("5. Save the file\n");
  printf("6. Load the file\n");
  printf("7. Quit\n");
  do {
    printf("\nEnter your choice: ");
    gets(s);
    c = atoi(s);
  } while(c<0 || c>7);
  return c;
}

/* Enter names and addresses. */
void enter(void)
{
  struct address *info;

  for(;;) {
    info = (struct address *)malloc(sizeof(list_entry));
    if(!info) {
      printf("\nout of memory");
      return;
    }

    inputs("enter name: ", info->name,30);
    if(!info->name[0]) break;  /* stop entering */
    inputs("enter street: ", info->street,40);
    inputs("enter city: ", info->city,20);
    inputs("enter state: ", info->state,3);
    inputs("enter zip: ", info->zip,10);
```

```
      dls_store(info, &start, &last);
   } /* entry loop */
}


/* This function will input a string up to
   the length in count and will prevent
   the string from being overrun.  It will also
   display a prompting message. */
void inputs(char *prompt, char *s, int count)
{
  char p[255];

  do {
    printf(prompt);
    gets(p);
    if(strlen(p)>count) printf("\ntoo long\n");
  } while(strlen(p)>count);
  strcpy(s, p);
}


/* Create a doubly linked list in sorted order.
*/
void dls_store(
  struct address *i,    /* new element */
  struct address **start, /* first element in list */
  struct address **last /* last element in list */
)
{
  struct address *old, *p;

  if(*last==NULL) {   /* first element in list */
    i->next = NULL;
    i->prior = NULL;
    *last = i;
    *start = i;
    return;
   }

  p = *start; /* start at top of list */

  old = NULL;
  while(p) {
    if(strcmp(p->name, i->name)<0){
      old = p;
      p = p->next;
    }
    else {
      if(p->prior) {
        p->prior->next = i;
        i->next = p;
        i->prior = p->prior;
        p->prior = i;
```

```
            return;
        }
        i->next = p; /* new first element */
        i->prior = NULL;
        p->prior = i;
        *start = i;
        return;
    }
  }
  old->next = i; /* put on end */
  i->next = NULL;
  i->prior = old;
  *last = i;
}

/* Remove an element from the list. */
void delete(struct address **start, struct address **last)
{
  struct address *info, *find();
  char s[80];

  printf("enter name: ");
  gets(s);
  info = find(s);
  if(info) {
    if(*start==info) {
      *start=info->next;
      if(*start) (*start)->prior = NULL;
      else *last = NULL;
    }
    else {
      info->prior->next = info->next;
      if(info!=*last)
          info->next->prior = info->prior;
      else
        *last = info->prior;
    }
    free(info);  /* return memory to system */
  }
}

/* Find an address. */
struct address *find( char *name)
{
  struct address *info;

  info = start;
  while(info) {
    if(!strcmp(name, info->name)) return info;
    info = info->next;  /* get next address */
  }
```

```
    printf("name not found\n");
    return NULL;  /* not found */
}

/* Display the entire list. */
void list(void)
{
  struct address *info;

  info = start;
  while(info) {
    display(info);
    info = info->next;  /* get next address */
  }
  printf("\n\n");
}

/* This function actually prints the fields in each address. */
void display(struct address *info)
{
    printf("%s\n", info->name);
    printf("%s\n", info->street);
    printf("%s\n", info->city);
    printf("%s\n", info->state);
    printf("%s\n", info->zip);
    printf("\n\n");
}

/* Look for a name in the list. */
void search(void)
{
  char name[40];
  struct address *info, *find();

  printf("enter name to find: ");
  gets(name);
  info = find(name);
  if(!info) printf("not found\n");
  else display(info);
}

/* Save the file to disk. */
void save(void)
{
  struct address *info;

  FILE *fp;

  fp = fopen("mlist", "wb");
  if(!fp) {
```

```
      printf("cannot open file\n");
      exit(1);
   }
   printf("\nsaving file\n");

   info = start;
   while(info) {
     fwrite(info, sizeof(struct address), 1, fp);
     info = info->next;  /* get next address */
   }
   fclose(fp);
}

/* Load the address file. */
void load()
{
   struct address *info;
   FILE *fp;

   fp = fopen("mlist", "rb");
   if(!fp) {
     printf("cannot open file\n");
     exit(1);
   }

   /* free any previously allocated memory */
   while(start) {
     info = start->next;
     free(info);
     start = info;
   }

   /* reset top and bottom pointers */
   start = last = NULL;

   printf("\nloading file\n");
   while(!feof(fp)) {
     info = (struct address *) malloc(sizeof(struct address));
     if(!info) {
       printf("out of memory");
       return;
     }
     if(1!=fread(info, sizeof(struct address), 1, fp)) break;
     dls_store(info, &start, &last);
   }
   fclose(fp);
}
```

BINARY TREES

The final data structure examined in this chapter is the *binary tree*. Although there are many different types of trees, binary trees are special because when they are sorted they lend themselves to rapid searches, insertions, and deletions. Each item in a tree consists of information, a link to the left member, and a link to the right member. Figure 2-11 shows a small tree.

You need to know special terminology to discuss trees. Computer scientists are not known for their grammar, and the terminology for trees is a classic case of mixed metaphors! The *root* is the

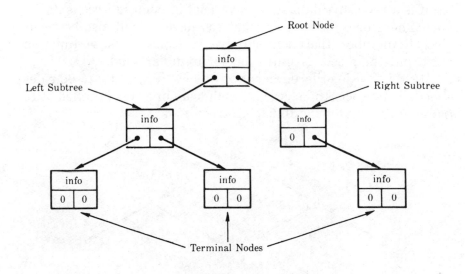

Figure 2-11.   A sample binary tree with a height of 3

first item in the tree. Each data item is called a *node* (sometimes called a *leaf*), and any piece of the tree is called a *subtree*. A node that has no subtrees attached to it is called a *terminal node*. The *height* of the tree is equal to the number of layers deep its roots grow. Throughout this discussion you will think of binary trees looking in memory the way they do on paper, but remember that a tree is only a way to structure data in memory, and memory is linear in form.

In a sense the binary tree is a special form of linked list. Items can be inserted, deleted, and accessed in any order, and the retrieval operation is nondestructive. Although trees are visually easy to understand, they present some very difficult programming problems of which this discussion will only scratch the surface.

Most functions that use trees are recursive because the tree itself is a recursive data structure. That is, each subtree is itself a tree. Therefore, the routines that you develop will also be recursive. Remember that nonrecursive versions of these functions exist, but their code is much harder to understand.

How a tree is ordered depends on how it is going to be referenced. The process of accessing each node in a tree is called a *tree traversal*. Consider the following tree:

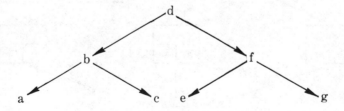

There are three ways to traverse a tree: *inorder*, *preorder*, and *postorder*. Using the inorder method, you visit the left subtree, the root, and then the right subtree. In preorder, you visit the root, the left subtree, and then the right subtree. With postorder, you visit the left subtree, the right subtree, and then the root. The order of access for the tree shown using each method is

inorder	a b c d e f g
preorder	d b a c f e g
postorder	a c b e g f d

Although a tree need not be sorted, most uses require it. Of course, what constitutes a sorted tree depends on how you will be traversing the tree. For the rest of this chapter, you will access the tree in inorder fashion. Therefore, a sorted binary tree is one where the subtree on the left contains nodes that are less than or equal to the root, while those on the right are greater than the root. The function **stree( )** will build a sorted binary tree.

```
struct tree *stree(
   struct tree *root,
   struct tree *r,
   char info)
{
   if(!r) {
     r = (struct tree *) malloc(sizeof(struct tree));
     if(!r) {
       printf("out of memory\n");
       exit(0);
     }
     r->left = NULL;
     r->right = NULL;
     r->info = info;
     if(!root) return r; /* first entry */
     if(info<root->info) root->left = r;
     else root->right = r;
     return r;
   }

   if(info<r->info) stree(r,r->left,info);
   else
       stree(r,r->right,info);
}
```

This algorithm simply follows the links through the tree, going left or right based on the **info** field. To use this function you need a global variable that holds the root of the tree. You must set this global to **NULL** initially and assign a pointer to the root on the first call to **stree( )**. Subsequent calls will not need to reassign the root. Assuming the name of this global is *rt*, to call the **stree( )** function you would use

```
/* call stree() */
if(!rt) rt=stree(rt, rt, info);
else stree(rt, rt, info);
```

In this way you can insert both the first and subsequent elements correctly.

stree( ) is a recursive algorithm, as are most tree routines. The same routine would be several times longer if you used straight iterative methods. You must call the function with a pointer to the root, the left or right node, and information. Although for the sake of clarity, only a character is used as the information, you could substitute any simple or complex data type you like.

To traverse the tree built using **stree( )** in inorder fashion, printing the **info** field of each node, you could use the function **inorder( )** shown here:

```
void inorder(struct tree *root)
{
  if(!root) return;

  inorder(root->left);
  printf("%c ", root->info);
  inorder(root->right);
}
```

This recursive function returns when your program encounters a terminal node (a null pointer). The functions to traverse the tree in preorder and postorder are shown here:

```
void preorder(struct tree *root)
{
  if(!root) return;

  printf("%c ", root->info);
  preorder(root->left);
  preorder(root->right);
}
```

```
void postorder(struct tree *root)
{
  if(!root) return;

  postorder(root->left);
  postorder(root->right);
  printf("%c ", root->info);
}
```

You can write a short but interesting program to build a sorted binary tree and print that tree sideways on the screen of your computer. To accomplish this you need to make only a small modification of the **inorder( )** function. The new function, called **print—tree( )**, which will print a tree in inorder fashion, is shown here:

```
void print_tree(struct tree *r, int l)
{
  int i;

  if(r==NULL) return;

  print_tree(r->left, l+1);
  for(i=0; i<l; ++i) printf("   ");
  printf("%c\n", r->info);
  print_tree(r->right, l+1);
}
```

The entire tree-printing program is given here. You should try entering various trees to see how each one is built.

```
/* This program displays a binary tree. */

#include <stdlib.h>
#include <stdio.h>

struct tree {
  char info;
  struct tree *left;
  struct tree *right;
};

struct tree *root;   /* first node in tree */
struct tree *stree(struct tree *root,
                   struct tree *r, char info);
void print_tree(struct tree *root, int l);

main()  /* printtree program */
{
```

```
  char s[80];

  root = NULL;  /* initialize the root */

  do {
    printf("enter a letter: ");
    gets(s);
    if(!root) root = stree(root, root, *s);
    else stree(root, root, *s);
  } while(*s);

  print tree(root, NULL);
  return 0;
}

struct tree *stree(
  struct tree *root,
  struct tree *r,
  char info)
{

  if(!r) {
    r = (struct tree *) malloc(sizeof(struct tree));
    if(!r) {
      printf("out of memory\n");
      exit(0);
    }
    r->left = NULL;
    r->right = NULL;
    r->info = info;
    if(!root) return r; /* first entry */
    if(info<root->info) root->left = r;
    else root->right = r;
    return r;
  }

  if(info<r->info) stree(r, r->left, info);
  else
    stree(r, r->right, info);
}

void print_tree(struct tree *r, int l)
{
  int i;

  if(!r) return;

  print_tree(r->left, l+1);
  for(i=0; i<l; ++i) printf("   ");
  printf("%c\n", r->info);
  print_tree(r->right, l+1);
}
```

You may not have thought about it, but this program is actually sorting the information you are giving it. This is essentially a variation on the insertion sort discussed in the previous chapter. For the average case its performance can be quite good, but the quicksort is still a better general-purpose sorting method because it uses less memory and has lower processing overhead. However, if you have to build a tree from scratch, or maintain an already sorted tree, you should always insert new entries in sorted order using the **stree( )** function.

If you have run the **Treeprint** program you have probably noticed that some trees are *balanced*—that is, each subtree is the same or nearly the same height as any other—and that others are very far out of balance. In fact, if you entered the tree **abcd**, it would have been built looking like this:

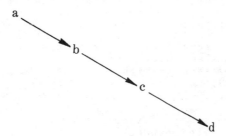

There would have been no left subtrees. This is called a *degenerate tree*, because it has degenerated into a linear list. If the data you are using as input to build a binary tree is fairly random, the tree produced will generally approximate a balanced tree. If the information is already sorted, however, the tree will be degenerate. (It is possible to readjust the tree with each insertion to keep the tree in balance, but the algorithms are fairly complex. Interested readers are referred to books on advanced programming algorithms.)

Search functions are easy to implement with binary trees. The following function returns a pointer to the node in the tree that matches the key; otherwise it returns null:

```
struct tree *search_tree(struct tree *root, char key)
{
  if(!root) return root;  /* empty tree */
  while(root->info!=key) {
    if(key<root->info) root = root->left;
    else root = root->right;
    if(root==NULL) break;
  }
  return root;
}
```

Unfortunately deleting a node from a tree is not as simple as searching the tree. The deleted node may be either the root, a left node, or a right node, and the node may have from zero to two subtrees attached to it. The process of rearranging the pointers lends itself to a recursive algorithm, as shown here:

```
struct tree *dtree(struct tree *root, char key)
{
  struct tree *p,*p2;

  if(root->info==key) { /* delete root */
    /* this means an empty tree */
    if(root->left==root->right){
      free(root);
      return NULL;
    }
    /* or if one subtree is null */
    else if(root->left==NULL) {
      p = root->right;
      free(root);
      return p;
    }
    else if(root->right==NULL) {
      p = root->left;
      free(root);
      return p;
    }
    /* or both tree present */
    else {
      p2 = root->right;
      p = root->right;
      while(p->left) p = p->left;
      p->left = root->left;
      free(root);
      return p2;
    }
  }
```

```
    if(root->info<key) root->right = dtree(root->right, key);
    else root->left = dtree(root->left, key);
    return root;
}
```

Remember to update the pointer to the root in the rest of your program's code; the node deleted could be the root of the tree.

Binary trees offer tremendous power, flexibility, and efficiency in database management programs because the information for the databases must reside on disk and access times are important. Because a balanced binary tree has, as a worst case, **$\log_2 n$** comparisons in searching, it is far better than a linked list, which must rely on a sequential search.

3

DYNAMIC ALLOCATION

Turbo C's dynamic allocation system has several uses. One is for creating variable length lists of information (in a database application, for example, as described in Chapter 2). Another is for supporting sparse arrays. A *sparse array* is one in which not all the elements of the array are actually present or necessary. You need to create an array like this when the array dimensions required by the application are larger than will fit in the memory of the machine, but not all array locations will actually be used. You should recall that arrays, especially multidimensional arrays, can consume vast quantities of memory because their storage needs are exponentially related to the number of dimensions. For example, a single-dimension, 100-character array needs only 100 bytes of memory; a 100×100, two-dimensional array needs 10,000; but a 100×100×100, three-dimensional array needs 1,000,000 bytes of memory—clearly too big for many computers. Dynamically allocated variables can also help you squeeze more performance out of a computer with limited RAM. Before exploring the ways that dynamic allocation can be used in your Turbo C programs, let's briefly review the dynamic allocation system.

THE TURBO C DYNAMIC
ALLOCATION SYSTEM

Before you can understand Turbo C's allocation system, you need to visualize how a program compiled by Turbo C organizes memory. Figure 3-1 shows conceptually how a program compiled by Turbo C appears in memory. (Although each of Turbo C's memory models organizes memory differently, the essence of this organization is correct.) The stack grows downward as it is used, so the amount of memory it needs is determined by how your program is designed. For example, a program with many recursive functions makes much greater demands on stack memory than one that does not have recursive functions because the former stores local variables on the stack. The memory required for the program and global data is fixed during the execution of the program. Memory to satisfy an allocation request is taken from the free memory area, starting just above the global variables and growing toward the stack. This region is called the heap. As you might guess, in fairly extreme cases the stack can run into allocated memory. (Or, if the program has been compiled for a large data model, the entire 64K segment used for the heap could become exhausted.) However, you can prevent this problem through a careful application of Turbo C's dynamic allocation functions.

malloc() and free()

Turbo C's dynamic allocation system contains several functions but the most important are **malloc()** and **free()**. These functions form the core of Turbo C's dynamic allocation system and are part of its standard library. They work together and use the heap to establish and maintain a list of available storage. Each time you make a memory request by using **malloc()**, a portion of the remaining free memory is allocated. Each time you call **free()** memory is returned to the system.

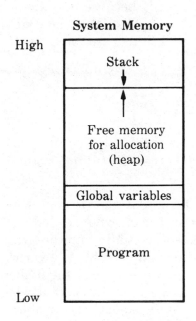

Figure 3-1.   A conceptual view of Turbo C's memory use

The **malloc( )** function has the prototype

void *malloc(unsigned *size*)

where *size* is the number of bytes you wish to allocate. If *size* bytes can be allocated, a pointer is returned to the first byte. Because **malloc( )** returns a **void** pointer, it can be assigned to any type of pointer. If there is not enough available memory to satisfy the **malloc( )** request, an allocation failure occurs and **malloc( )** returns **NULL**. It is very important to confirm that the pointer returned by **malloc( )** is valid before you use it. Simply put, using a null pointer on the left side of an assignment statement generally causes a system crash because you are overwriting some important memory locations. The following code shows the proper way to allocate memory, in this case for a **float**:

```
float *f;

f = malloc(sizeof(float));

if(!f) {
  printf("memory allocation error");
  exit(1);   /* or call error handling routine */
}
```

As the foregoing fragment shows, you should use **sizeof** to determine the exact number of bytes needed for the type of data you will be storing instead of adding up the bytes manually. This not only makes your program portable to a variety of systems but also makes it easier to maintain when the dynamically allocated object changes. This is especially important when you are using dynamic allocation to store structure variables. Because many computers require that data be aligned on even word boundaries, the actual size of a structure may be 1 or more bytes larger than the sum of the sizes of the individual fields.

The function **free( )** is the opposite of **malloc( )** because it returns previously allocated memory to the system. Once the memory has been released, it can be reused by a subsequent call to **malloc( )**. The **free( )** function is declared as

    free(void *p);

The only really important thing to remember is that you must *never* call **free( )** with an invalid argument. If an invalid argument is used the free list could be destroyed, which would stop the allocation system.

It is good programming practice to include the header file **stdlib.h** in any program that uses Turbo C's allocation system because it declares the allocation functions and ensures proper type checking.

Your program can determine approximately how much free memory is available for allocation by using Turbo C's **coreleft( )** function, which has the following prototype when used with small data models:

unsigned coreleft(void);

If you compile using a large data model, the function returns an **unsigned long.** Its prototype is found in **stdlib.h.**

The **coreleft( )** function returns only an approximation of the amount of free memory because it cannot predict a program's stack usage.

This program displays the amount of available free memory. It assumes that a small data model is used.

```
#include <stdlib.h>
#include <stdio.h>

main()
{
  printf("free RAM: %u", coreleft());
}
```

SPARSE ARRAY PROCESSING

Numerous applications require sparse array processing. Many are scientific and engineering problems that are easily understood only by people in those fields. However, one very familiar application commonly uses sparse arrays: a spreadsheet program. Even though the matrix of the average spreadsheet is very large, say 999 by 999, only a portion of that may actually be in use at one time. Spreadsheets use the matrix to hold formulas, values and strings associated with each location. The general idea behind a sparse array is that storage for each element is allocated from the pool of free memory as it is needed. Although only a small portion of the elements are actually in use, the array may appear larger than would normally fit in the memory of the computer.

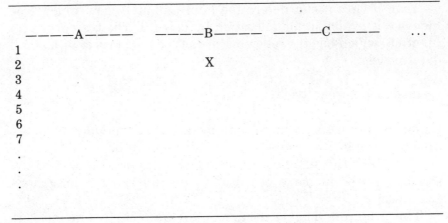

Figure 3-2.   The organization of a sample worksheet

The rest of this discussion will use the two terms *logical array* and *physical array* and the concept of a spreadsheet to illustrate sparse array processing. The logical array is the array that you think of as existing in the system. For example, the spreadsheet matrix is a logical array. The physical array is the array that actually exists inside the computer. It is the job of the sparse array support routines to link these two arrays.

There are four distinct techniques for creating a sparse array: the linked list, the binary tree, the pointer array, and hashing. All examples assume that the spreadsheet matrix is organized as shown in Figure 3-2, where the *X* is located in cell B2.

THE LINKED LIST
SPARSE ARRAY

When a sparse array is implemented by using a linked list, a structure is used to hold the information, its logical position in the array, and links to the previous and next elements. Each structure is placed in the list with the elements inserted in sorted order based on the array index. The array is accessed by following the links.

For example, this structure can be used as the basis for a sparse array to be used in a spreadsheet program:

```
struct cell {
  char cell_name[9];  /* cell name e.g., A1, B34 */
  char  formula[128]; /* info e.g.,. 10/B2 */
  struct cell *next;  /* pointer to next entry */
  struct cell *prior;  /* pointer to previous record */
} list_entry;
```

Here, the field **cell—name** holds a string that contains the cell name, such as A1, B34, Z19, and the like. The *formula* string holds the formula assigned to each spreadsheet location. While an entire spreadsheet program is far too large to use as an example, the key functions that support the linked list sparse array are examined here. Remember that there are many ways to implement a spreadsheet program; the data structure and routines used here are only examples of sparse array techniques. The following global variables point to the beginning and end of the linked array list:

```
struct cell *start;  /* first element in list */
struct cell *last;   /* last element in list */
```

When you enter a formula into a cell in most spreadsheets, you create a new element in the sparse array. If the spreadsheet uses a linked list, that new cell is inserted by using a function similar to **dls—store( )**, which was developed in Chapter 2. Remember that the list is sorted using the cell name; that is, A12 precedes A13, and so on.

```
/* Store cells in sorted order. */
void dls_store(struct cell *i,
               struct cell **start,
               struct cell **last)
{
  struct cell *old, *p;

  if(!*last) {  /* first element in list */
    i->next = NULL;
    i->prior = NULL;
```

```
    *last = i;
    *start = i;
    return;
}

p = *start; /* start at top of list */

old = NULL;
while(p) {
  if(strcmp(p->cell_name, i->cell_name)<0){
    old = p;
    p = p->next;
  }
  else { /* is a middle element */
    if(p->prior) {
      p->prior->next = i;
      i->next = p;
      i->prior = p->prior;
      p->prior = i;
      return;
    }
    i->next = p; /* new first element */
    i->prior = NULL;
    p->prior = i;
    *start = i;
    return;
  }
}
old->next = i; /* put on end */
i->next = NULL;
i->prior = old;
*last = i;
return;
}
```

To remove a cell from the spreadsheet you remove the proper structure from the list and return the memory to the system by using **free( )**. The **delete( )** function shown here will remove a cell from the list when given the cell's name.

```
void delete(char *cell_name,
            struct cell **start,
            struct cell **last)
{
  struct cell *info;

  info = find(cell_name, *start);
  if(info) {
```

```
    if(*start==info) {
      *start = info->next;
      if(*start) (*start)->prior = NULL;
      else *last = NULL;
    }
    else {
      if(info->prior) info->prior->next = info->next;
      if(info!=*last)
          info->next->prior = info->prior;
      else
        *last = info->prior;
    }
    free(info);  /* return memory to system */
  }
}
```

The final function needed to support a linked list sparse array is **find( )**, which will locate any specific cell. The **find( )** fuction requires a linear search to locate each item and, as you saw in Chapter 1, the average number of comparisons in a linear search is $n/2$, where n is the number of elements in the list. Here is **find( )**:

```
struct cell *find(char *cell_name,
                  struct cell *start)
{
  struct cell *info;

  info = start;
  while(info) {
    if(!strcmp(cell_name, info->cell_name)) return info;
    info = info->next;  /* get next cell */
  }
  printf("cell not found\n");
  return NULL;  /* not found */
}
```

To demonstrate these routines, you can use the following program, which lets you enter three cell names and then lets you find and delete them:

```
/* Demonstrate the linked list approach to sparse arrays. */
#include <stdlib.h>
#include <stdio.h>
#include <string.h>
```

```
struct cell {
  char cell_name[9];   /* cell name e.g., A1, B34 */
  char  formula[128]; /* info e.g.,. 10/B2 */
  struct cell *next;   /* pointer to next entry */
  struct cell *prior;  /* pointer to previous record */
} ;

struct cell *start;  /* first element in list */
struct cell *last;   /* last element in list */

void dls_store(struct cell *i,
               struct cell **start,
               struct cell **last);
void delete(char *cell_name,
            struct cell **start,
            struct cell **last);
struct cell *find(char *cell_name,
                  struct cell *start);

main()
{
  struct cell *info;
  int i;
  char s[80];

  start = last = NULL;

  for(i=0; i<3; i++) {
    info = malloc(sizeof(struct cell));
    if(!info) exit(1);  /* allocation failure */
    printf("Enter a legal cell name: ");
    gets(info->cell_name);
    dls_store(info, &start, &last);
  }

  /* examine and delete */
  for(;;) {
    printf("enter cell name (CR to quit): ");
    gets(s);
    if(!*s) break;
    info = find(s, start);
    if(info) {
      printf("is found, deleting...\n");
      delete(s, &start, &last);
    }
  }
  return 0;
}

/* Store cells in sorted order. */
void dls_store(struct cell *i,
               struct cell **start,
               struct cell **last)
```

```
{
  struct cell *old, *p;

  if(!*last) {   /* first element in list */
    i->next = NULL;
    i->prior = NULL;
    *last = i;
    *start = i;
    return;
  }

  p = *start; /* start at top of list */

  old = NULL;
  while(p) {
    if(strcmp(p->cell_name, i->cell_name)<0){
      old = p;
      p = p->next;
    }
    else { /* is a middle element */
      if(p->prior) {
        p->prior->next = i;
        i->next = p;
        i->prior = p->prior;
        p->prior = i;
        return;
      }
      i->next = p; /* new first element */
      i->prior = NULL;
      p->prior = i;
      *start = i;
      return;
    }
  }
  old->next = i; /* put on end */
  i->next = NULL;
  i->prior = old;
  *last = i;
  return;
}

void delete(char *cell_name,
            struct cell **start,
            struct cell **last)
{
  struct cell *info;

  info = find(cell_name, *start);
  if(info) {
    if(*start==info) {
      *start = info->next;

      if(*start) (*start)->prior = NULL;
      else *last = NULL;
```

```
    }
    else {
      if(info->prior) info->prior->next = info->next;
      if(info!=*last)
          info->next->prior = info->prior;
      else
        *last = info->prior;
    }
    free(info);   /* return memory to system */
  }
}

struct cell *find(char *cell_name,
                  struct cell *start)
{
  struct cell *info;

  info = start;
  while(info) {
    if(!strcmp(cell_name, info->cell_name)) return info;
    info = info->next;  /* get next cell */
  }
  printf("cell not found\n");
  return NULL;  /* not found */
}
```

Analysis of the Linked List Approach

The principal advantage of the linked list method is that it is very memory efficient. It has one major drawback, however; it must use a linear search to access each cell in the list. Without using additional information, which requires additional memory overhead, there is no way to perform a binary search to locate a cell. Even the store routine uses a linear search to find the proper place to insert a new cell in the list. These problems are solved by using a binary tree to support the sparse array.

THE BINARY TREE APPROACH TO SPARSE ARRAYS

In essence, the binary tree is simply a modified doubly linked list. Its major advantage over a list is that it can be searched quickly, so insertions and searches can be very fast. In applications where a linked list structure is desired but fast search times are also needed, the binary tree is perfect.

To use a binary tree to support the spreadsheet example, the structure **cell** must be changed as shown:

```
struct cell {
  char cell_name[9];  /* cell name e.g., A1, B34 */
  char  formula[128]; /* info e.g., 10/B2 */
  struct cell *left;   /* pointer to left subtree */
  struct cell *right;  /* pointer to right subtree */
} ;
```

You can modify the **stree( )** function from Chapter 2 to build a tree based on the cell name. Notice that it assumes that the parameter *new* is a pointer to a new entry in the tree.

```
struct cell *stree(
        struct cell *root,
        struct cell *r,
        struct cell *new)
{
  if(!r) {      /* first node in subtree */
    new->left = NULL;
    new->right = NULL;
    if(!root) return new;  /* first entry in tree */
    if(strcmp(new->cell_name, root->cell_name)<0)
      root->left = new;
    else
      root->right = new;
    return new;
  }

  if(strcmp(r->cell_name, new->cell_name)<=0)
    stree(r, r->right, new);
  else
    stree(r, r->left, new);

  return root;
}
```

The **stree( )** function must be called with a pointer to the root node for the first two parameters and a pointer to the new cell for the third. It will return a pointer to the root.

To delete a cell from the spreadsheet, you can modify the **dtree( )** function as shown here to accept the name of the cell as a key.

```
struct cell *dtree(
        struct cell *root,
        char *key)
{
   struct cell *p, *p2;

   if(!strcmp(root->cell_name, key)) { /* delete root */
     /* this means an empty tree */
     if(root->left==root->right){
       free(root);
       return NULL;
     }
     /* or if one subtree is null */
     else if(root->left==NULL) {
       p = root->right;
       free(root);
       return p;
     }
     else if(root->right==NULL) {
       p = root->left;
       free(root);
       return p;
     }
     /* or both tree present */
     else {
       p2 = root->right;
       p = root->right;
       while(p->left) p = p->left;
       p->left = root->left;
       free(root);
       return p2;
       }
     }
     if(strcmp(root->cell_name, key)<=0)
       root->right = dtree(root->right, key);
     else root->left = dtree(root->left, key);
     return root;
}
```

Finally, you can use a modified **search( )** function to locate any cell in the spreadsheet quickly, given its cell name.

```
struct cell *search_tree(
        struct cell *root,
        char *key)
{
   if(!root) return root;  /* empty tree */
   while(strcmp(root->cell_name, key)) {
```

```
     if(strcmp(root->cell_name, key)<=0)
       root = root->right;
     else root = root->left;
     if(root==NULL) break;
   }
   return root;
}
```

The following program demonstrates the use of the binary tree sparse array functions:

```
/* Demonstrate the binary tree sparse array functions. */
#include <stdlib.h>
#include <stdio.h>
#include <string.h>

struct cell {
  char cell_name[9];   /* cell name e.g., A1, B34 */
  char  formula[128]; /* info e.g., 10/B2 */
  struct cell *left;  /* pointer to left subtree */
  struct cell *right;  /* pointer to right subtree */
} ;

struct cell *root;


struct cell *stree(
        struct cell *root,
        struct cell *r,
        struct cell *new);
struct cell *dtree(
        struct cell *root,
        char *key);
struct cell *search_tree(
        struct cell *root,
        char *key);

main()
{
  struct cell *info;
  int i;
  char s[80];

  root = NULL;

  for(i=0; i<3; i++) {
    info = malloc(sizeof(struct cell));
    if(!info) exit(1);  /* allocation failure */
```

```
    printf("Enter a legal cell name: ");
    gets(info->cell_name);
    if(!root) root = stree(root, root, info);
    else stree(root, root, info);
  }

  /* examine and delete */
  for(;;) {
    printf("enter cell name (CR to quit): ");
    gets(s);
    if(!*s) break;
    info = search_tree(root, s);
    if(info) {
      printf("is found, deleting...\n");
      root = dtree(root, s);
    }
    else printf("not found\n");
  }
  return 0;
}

struct cell *stree(
        struct cell *root,
        struct cell *r,
        struct cell *new)
{
  if(!r) {     /* first node in subtree */
    new->left = NULL;
    new->right = NULL;
    if(!root) return new;  /* first entry in tree */
    if(strcmp(new->cell_name, root->cell_name)<0)
      root->left = new;
    else
      root->right = new;
    return new;
  }

  if(strcmp(r->cell_name, new->cell_name)<=0)
    stree(r, r->right, new);
  else
    stree(r, r->left, new);

  return root;
}

struct cell *dtree(
        struct cell *root,
        char *key)
{
```

```
        struct cell *p, *p2;

        if(!strcmp(root->cell_name, key)) { /* delete root */
          /* this means an empty tree */
          if(root->left==root->right){
            free(root);
            return NULL;
          }
          /* or if one subtree is null */
          else if(root->left==NULL) {
            p = root->right;
            free(root);
            return p;
          }
          else if(root->right==NULL) {
            p = root->left;
            free(root);
            return p;
          }
          /* or both tree present */
          else {
            p2 = root->right;
            p = root->right;
            while(p->left) p = p->left;
            p->left = root->left;
            free(root);
            return p2;
          }
        }
        if(strcmp(root->cell_name, key)<=0)
          root->right = dtree(root->right, key);
        else root->left = dtree(root->left, key);
        return root;
}

struct cell *search_tree(
          struct cell *root,
          char *key)
{
  if(!root) return root;  /* empty tree */
  while(strcmp(root->cell_name, key)) {
    if(strcmp(root->cell_name, key)<=0)
      root = root->right;
    else root = root->left;
    if(root==NULL) break;
  }
  return root;
}
```

Analysis of the Binary Tree Approach

The most important advantage of a binary tree over a linked list is that it accelerates insert and search times. Remember that a sequential search requires an average of $n/2$ comparisons, where n is the number of elements in the list, but a binary search requires only $\log_2 n$ comparisons. Moreover, the binary tree is as memory efficient as a doubly linked list. However, there is an even better alternative in some situations.

THE POINTER ARRAY APPROACH TO SPARSE ARRAYS

Suppose that the spreadsheet had the dimensions 26 by 100 (A1 through Z100), or 2600 elements total. In theory the following array of structures could be used to hold the spreadsheet entries:

```
struct cell {
  char cell_name[9];
  char  formula[128];
} list_entry[2600];    /* 2,600 cells */
```

The problem here is that 2600 times 137 (the raw size of the structure; some machines will require an even amount) requires 356,200 bytes of memory. This is too large for many systems. And on processors that use a segment architecture, such as the 8086, memory access to such a large array will be very slow because 32-bit pointers will be required. So this approach is often not practical. However, you could create an array of pointers to structures that would require significantly less permanent storage than an entire array but would offer superior performance over the linked list and binary tree methods. For example:

```
struct cell {
  char cell_name[9];
  char  formula[128];
} list_entry;

struct cell *sheet[2600]; /* array of 2,600 pointers */
```

Now you can use this smaller array to hold pointers to the information structures. As you make each entry, a pointer to the information is stored in the proper location in the array. Figure 3-3 shows how this might appear in memory, with the pointer array providing support for the sparse array.

Before the pointer array can be used, each element must first must be initialized to **NULL**, indicating that there is no entry in that location. The function that does this is

```
void init_sheet()
{
  register int t;

  for(t=0; t<2600; ++t) sheet[t] = NULL;
}
```

When the spreadsheet user enters a formula for a cell, the cell location, defined by its name, is used to produce an index for the pointer array *sheet*. The index is derived from the cell name by converting the name into a number, as shown here in **store( )**. When computing the index, **store( )** assumes that all cell names start with a capital letter and are followed by an integer (e.g., B34, C19).

```
void store(struct cell *i)
{
  int loc;
  char *p;

  /* compute location given point name */
  loc = (*(i->cell_name)-'A');
  p = &(i->cell_name[1]);
  loc += (atoi(p)-1) * 26;    /* WIDTH * rows */

  if(loc>=2600) {
```

```
    printf("cell out of bounds\n");
    return;
  }
  sheet[loc] = i; /* place pointer in the array */
}
```

Because each cell name is unique, each index is also unique. For example, the cell name B10 is transformed into $2+(9*26)$, or 236. If you compare this procedure to the linked list or binary tree versions, you will see how much shorter and simpler it is.

The **delete( )** function also becomes very short. Called with the index of the cell to remove, it simply changes the pointer to the element to zero and returns the memory to the system.

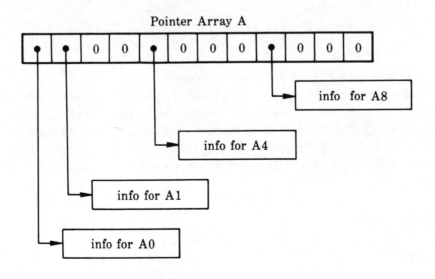

Figure 3-3. A pointer array as support for a sparse array

```
void delete(struct cell *i)
{
  int loc;
  char *p;

  /* compute location given point name */
  loc = (*(i->cell_name)-'A');
  p = &(i->cell_name[1]);
  loc += (atoi(p)-1) * 26;    /* WIDTH * rows */

  if(loc>=2600) {
    printf("cell out of bounds\n");
    return;
  }
  if(!sheet[loc]) return; /* don't free a null pointer */

  free(sheet[loc]);  /* return memory to system */
  sheet[loc] = NULL;
}
```

Compared to the linked list version, this code is much faster and simpler.

The process of locating a given cell is trivial because the cell name directly produces the array index; therefore, the **find( )** function becomes

```
struct cell *find(char *cell_name)
{
  int loc;
  char *p;

  /* compute location given name */
  loc = (*(cell_name)-'A');
  p = &(cell_name[1]);
  loc += (atoi(p)-1) * 26;    /* WIDTH * rows */

  if(loc>=2600 || !sheet[loc]) {  /* no entry in that cell */
    printf("cell not found\n");
    return NULL;  /* not found */
  }
  else return sheet[loc];
}
```

The following program demonstrates the pointer array method of supporting sparse arrays.

```c
/* Pointer array approach to sparse arrays. */
#include <stdlib.h>
#include <stdio.h>

struct cell {
  char cell_name[9];
  char  formula[128];
} ;

struct cell *sheet[2600]; /* array of 2,600 pointers */

void init_sheet(void);
void store(struct cell *i);
void delete(struct cell *i);
struct cell *find(char *cell_name);

main()
{
  struct cell *info;
  int i;
  char s[80];

  init_sheet();

  for(i=0; i<3; i++) {
    info = malloc(sizeof(struct cell));
    if(!info) exit(1);  /* allocation failure */
    printf("Enter a legal cell name: ");
    gets(info->cell_name);
    store(info);
  }

  /* examine and delete */
  for(;;) {
    printf("enter cell name (CR to quit): ");
    gets(s);
    if(!*s) break;
    info = find(s);
    if(info) {
      printf("is found, deleting...\n");
      delete(info);
    }
  }
  return 0;
}

void init_sheet(void)
{
  register int t;

  for(t=0; t<2600; ++t) sheet[t] = NULL;
}

void store(struct cell *i)
{
```

```
    int loc;
    char *p;

    /* compute location given point name */
    loc = (*(i->cell_name)-'A');
    p = &(i->cell_name[1]);
    loc += (atoi(p)-1) * 26;    /* WIDTH * rows */

    if(loc>=2600) {
      printf("cell out of bounds\n");
      return;
    }
    sheet[loc] = i; /* place pointer in the array */
 }


void delete(struct cell *i)
{
    int loc;
    char *p;

    /* compute location given point name */
    loc = (*(i->cell_name)-'A');
    p = &(i->cell_name[1]);
    loc += (atoi(p)-1) * 26;    /* WIDTH * rows */

    if(loc>=2600) {
      printf("cell out of bounds\n");
      return;
    }

  if(!sheet[loc]) return; /* don't free a null pointer */

  free(sheet[loc]);   /* return memory to system */
  sheet[loc] = NULL;
}


struct cell *find(char *cell_name)
{
    int loc;
    char *p;

    /* compute location given name */
    loc = (*(cell_name)-'A');
    p = &(cell_name[1]);
    loc += (atoi(p)-1) * 26;    /* WIDTH * rows */

    if(loc>=2600 || !sheet[loc]) { /* no entry in that cell */
      printf("cell not found\n");
      return NULL;  /* not found */
    }
    else return sheet[loc];
}
```

Analysis of the Pointer
Array Approach

The pointer array provides much faster accessing of array elements than either a linked list or binary tree. Unless the array is very sparse, the memory used by the pointer array is generally not a significant drain on the free memory of the system. However, remember that the pointer array itself uses some memory for every location, whether the pointers are pointing to actual information or not. This may be a serious limitation for certain applications, but generally it is not a problem.

HASHING

Hashing is the process of extracting the index of an array element directly from the information that will be stored there. The index generated is called the *hash*. Hashing has generally been applied to disk files to decrease access time. However, the same general methods can be used as a means of implementing sparse arrays. The procedure used with the foregoing pointer array example used a special form of hashing called *direct indexing*, in which each key maps onto only one array location. That is, each hashed index is unique. Note that the pointer array approach does not require a direct indexing hash; it was just an obvious approach given the spreadsheet problem. In actual practice, however, there are few such direct hashing schemes, and a more flexible method is required. In this section you will see how hashing can be generalized to allow greater power and flexibility.

If you think about the spreadsheet example, it is clear that even the most rigorous environments will not use every cell in the sheet. For the sake of this example, suppose that no more than 10 percent of the potential locations will be occupied by actual entries. This means that if the spreadsheet has the dimensions 26×100 (2600 locations), only about 260 will ever actually be used at one time. Therefore, the largest array necessary to hold all the entries will be only 260 elements in size. The problem then becomes: How do you map and access the logical array locations on this smaller physical array, and what happens when this array is full?

When the user enters a formula for a cell in the spreadsheet (the logical array), the cell location (defined by its name) is used to produce an index (a hash) into the smaller physical array, sometimes called the *primary array*. The index is derived from the cell name by converting the name into a number as was done in the pointer array example. However, this number is then divided by 10 to produce an initial entry point into the array. (Note that in this example the physical array is only 10% as big as the logical array.) If the location referenced by this index is free, the logical index and the value are stored there. However, since ten logical locations actually map onto one physical location, hash collisions can occur. When this happens, a linked list—sometimes called the *collision list*—is used to hold the entry. A separate collision list is associated with each entry in the primary array. Of course, these lists are zero length until a collision occurs. This situation is depicted in Figure 3-4.

To find an element in the physical array, a hashing program first transforms the element's logical array index into its hash value and checks the physical array at the index generated by the hash to see if the logical index stored there matches the one you want. If it does, the program returns the information. Otherwise it follows the collision list until either it finds the proper index or it reaches the end of the chain.

To understand how this procedure would actually be applied to the spreadsheet program you need to know the definitions of two array structures. The *primary* array is the one indexed by the hash algorithm. The *collision* array is used to hold the hash chain generated when collisions occur.

```
#define MAX 260

struct htype {
   int index; /* actual index */
   int val;  /* actual value of the array element */
   int next; /* index of next value with same hash */
} primary[MAX];
```

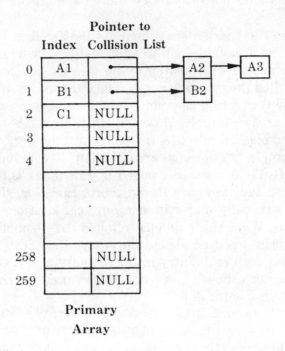

given entries in this order: A1
                            A2
                            B1
                            B2
                            A3
                            C1

Figure 3-4.   A hashing example

Before this array can be used, it must be initialized. The following function initializes the **index** field to −1, a value that by definition cannot be generated, to indicate an empty element. A **NULL** in the **next** field indicates the end of a hash chain.

```
/* Initialize the hash array. */
void init()
{
  register int i;

  for (i=0; i<MAX; i++) {
    primary[i].index = -1;
    primary[i].next = NULL;  /* null chain */
    primary[i].val = 0;
  }
}
```

The **store()** procedure converts a cell name into a hashed index to the primary array. Notice that if the location directly pointed to by the hashed value is occupied, it automatically adds the entry to the collision list by using a modified version of **slstore()**, developed in Chapter 2. It is necessary to store the logical index because it will be needed when you access that element again. These functions are shown here:

```
/* Compute hash and store value. */
void store(char *cell_name, int v)
{
  int h, loc;
  struct htype *p;

  /* produce the hash value */
  loc = *cell_name-'A';
  loc += (atoi(&cell_name[1])-1) * 26;  /* WIDTH * rows */
  h = loc/10;

  /* store in the location unless full or
     store there if logical indexes agree - i.e., update.
  */
  if(primary[h].index==-1 || primary[h].index==loc) {
    primary[h].index = loc;
    primary[h].val = v;
    return;
  }
```

```
/* otherwise, create or add to collision list */
p = malloc(sizeof(struct htype));
if(!p) {
  printf("out of memory\n");
  return;
}
p->index = loc;
p->val = v;
slstore(p, &primary[h]);
}

/* Add elements to the collision list. */
void slstore(struct htype *i,
             struct htype *start)
{
  struct htype *old, *p;

  old = start;
  /* find end of list */
  while(start) {
    old = start;
    start = start->next;
  }
  /* link in new entry */
  old->next = i;
  i->next = NULL;
}
```

To find the value of an element, your program first computes
the hash and then checks to see if the logical index stored in the
physical array matches that of the index of the requested logical
array. If it does, the program returns that value; otherwise, it
searches the collision chain. The **find( )** function, which performs
these tasks, is shown here:

```
/* Compute hash and return value. */
int find(char *cell_name)
{
  int h, loc;
  struct htype *p;

  /* produce the hash value */
  loc = *cell_name-'A';
  loc += (atoi(&cell_name[1])-1) * 26;   /* WIDTH * rows */
  h = loc/10;

  /* return the value if found */
  if(primary[h].index==loc)  return(primary[h].val);
  else { /* look in collision list */
```

```
    p = primary[h].next;
    while(p) {
      if(p->index == loc) return p->val;
      p = p->next;
    }
    printf("not in array\n");
    return -1;
  }
}
```

Try creating a deletion function as an exercise. *Hint:* Just reverse the insertion process.

The following program demonstrates the hash routines:

```
/* A simple hashing example. */
#include <stdlib.h>
#include <stdio.h>

#define MAX 260

struct htype {
  int index; /* actual index */
  int val;  /* actual value of the array element */
  struct htype *next; /* pointer to collision list */
} primary[MAX];

void init(void);
void store(char *cell_name, int v);
int find(char *cell_name);
void slstore(struct htype *i,
             struct htype *start);

main()
{
  int i, val;
  char s[80];

  for(i=0; i<3; i++) {
    printf("Enter a legal cell name: ");
    gets(s);
    printf("enter an integer value: ");
    scanf("%d%*c", &val);
    store(s, val);
  }

  /* examine */
  for(;;) {
    printf("enter cell name (CR to quit): ");
    gets(s);
```

```
      if(!*s) break;
      printf("value is: %d\n", find(s));
   }
   return 0;
}

/* Init the hash array. */
void init(void)
{
   register int i;

   for (i=0; i<MAX; i++) {
      primary[i].index = -1;
      primary[i].next = NULL;   /* null chain */
      primary[i].val = 0;
   }
}

/* Compute hash and store value. */
void store(char *cell_name, int v)
{
   int h, loc;
   struct htype *p;

   /* produce the hash value */
   loc = *cell_name-'A';
   loc += (atoi(&cell_name[1])-1) * 26;   /* WIDTH * rows */
   h = loc/10;

   /* store in the location unless full or
      store there if logical indexes agree - i.e., update.
   */
   if(primary[h].index==-1 || primary[h].index==loc) {
      primary[h].index = loc;
      primary[h].val = v;
      return;
   }

   /* otherwise, create or add to collision list */
   p = malloc(sizeof(struct htype));
   if(!p) {
      printf("out of memory\n");
      return;
   }
   p->index = loc;
   p->val = v;
   slstore(p, &primary[h]);
}

/* Compute hash and return value. */
int find(char *cell_name)
{
```

```
    int h, loc;
    struct htype *p;

    /* produce the hash value */
    loc = *cell_name-'A';
    loc += (atoi(&cell_name[1])-1) * 26;    /* WIDTH * rows */
    h = loc/10;

    /* return the value if found */
    if(primary[h].index==loc)  return(primary[h].val);
    else { /* look in collision list */
      p = primary[h].next;
      while(p) {
        if(p->index == loc) return p->val;
        p = p->next;
      }
      printf("not in array\n");
      return -1;
    }
}




/* Add elements to the collision list. */
void slstore(struct htype *i,
             struct htype *start)
{
  struct htype *old;

  old = start;
  /* find end of list */
  while(start) {
    old = start;
    start = start->next;
  }
  /* link in new entry */
  old->next = i;
  i->next = NULL;
}
```

Remember that the hashing algorithm used here is very simple. Generally a more complex method is used to provide a more even distribution of indexes in the primary array and avoid the creation of very long hash chains. The basic principle is the same, however.

Analysis of Hashing

In its best case each physical index created by the hash is unique, and access times approximate those of direct indexing. This means that no collision lists are created and all lookups are essentially direct accesses. However, this case is quite rare because it requires that the logical indexes be evenly distributed throughout the logical index space. In the worst case (also rare), a hashed scheme degenerates into a linked list. This can happen when the hashed values of the logical indexes are all the same. In the average case (the most likely) the hash method can access any specific element in a time equal to that of using a direct index plus some constant that is proportional to the average length of the hash chains. The most critical factor in using hashing to support a sparse array is to make sure that the hashing algorithm evenly spreads the physical index to avoid long collision lists.

CHOOSING AN APPROACH

When deciding whether to use a linked list, a binary tree, a pointer array, or hashing to implement a sparse array there are two main considerations: speed and memory efficiency.

When the array is very sparse, the most memory efficient approaches are the linked list and binary tree implementations because only the array elements that are actually in use have memory allocated to them. The links themselves require very little additional memory and generally have a negligible effect. The pointer array design requires that the entire pointer array exists even if some of its elements are not used. Not only must the entire pointer array fit in memory, but also enough memory must be left over for the application to use. This could be a serious problem for certain applications, but it may be no problem at all for others. Usually you can decide this issue by calculating the approximate amount of free memory and determining whether it is sufficient for your program. The hashing method lies somewhere between the pointer array and the linked list and binary tree approaches. Although it requires all of the physical array to exist even if it is not all used, hashing may still require less memory than a pointer array, which needs at least one pointer for each logical array location.

When the array is fairly full, the pointer array makes the best use of memory. Binary trees and linked lists need two pointers for each element, whereas the pointer array only needs one. For example, if a 1000-element array were full and the pointers were 2 bytes long, both the binary tree and the linked list would use 4000 bytes for pointers, but the pointer array would need only 2000. The hashing method "wastes" even more memory to support the array.

In terms of execution speed the pointer array is by far the fastest. Often, as in the spreadsheet example, there is an easy way to index the pointer array and link it with the sparse array elements. This makes accessing the elements of the sparse array nearly as fast as it would be if it were a normal array. The linked list version is very slow by comparison because it must use a linear search to locate each element. Even if extra information were added to allow faster accessing of elements, the linked list would be slower than the pointer array's direct accessing capability. The binary tree certainly speeds up the search time, but when compared with the pointer array's direct indexing capability it still seems sluggish. If the hashing algorithm is properly chosen, the hashing method can often beat the binary tree in access times, but it will never be faster than the pointer array approach.

The rule of thumb is to use a pointer array when possible because it is the fastest in terms of access time. But if memory use is critical, use the linked list or binary tree approach.

REUSABLE BUFFERS

When memory is scarce, dynamic allocation can be used in place of normal variables. For example, consider two processes, **A( )** and **B( )**, inside one program. Assume that **A( )** requires 60 percent of free memory, and that **B( )** needs 55 percent of free memory. If both **A( )** and **B( )** derive their storage needs from local variables, **A( )** cannot call **B( )**, and vice versa, because more than 100 percent of memory would be required. If **A( )** never calls **B( )**, there is no trouble. The problem arises when you want **A( )** to be able to call **B( )**! The only way this can occur is for both to use dynamic storage and to free their allocated memory before calling the other.

For example, imagine that there are 10,000 bytes of free memory left in a computer that is running a program with the following two functions in it:

```
A()
{
  char a[6000];
  .
  .
  .
  B();
  .
  .
  .
}

B()
{
  char b[5500];
  .
  .
  .
}
```

Here, **A( )** and **B( )** both have local variables requiring more than half the free memory. In this case there is no way that **B( )** can execute because there is not enough memory available to allocate the 5500 bytes needed for the local array *b*.

Such a situation is often insurmountable, but in certain specific instances, you can work around it. If **A( )** does not need to preserve the contents of the array a while **B( )** is executing, **A( )** and **B( )** can share the memory. The way to do this is to allocate **A( )** and **B( )**'s arrays dynamically. Then **A( )** could free the memory prior to the call to **B( )** and reallocate it later if needed. Here is the way the code would look:

```
A()
{
    char *a;

    s = malloc(6000);
    .
    .
    .
    free(s); /* free memory for B(*/
    B();
    s = malloc(6000);
    .
    .
    .
    free(s); /* all done */
}

B()
{
    char *b;

    b = malloc(5500);
    .
    .
    .
    free(5500);
}
```

Here only the pointer **a** is in existence while **B( )** is executing.

Although you will rarely need to do something like this, the technique is useful because it is often the only way around this type of problem.

THE "UNKNOWN MEMORY DILEMMA"

If you are a professional programmer, you almost certainly have faced the "unknown memory dilemma." This problem occurs when you write a program that has some aspect of its performance based on the amount of memory inside the computer running it. Examples of programs that exhibit this problem are spreadsheets, in-RAM mailing list programs, and sorts. For example, an in-memory sort that can handle 10,000 addresses in 256K may be able to sort only 5000 addresses in 128K. If this program is going to be used on computers of unknown memory sizes, you cannot use a fixed size array to hold the sort information because the program would not work on machines with small memory (the array would not fit), or it would not allow users with more memory to use their extra capacity. The solution to this problem is to use dynamic allocation to hold the information.

A text editing program illustrates the unknown memory dilemma and solution quite well. Many text editors do not have a fixed number of characters that they can hold, but use all the available memory to store the text you type in. As you enter each line, the program allocates storage and maintains a linked list. When you delete a line, the program returns memory to the system. One way to implement such a text editor would be to use the following structure for each line:

```
struct line {
  char text[81];
  int num;  /* line number of line */
  struct line *next;  /* pointer to next entry */
  struct line *prior;  /* pointer to previous record */
} ;

struct line *start;  /* pointer to first entry in list */
 truct line *last;  /* pointer to last entry */
```

For the sake of simplicity the editor always allocates enough memory for each line to be 80 characters long with a null termi-

nator. The element *num* will hold the line number for each line of
text. This allows you to use the standard sorted doubly linked list
storage function **dls—store( )** to create and maintain the text file
as a linked list.

The entire program for a simple text editor is shown below. It
supports only the insertion of lines (at any point based on the line
number specified) and the deletion of any line. You can also list
the text and store it in a disk file.

The general means of operation for the editor is based on a
sorted linked list of text lines. The sort key is the line number of
each line. This makes it possible to insert and delete text easily at
any point by specifying the starting line number. The only function that may not be intuitive is **patchup( )**. It renumbers the
element *num* for each line of text as needed when insertions or
deletions cause the line number to be changed.

The key point of this example is that the amount of text that
the editor can hold is directly based on the amount of free
memory in the user's system. Thus the editor automatically uses
additional memory without having to be reprogrammed. This is,
perhaps, the single most important reason to use dynamic allocation when faced with the unknown memory dilemma.

The program shown is very limited, but the basic text editing
support is solid and you might enjoy enhancing it to create a custom text editor.

```
/* A very simple editor that uses dynamic allocation. */

#include <stdio.h>
#include <stdlib.h>

struct line {
  char text[81];
  int num;                /* line number of line */
  struct line *next;      /* pointer to next entry */
  struct line *prior;     /* pointer to previous record */
} ;

struct line *start;  /* pointer to first entry in list */
struct line *last;   /* pointer to last entry */

struct line *dls_store(struct line *), *find(int);
```

```
int menu_select(void), enter(int);
void patchup(int, int), delete(void), list(void);
void save(char *), load(char *);

main(int argc, char *argv[])
{
   char s[80], choice, fname[80];
   int linenum=1;

   start = NULL; last = NULL; /* zero length list */

   if(argc==2) load(argv[1]); /* read file on command line */

   for(;;) {
       choice = menu_select();
       switch(choice) {
         case 1: printf("Enter line number: ");
           gets(s);
           linenum = atoi(s);
           enter(linenum);
           break;
         case 2: delete();
           break;
         case 3: list();
           break;
         case 4: printf("enter filename: ");
           gets(fname);
           save(fname);   /* write to disk */
           break;
         case 5: printf("enter filename: ");
           gets(fname);
           load(fname);   /* read from disk */
           break;
         case 6: return 0;
       }
   }
}

/* Select a menu option. */
menu_select(void)
{
   char s[80];
   int c;

   printf("1. Enter text\n");
   printf("2. Delete a line\n");
   printf("3. List the file\n");
   printf("4. Save the file\n");
   printf("5. Load the file\n");
   printf("6. Quit\n");
   do {
```

```
      printf("\nEnter your choice: ");
      gets(s);
      c = atoi(s);
   } while(c<0 || c>6);
   return c;
}

/* Enter text at the specified line number. */
enter(int linenum)
{
   struct line *info;

   for(;;) {
     info = malloc(sizeof(struct line));
     if(!info) {
       printf("\nout of memory");
       exit(1);
     }

     printf("%d : ", linenum);
     gets(info->text);
     info->num = linenum;
     if(*info->text) {
       if(find(linenum)) patchup(linenum, 1); /* fix up
                                       old line nums */
       if(*info->text) start = dls_store(info);
     }
     else break;
     linenum++;
   }
   return linenum;
}

/* When text is inserted into middle of file
   line numbers below it must be increased by one
   and those after deleted lines must be decreased
   by 1.
*/
void patchup(int n, int incr)
{
   struct line *i;

   i = find(n);

   while(i) {
     i->num = i->num+incr;
     i = i->next;
   }
}

/* Store in sorted order by line number. */
```

```
struct line *dls_store(struct line *i)
{
  struct line *old, *p;

  if(!last) {  /* first element in list */
    i->next = NULL;
    i->prior = NULL;
    last = i;
    return i;
  }

  p = start; /* start at top of list */

  old = NULL;
  while(p) {
    if(p->num < i->num){
      old = p;
      p = p->next;
    }
    else {
      if(p->prior) {
        p->prior->next = i;
        i->next = p;
        p->prior = i;
        return start;
      }
      i->next = p; /* new first element */
      i->prior = NULL;
      p->prior = i;
      return  i;
    }
  }
  old->next = i; /* put on end */
  i->next = NULL;
  i->prior = old;
  last = i;
  return start;
}

/* Delete a line. */
void delete(void)
{
  struct line *info;
  char s[80];
  int linenum;

  printf("enter line number ");
  gets(s);
  linenum = atoi(s);
```

```
    info = find(linenum);
      if(info) {
      if(start==info) {
        start = info->next;
        if(start) start->prior = NULL;
        else last = NULL;
      }
      else {
        info->prior->next = info->next;
        if(info!= last)
            info->next->prior = info->prior;
        else
          last = info->prior;
      }
      free(info);   /* return memory to system */
      patchup(linenum+1, -1); /* decrement line numbers */
    }
}

/* Find a line of text. */
struct line *find(int linenum)
{
  struct line *info;

  info = start;
  while(info) {
    if(linenum==info->num) return info;
    info = info->next;  /* get next address */
  }
  return NULL;  /* not found */
}

/* List the text. */
void list(void)
{
  struct line *info;

  info = start;

  while(info) {
    printf("%d: %s\n", info->num, info->text);
    info = info->next;  /* get next address */
  }
  printf("\n\n");
}

/* Save the file. */
void save(char *fname)
{
```

```
  struct line *info;
  char *p;

  FILE *fp;

  if((fp=fopen(fname, "wb"))==NULL) {
    printf("cannot open file\n");
    exit(1);
  }
  printf("\nsaving file\n");

  info = start;
  while(info) {
    p = info->text;  /* convert to char pointer */
    while(*p) putc(*p++, fp);  /* save byte at a time */
    putc('\r', fp);  /* terminator */
    putc('\n', fp);  /* terminator */
    info = info->next;  /* get next line */
  }
  fclose(fp);
}

/* Load the file. */
void load(char *fname)
{
  register int size, lnct;
  struct line *info, *temp;
  char *p;
  FILE *fp;

  if((fp=fopen(fname, "rb"))==NULL) {
    printf("cannot open file\n");
    return;
  }
  while(start) {   /* free any previous edit */
    temp = start;
    start = start->next;
    free(temp);
  }

  printf("\nloading file\n");

  size = sizeof(struct line);
  start = malloc(size);
  if(!start) {
    printf("out of memory\n");
    return;
  }
  info = start;
  p = info->text;  /* convert to char pointer */
  lnct = 1;
  while((*p=getc(fp))!=EOF) {
    p++;
    while((*p=getc(fp))!='\r') p++;
    getc(fp); /* throw away the \n */
```

```
  *p = '\0';
  info->num = lnct++;
  info->next = malloc(size); /* get memory for next */
  if(!info->next) {
    printf("out of memory\n");
    return;
  }
  info->prior = temp;
  temp = info;
  info = info->next;
  p = info->text;
}
temp->next = NULL;  /* last entry */
last = temp;
free(info);
start->prior = NULL;
fclose(fp);
}
```

FRAGMENTATION

Because **malloc( )** and **free( )** are not technically part of the C language, but part of the C library, their exact implementation varies from compiler to compiler. Even though Turbo C's dynamic allocation routines are very reliable, *fragmentation* of memory can occur under all implementations of **malloc( )** and **free( )**. Over time fragmentation can cause allocation requests to fail even though there is actually enough free memory to fill the request.

Fragmentation is essentially a situation in which pieces of free memory lie between pieces of allocated memory. Although this is often fine when one of the pieces of free memory is still large enough to fill allocation requests, it becomes a problem when the pieces are too little to fill a request by themselves, even though there would be sufficient memory if they were added together. Figure 3-5 shows how a sequence of calls to **malloc( )** and **free( )** can produce this situation.

You can avoid some types of fragmentation if the dynamic allocation functions combine adjacent regions of memory. For example, if memory regions A, B, C, and D were allocated, and then regions B and C were freed, in theory B and C could be combined because they are next to each other. If B and D were freed, how-

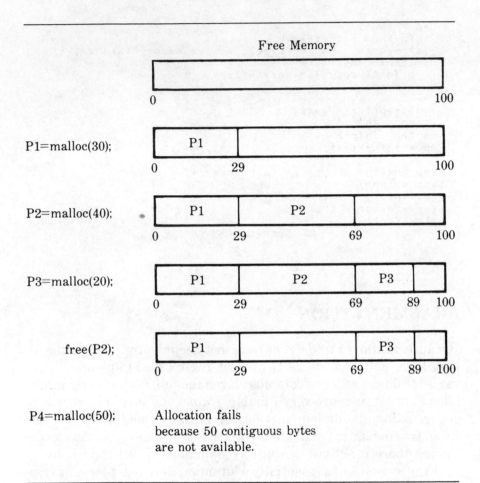

Figure 3-5. Fragmentation in dynamic allocation

ever, they could not be combined because C lies between them and is still in use.

You might be inclined to suggest moving C's contents to D and combining B and C. The trouble with this is that your program would have no way of knowing that what was in C had been moved to D!

Fragmentation is difficult to eliminate. Sometimes it is possible to pack several small requests into one large request to avoid developing very small fragments. Another solution is to write all the information out to a temporary disk file, free all memory, and then read the information back in. Freeing all of memory allows the allocation system to combine small pieces.

4

USING SYSTEM RESOURCES

As powerful as Turbo C is, there are times when you will want to bypass Turbo C's highest level functions and access the resources of both the operating system and the host environment directly. For example, you often need to use a specific device or operating system function in an unusual way, one not allowed by a standard library function. To achieve increased performance, you may sometimes need to bypass a standard library routine and directly manipulate a device or operating function yourself. For example, you can output text faster by using an operating system call than you can by using **printf( )**.

This chapter examines a number of special Turbo C functions that allow your programs to access the resources of your computer by executing BIOS or DOS functions. In most cases you will examine these services from two points of view. First, you will see how to access these resources directly, and then you will learn about some special Turbo C library functions that allow you to access the hardware of the computer. Using this approach will help you learn the full resources of your system and gain insight into some of Turbo C's more exotic library functions.

Each processor and operating system has its own methods of accessing system resources. The remainder of this chapter assumes you are using the DOS operating system and the 8086 family of processors. (The term *8086* is used in this chapter to include the 8088, 80186, 80286, and the 80386 running in 8086 emulation mode.) An explanation of the detailed workings of the 8086 processor is beyond the scope of this book, but the following will give you a brief overview.

THE 8086 FAMILY OF PROCESSORS

The 8086 family of processors contains 14 registers into which information is placed for processing or program control. The registers fall into the following categories:

- General-purpose registers
- Base pointer and index registers
- Segment registers
- Special-purpose registers

All the registers in the 8086 CPU are 16 bits (2 bytes) wide.

The *general-purpose registers* are the "workhorse" registers of the CPU. Values are placed in these registers for processing, including arithmetic operations, such as adding or multiplying; comparisons, such as equality, less than, and greater than; and branch (jump) instructions. Each of the general-purpose registers can be accessed as (1) a 16-bit register or (2) two 8-bit registers.

The *base pointer and index registers* are used to provide support for such things as relative addressing and block move instructions.

The *segment registers* are used to support the 8086's segmented memory scheme. The CS register holds the beginning address of the current code segment, the DS register holds the beginning address of the current data segment, the ES register holds the beginning address of the extra segment, and the SS register holds the beginning address of the stack segment.

Finally, the *special-purpose registers* are the flag register, which holds the state of of the CPU, and the instruction pointer, which points to the next instruction for the CPU to execute.

Figure 4-1 shows the layout of the 8086 registers.

THE 8086 INTERRUPTS

An interrupt is a special type of instruction that halts the execution of the current program, saves the current state of the system on the stack, and then jumps to an interrupt-handling routine that is determined by the number of the interrupt. After the interrupt routine has finished, it performs an *interrupt return*, which causes the previously executing program to resume. There are two basic types of interrupts: those generated by hardware and those generated by software. It is the latter type that is of interest at this time.

The 8086 CPU allows a program to execute a software interrupt via the **INT** instruction. The number that follows the instruction determines the number of the interrupt. For example, **INT 21h** causes interrupt 21h to be executed. The number of the interrupt is used to find the proper interrupt handler. The 8086 reserves the first 1K of memory for use as an *interrupt vector table*. This table contains the addresses (in segment/offset form) of the interrupt handlers. Each address requires 4 bytes, so the 8086 supports 256 interrupt vectors. For example, the **INT 5** instruction tells the CPU to use the address found at the **5*4** byte in memory as the location of the interrupt routine. (**INT 5** calls the print screen utility.) This situation is depicted in Figure 4-2.

Many of the interrupts are used by either BIOS or DOS as a means of accessing various functions that are part of the operating system. Each interrupt is associated with a category of functions that it accesses, and these functions are determined by the value of the AH register. If additional information is needed, it is passed in the AL, BX, CX, and DX registers. The BIOS provides

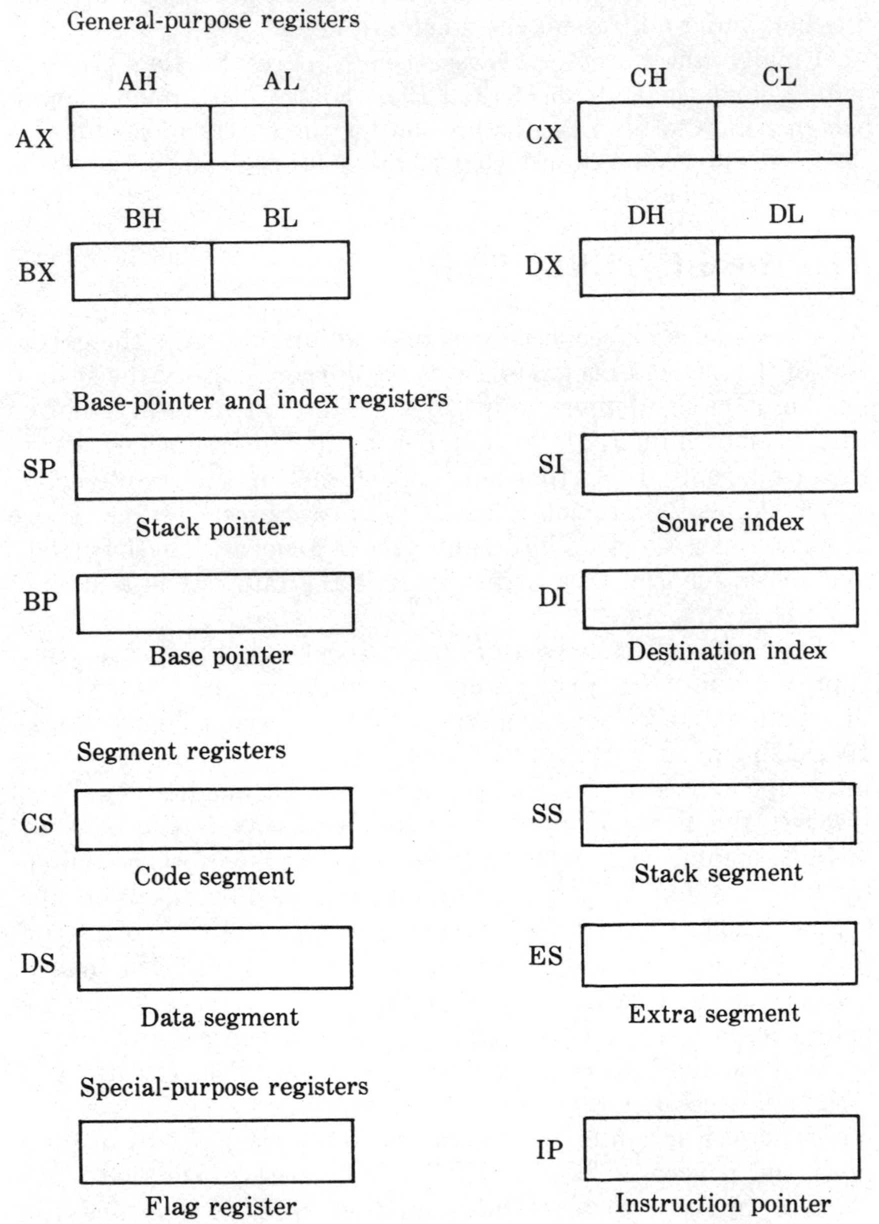

General-purpose registers

	AH	AL			CH	CL
AX				**CX**		

	BH	BL			DH	DL
BX				**DX**		

Base-pointer and index registers

SP

Stack pointer

BP

Base pointer

SI

Source index

DI

Destination index

Segment registers

CS

Code segment

DS

Data segment

SS

Stack segment

ES

Extra segment

Special-purpose registers

Flag register

IP

Instruction pointer

Figure 4-1.   The 8086 CPU registers

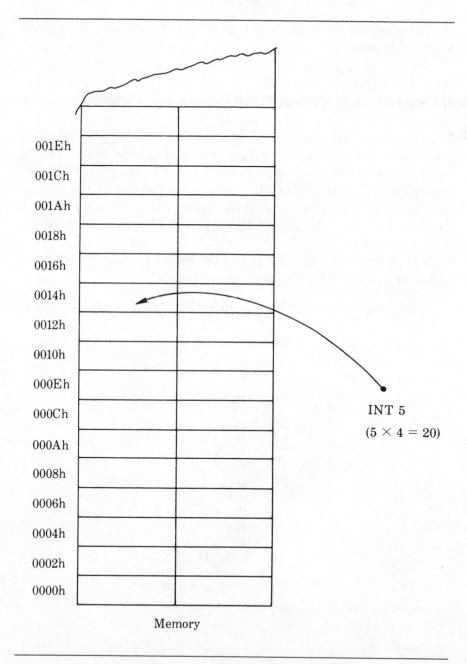

Figure 4-2.   The interrupt vector table for the 8086

the lowest-level routines, which DOS uses to provide the higher-level functions.

ACCESSING SYSTEM RESOURCES IN THE BIOS

The 12 BIOS interrupts are shown in Table 4-1. Many of these interrupts are associated with a number of options, which can be accessed depending on the value of the AH register when the interrupt is called. Table 4-2 shows a partial list of the options available for several of these interrupts. (For a complete list and explanation, refer to the *IBM Technical Reference Manual* for your computer.)

The Turbo C library routine called **int86( )** is used to execute a software interrupt. It has the prototype

int int86(int *intnum*, union REGS **in*, union REGS **out*)

Table 4-1.   ROM-BIOS Interrupts

Interrupt	Function
5h	Print screen utility
10h	Video I/O
11h	Equipment list
12h	Memory size
13h	Disk I/O
14h	Serial port I/O
15h	Cassette control
16h	Keyboard I/O
17h	Printer I/O
18h	Execute ROM BASIC
19h	Execute bootstrap loader
1Ah	Time and date

Table 4-2.   Common BIOS Routines

Video I/O Functions — Interrupt 10h

AH Register	Function
0	Set video mode
	AL: video mode (see Table 4-3)
1	Set cursor lines
	CH: start of line
	CL: end of line
2	Set cursor position
	DH: row
	DL: column
	BH: video page number
3	Read cursor position
	BH: video page number
	Returns:
	DH: row
	DL: column
	CH: start of cursor
	CL: end of cursor
4	Read light pen position
	Returns:
	if AH=0, pen not triggered
	if AH=1, pen triggered
	DH: row
	DL: column
	CH: raster line
	BX: pixel column
5	Set active video page
	AL may be 0-7
6	Scroll page up
	AL: number of lines to scroll, 0 for all
	CH: row of upper left corner of scroll
	CL: column of upper left corner of scroll
	DH: row of lower right corner of scroll
	DL: column of lower right corner of scroll
	BH: attribute to be used on blank line

Table 4-2. Common BIOS Routines (*continued*)

Video I/O Functions—Interrupt 10h

AH Register	Function
7	Scroll page down (same as 6)
8	Read character at cursor position 　BH: video page Returns: 　AL: character read 　AH: attribute
9	Write character and attribute at cursor position 　BH: video page 　BL: attribute 　CX: number of characters to write 　AL: character
Ah	Write character at current cursor position 　BH: video page 　BL: color attribute (graphics only) 　CX: number of characters to write 　AL: character
Bh	Set color palette 　BH: palette number 　BL: color
Ch	Write a pixel 　DX: row number 　CX: column number 　AL: color
Dh	Read a pixel 　DX: row number 　CX: column number Returns: 　AL: color
Eh	Write character to screen and advance cursor 　AL: character

---

Table 4-2.   Common BIOS Routines (*continued*)

Video I/O Functions—Interrupt 10h

AH Register	Function
	BL: foreground color
	BH: video page
Fh	Read video state
	Returns:
	AL: current mode
	AH: number of columns on screen
	BH: current active video page

Equipment List—Interrupt 11h

AH Register	Function
—	Read equipment list
	Returns:
	AX: list of equipment installed
	bit 0: 1 if diskettes present
	bit 1: 1 if 8087/80287 installed
	bits 2,3: system board RAM, 11=64K
	bits 4,5: initial video mode, 10=80 column color, 11=monochrome, 01=40 column
	bits 6,7: number of disk drives, 0=1
	bit 8: DMA chip installed if 0
	bits 9,10,11: number of RS-232 ports
	bit 12: 1=game adapter installed
	bit 13: 1=serial printer (PCjr only)
	bits 14,15: number of printers

Memory Size—Interrupt 12h

AH Register	Function
-	Returns the number of kilobytes of RAM that are resident in the system
	Returns:
	AX: number of kilobytes of RAM

Table 4-2.   Common BIOS Routines (*continued*)

Disk I/O Functions—Interrupt 13h

AH Register	Function
0	Reset disk system
1	Read disk status
	Returns:
	AL: status (see *IBM Technical Reference Manual*)
2	Read sectors into memory
	DL: drive number
	DH: head number
	CH: track number
	CL: sector number
	AL: number of sectors to read
	ES:BX: address of buffer
	Returns:
	AL: number of sectors read
	AH: 0 on success; otherwise, status
3	Write sectors to disk
	(same as 2)
4	Verify
	(same as 2)
5	Format a track
	DL: drive number
	DH: head number
	CH: track number
	ES:BX: sector information

Keyboard I/O Functions—Interrupt 16h

AH Register	Function
0	Read scan code
	Returns:
	AH: position code
	AL: character code

Table 4-2.   Common BIOS Routines (*continued*)

Keyboard I/O Functions—Interrupt 16h

AH Register	Function
1	Get status of buffer
	Returns:
	ZF: if 1, then buffer empty
	if 0, then characters waiting with next char in
	AX as described above
2	Get status of keyboard
	AL: bit 0: 1 if right shift key pressed
	bit 1: 1 if left shift key pressed
	bit 2: 1 if CONTROL key pressed
	bit 3: 1 if ALT key pressed
	bit 4: 1 if SCROLL LOCK pressed
	bit 5: 1 if NUM LOCK pressed
	bit 6: 1 if CAPS LOCK pressed
	bit 7: 1 if Insert pressed

BIOS Printer I/O Functions—Interrupt 17h

AH Register	Function
0	Print a character
	AL: character
	DX: printer number
	Returns:
	AH: status
1	Initialize printer
	DX: printer number
	Returns:
	AH: status
2	Read status
	DX: printer number
	Returns:
	AH: status

where *intnum* is the number of the interrupt, *in* is a union containing the registers that will be used to pass information to the interrupt handlers, and *out* is the union that will hold any values returned by the interrupt routine. However, **int86( )** will also return the value of the AX register. The type **REGS** is supplied in the header **dos.h**, as shown here:

```
/*
        Copyright (c) Borland International Inc. 1987
        All Rights Reserved.
*/


struct WORDREGS
        {
        unsigned int     ax, bx, cx, dx, si, di, cflag;
        };

struct BYTEREGS
        {
        unsigned char    al, ah, bl, bh, cl, ch, dl, dh;
        };

union   REGS    {
        struct  WORDREGS x;
        struct  BYTEREGS h;
        };
```

As you can see, **REGS** is a union of two structures. Using the **WORDREGS** structure allows you to access the registers of the CPU as 16-bit quantities. **BYTEREGS** gives you access to the individual 8-bit registers.

The **int86( )** function is used in the examples in this section to access the various BIOS functions. The sections that follow examine a few of the more common BIOS functions. Many of the BIOS functions are available through parallel Turbo C library functions. When such an equivalent Turbo C function exists, it will also be discussed.

Changing the Screen Mode

Suppose that you wish to change the screen mode during the execution of a program. The IBM line of systems commonly supports 19 video modes (see Table 4-3).

By using the **int86( )** function you can create the function called **mode( )**, which will change the mode of the screen to the specified type:

```
#include <dos.h>

void mode(int mode_code)
{
  union REGS r;

  r.h.al = mode_code;
  r.h.ah = 0;
  int86(0x10, &r, &r);
}
```

Turbo C's library contains the function **initgraph( )**, which can also be used to set the screen mode (although it uses a substantially different approach). However, since graphics functions are the subject of Chapter 6, discussion of **initgraph( )** is deferred until then.

Clearing the Screen

It is easy to create a function that clears the screen by calling the BIOS interrupt 10h, function 6, as shown here:

```
#include <dos.h>

/* Clear the screen. */
void cls()
{
```

```
union REGS r;

r.h.ah=6; /* screen scroll code */
r.h.al=0; /* clear screen code */
r.h.ch=0; /* start row */
r.h.cl=0; /* start column */
r.h.dh=24; /* end row */
r.h.dl=79; /* end column */
r.h.bh=7;  /* blank line is blank */
int86(0x10, &r, &r);
}
```

The value placed in AL determines the number of lines to scroll the screen given the starting and ending coordinates. If AL is 0, however, the entire screen is erased. The BH register is used to determine the attribute of a blank line. This code used 7, which means that blank lines will be black.

Table 4-3.   Most Common Screen Modes Available for Various IMB PCs

Mode	Type	Dimensions	Adapters
0	text, b/w	40×25	CGA, EGA, VGA
1	text, 16 colors	40×25	CGA, EGA, VGA
2	text, b/w	80×25	CGA, EGA, VGA
3	text, 16 colors	80×25	CGA, EGA, VGA
4	graphics, 4 colors	320×200	CGA, EGA, VGA
5	graphics, 4 gray tones	320×200	CGA, EGA, VGA
6	graphics, b/w	640×200	CGA, EGA, VGA
7	text, b/w	80×25	monochrome
8	graphics, 16 colors	160×200	PCjr
9	graphics, 16 colors	320×200	PCjr
10	graphics, 4 colors PCjr, 16 colors EGA, VGA	640×200	PCjr, EGA, VGA
13	graphics, 16 colors	320×200	EGA, VGA
14	graphics, 16 colors	640×200	EGA, VGA
15	graphics, 4 colors	640×350	EGA, VGA
16	graphics, 16 colors	640×350	VGA
17	graphics, 2 colors	640×480	VGA
18	graphics, 16 colors	640×480	VGA
19	graphics, 256 colors	620×200	VGA

Turbo C's equivalent function is called **clrscr( )** and has the prototype

void clrscr(void);

Its prototype is in **conio.h.**

Cursor Positioning

Another useful function is **goto—xy( )**, which locates the cursor at the specified x and y coordinates. This function uses the BIOS interrupt 0x10, function 2, which places the cursor at the location specified by the DL and DH registers. The **goto—xy( )** function is shown here:

```
#include <dos.h>

/* Send the cursor to x,y. */
void goto_xy(int x, int y)
{
  union REGS r;

  r.h.ah=2; /* cursor addressing function */
  r.h.dl=y; /* column coordinate */
  r.h.dh=x; /* row coordinate */
  r.h.bh=0; /* video page */
  int86(0x10, &r, &r);
}
```

For the IBM PC, 0,0 is the upper left corner of the screen.

To see how this function works, try the following short program, which first clears the screen and then prints Xs diagonally across the screen:

```
/* Clear the screen and print Xs. */

#include <dos.h>
#include <stdio.h>
#include <stdlib.h>

void cls(void), goto_xy(int x, int y);

main()
```

```
{
  register int x,y;

  cls();
  for(x=0, y=0; x<25; x++, y+=3) {
    goto_xy(x,y);
    printf("X");
  }
  return 0;
}


/* clear the screen */
void cls(void)
{
  union REGS r;

  r.h.ah=6; /* screen scroll code */
  r.h.al=0; /* clear screen code */
  r.h.ch=0; /* start row */
  r.h.cl=0; /* start column */
  r.h.dh=24; /* end row */
  r.h.dl=79; /* end column */
  r.h.bh=7;  /* blank line is blank */
  int86(0x10, &r, &r);
}

/* Send the cursor to x,y. */
void goto_xy(int x, int y)
{
  union REGS r;

  r.h.ah=2; /* cursor addressing function */
  r.h.dl=y; /* column coordinate */
  r.h.dh=x; /* row coordinate */
  r.h.bh=0; /* video page */
  int86(0x10, &r, &r);
}
```

Turbo C's nearly equivalent function is called **gotoxy()**. Its prototype is

void gotoxy(int x, int y);

and its prototype is in **conio.h**. The only difference between the two versions is that **gotoxy()** uses the coordinates 1,1 as the upper left corner.

Using the Scan Codes from the PC Keyboard

One of the most frustrating experiences you will encounter while working with the IBM PC and its clones is trying to use the arrow keys (as well as INS, DEL, PGUP, PGDN, END, and HOME) and the function keys. The problem is that these keys do not return the normal 8-bit (1-byte) character the way the rest of the keyboard does. When you press a key on the IBM PC, you are actually generating a 2-byte (16-bit) value called a *scan code*. The scan code consists of two pieces: the low-order byte that contains the ASCII code for a normal key; and a high-order byte that contains the key's position on the keyboard. However, the character code for a special key is 0. This means that you must use the position code to determine which key was pressed. The standard input functions, such as **getch()**, do not return the position codes. Therefore, you need to use a special input function when your program must read the position codes.

The **get_key()** function calls interrupt 16h, which returns the scan code of any key that is pressed. After a call to interrupt 16h, function 0, the position code is in AH, and the character code is in AL. As shown here, the function returns these codes as an integer:

```
#include <dos.h>

/* Read the 16-bit scan code of a key. */
get_key(void)
{
  union REGS r;

  r.h.ah = 0;
  return int86(0x16, &r, &r);
}
```

The trick to using **get_key()** is that when you press a special key, the character code is 0. In this case you then decode the position code to determine which key was actually typed. To use **get_key()** for all keyboard input requires the calling routine to make decisions based on the contents of AH and AL. This short program illustrates one way to do this:

```
#include <dos.h>
#include <stdio.h>
#include <stdlib.h>

int get_key(void);

main()  /* scan code example */
{
  union scan {
    int c;
    char ch[2];
  } sc;

  do { /* read the keyboard */
    sc.c=get_key();
    if(sc.ch[0]==0)  /* is special key */
      printf("special key number %d",sc.ch[1]);
    else /* regular key */
      printf("%c",sc.ch[0]);
  } while(sc.ch[0]!='q');
  return 0;
}

/* Read the 16-bit scan code of a key. */
get_key(void)
{
  union REGS r;

  r.h.ah = 0;
  return int86(0x16, &r, &r);
}
```

Notice the use of **union** to allow the decoding of the two halves of the scan code returned by **get_key( )**.

There are basically two ways to decode a scan code. The first is to look in the *IBM Technical Reference Manual;* the other is to use the short program shown above and determine the values experimentally. The latter method is more fun! To help you get started, here are the scan codes for the arrow keys:

Left   75

Right   77

Up   72

Down   80

To integrate the special keys with the normal keys will require special input functions and bypassing the normal **gets( )**, **scanf( )**, and **getche( )** functions found in the library. This is unfortunate, but it is the only way. However, the reward is that your program will appear very professional and be much easier to use.

Turbo C provides a function similar to **get_key( )**. It is called **bioskey( )** and has the prototype

int bioskey(int *mode*);

where *mode* determines what **bioskey( )** returns. If *mode* is 0, **bioskey( )** returns the scan code for the key pressed with the low-order byte holding the character code and the high-order byte containing the position code. If *mode* is 1, **bioskey( )** returns true if a key has been pressed; false otherwise. If *mode* is 2, **bioskey( )** returns the status of the shift keys. They are encoded as shown here:

Bit	Meaning When Set
0	right shift key pressed
1	left shift key pressed
2	CONTROL key pressed
3	ALT key pressed
4	SCROLL LOCK on
5	NUM LOCK on
6	CAPS LOCK on
7	Insert on

The prototype for **bioskey( )** is in **bios.h**.

The following program uses **bioskey( )** to display the status of the various shift keys:

```
/* This program displays the status of the shift
   keys.
*/
#include <bios.h>
#include <stdio.h>
#include <stdlib.h>

main()
{
  struct shift {
    unsigned rightshift: 1;
```

```
    unsigned leftshift: 1;
    unsigned control: 1;
    unsigned alt: 1;
    unsigned scroll: 1;
    unsigned num: 1;
    unsigned caps: 1;
    unsigned insert: 1;
  };

  union {
    struct shift status;
    unsigned i;
  } key;

  key.i = bioskey(2);

  if(key.status.rightshift) printf("right shift\n");
  if(key.status.leftshift) printf("left shift\n");
  if(key.status.control) printf("control\n");
  if(key.status.alt) printf("alt\n");
  if(key.status.scroll) printf("scroll lock\n");
  if(key.status.num) printf("num lock\n");
  if(key.status.caps) printf("caps lock\n");
  if(key.status.insert) printf("insert\n");

  return 0;
}
```

Restarting the Computer

One of the more exotic BIOS interrupts is number 19H. When this interrupt occurs, it causes BIOS to activate the initial program load sequence; that is, it reboots the computer. You might want to use this in case a catastrophic error occurs—for example, if memory becomes corrupted—and you want to make sure that the system is left in a safe state. The following program causes the system to reboot:

```
#include <dos.h>

main()
{
  union REGS r;

  int86(0x19, &r, &r);
}
```

ACCESSING DOS RESOURCES

DOS contains various higher-level functions than those found, for the most part, in the BIOS routines (although there is some overlap). All the DOS functions are accessed through interrupt 21h using the AH register to pass the specific DOS function number requested. Table 4-4 shows a partial list of the DOS functions.

Although it is possible to access the DOS functions using **int86()** as you did for the BIOS functions, Turbo C includes a specific function for this purpose that is more convenient. The function is called **bdos()**. It is used to perform an interrupt 21h call to access DOS. The **bdos()** function is declared as

int bdos(int *fnum*, unsigned *Reg—DX*, unsigned *Reg—AL*)

where *fnum* is the number of the DOS function. The values of *Reg—DX* and *Reg—AL* are assigned to the DX and AL registers respectively. The function returns the value of the AX register. The prototype for **bdos()** is in **dos.h**.

Table 4-4.   High Level DOS Function Calls—Interrupt 21h (Partial List)

AH Register	Function
1	Read character from the keyboard Returns: AL: character
2	Display a character on the screen DL: character
3	Read a character from async port Returns: AL: character

Table 4-4.   High Level DOS Function Calls—Interrupt 21h (Partial List) *(continued)*

AH Register	Function
4	Write a character to async port DL: character
5	Print a character to list device DL: character
7	Read character from keyboard but do not display it Returns: AL: character
B	Check keyboard status Returns: AL: 0FFh if key struck; 0 otherwise
D	Reset disk
E	Set default drive DL: drive number (0=A, 1=B,...)
11	Search for filename DX: address of FCB Returns: AL: 0 if found, FFh if not with name in disk transfer address
12	Find next occurrence of filename (same as 11)
1A	Set disk transfer address DX: disk transfer address
2A	Get system date Returns: CX: year (1980-2099) DH: month (1-12) DL: day (1-31)
2B	Set system date CX: year (1980-2099) DH: month (1-12) DL: day (1-31)

Table 4-4. High Level DOS Function Calls—Interrupt 21h (Partial List) *(continued)*

AH Register	Function
2C	Get system time
	Returns:
	CH: hours (0-23)
	CL: minutes (0-59)
	DH: seconds (0-59)
	DL: hundredths of seconds (0-99)
2D	Set system time
	CH: hours (0-23)
	CL: minutes (0-59)
	DH: seconds (0-59)
	DL: hundredths of seconds (0-99)
30	Get DOS version number
	AH: minor number
	AL: major number

Displaying the DOS Version Number

It is sometimes useful for a program to know what version of DOS it is being run under. To accomplish this, you use the DOS function 30h, which returns both the major version number in AL and the minor version number in AH. The following program displays the current version of DOS:

```
#include <dos.h>
#include <stdio.h>
#include <stdlib.h>

main()
{

  int ver;
  int major, minor;
  ver = bdos(0x30, 0, 0);
  major = ver & 0xFF;
  minor = ver>>8;

  printf("DOS version %d.%d", major, minor);

  return 0;
}
```

Using the Printer

Using DOS function 5, you can easily create a function that sends characters to the printer. The short function **prints( )**, shown here, will print a null-terminated string to the printer:

```
#include <dos.h>

/* Send a string to the printer. */
void prints(char *s)
{
  while(*s) bdos(0x5, *s++, 0);
}
```

If you wish, you can also use Turbo C's **biosprint( )** library function to output to the printer, which uses a BIOS- rather than DOS-level printer output routine. It has the prototype

int biosprint(int *mode*, int *value*, int *port*);

where *mode* determines what **biosprint( )** does. If *mode* is 0, **biosprint( )** sends *value* to the printer; if *mode* is 1, it initializes the printer; and if *mode* is 2, it returns the printer's status. The value of *port* determines which printer is used, with 0 specifying LTP1, 1 specifying LPT2, and so on. The prototype of **biosprint( )** is in **bios.h**.

Reading and Writing the Serial Port

To access the serial port, use DOS function 3 to read a character and function 4 to write a character, as shown by the following functions:

```
#include <dos.h>

/* Send a character out the port. */
void put_async(char ch)
{
  bdos(0x4, ch, 0);
}

/* Return a character read from the port. */
char get_async()
{
  return((char) bdos(0x3, 0, 0));
}
```

Notice the use of the **char** cast to ensure that only the value in AL is passed to any calling routine. These functions automatically use the default serial port. If you change the port using the DOS MODE command, these functions automatically use the new port instead.

Turbo C includes a library function called **bioscom( )**, which can also be used to access the serial port using BIOS rather than DOS functions. It has the prototype

int bioscom(int *mode*, char *val*, int *port*);

where *mode* determines the operation of **bioscom( )** as shown here:

Mode	Function
0	Initializes the port
1	Transmits a byte
2	Receives a byte
3	Returns the status of the port

The serial port to be accessed is specified by *port* with 0 indicating COM1, 1 meaning COM2, and so on.

The prototype for **bioscom( )** is in **bios.h.**

Before using the serial port, you will probably want to initialize it to a setting other than the default setting given to it when DOS begins execution. When *mode* is 0, the value of *val* is used to initialize the port. Refer to the *Turbo C Reference Guide* for details on how to construct the proper initialization value.

Listing the Disk Directory

It is often useful for your program to be able to access the disk directory. For example, it might be valuable to confirm the existence of a certain file or to allow the user to choose a file from a list. It is possible to access the directory using DOS functions. However, it is much easier to use Turbo C's built-in directory functions **findfirst( )** and **findnext( )**, whose prototypes are

```
int findfirst(char *fname, struct ffblk *ptr, int attrib)
int findnext(struct ffblk *ptr);
```

The prototypes for **findfirst( )** and **findnext( )** are in **dir.h.** However, you will also need to include the **dos.h** header, which contains macros that can be used as values for *attrib*.

The **findfirst( )** function searches for the first filename that matches that pointed to by *fname*. The filename can include both a drive specifier and a pathname. The filename can also include the wild card characters * and ?. If a match is found, the structure pointed to by *ptr* is filled with information about the file.

The *ffblk* structure is defined as

```
struct ffblk {
  char ff_reserved[2];   /* used by DOS */
  char ff_attrib;        /* attribute of file */
  int ff_ftime;          /* creation time */
  int ff_fdate;          /* create date */
  long ff_fsize;         /* size in bytes */
  char ff_name[13];      /* filename */
};
```

The *attrib* parameter determines what type of file will be found by **findfirst( )**. If *attrib* is 0, all types of files that match the desired filename are acceptable. To cause a more selective search, *attrib* can be one of the following macros:

Macro	Meaning
FA—RDONLY	Read only file
FA—HIDDEN	Hidden file
FA—SYSTEM	System file
FA—LABEL	Volume label
FA—DIREC	Subdirectory
FA—ARCH	Archive bit set

The **findnext( )** function continues a search started by **findfirst( )** and uses the structure initialized by **findfirst( )**. Each time you call **findnext( )**, it returns information about another file that fits the specified filename.

Both the **findfirst( )** and **findnext( )** functions return 0 on success and −1 on failure.

It is possible to list the directory of a disk using **findfirst( )** and **findnext( )** using this process. First, call **findfirst( )** with *fname* pointing to the mask *.*. Next, repeatedly call **findnext( )** until it returns a −1. The following program illustrates this process. It displays the contents of the current directory along with the size of each file.

```
#include <dir.h>
#include <stdio.h>
```

```
main()
{
  struct ffblk f;
  register int done, i;

  done = findfirst("*.*", &f, 0);
  i = 1;
  while(!done) {
    if(!(i%4)) {
      printf("\n");
      i = 1;
    }
    printf("%14s %6ld", f.ff_name, f.ff_fsize);
    i++;
    done = findnext(&f);
  }

  return 0;
}
```

FINAL THOUGHTS ON USING SYSTEM RESOURCES

This chapter has only scratched the surface of what can be done through creative use of system resources. To fully integrate your program with the operating system, you will need to have access to information that describes all the functions in detail. You should also explore several of Turbo C's DOS and BIOS functions.

You should remember two things before using operating system functions:

1. They can make your program look and feel very professional. Bypassing some of Turbo C's built-in functions in favor of the operating system functions can create programs that run faster and use less memory, and you will have access to functions that are not available in Turbo C's library.

2. You create more trouble for yourself when you use the operating system functions instead of Turbo C's standard functions because your code is no longer portable. You may also become

dependent on specific versions of a given operating system, creating compatibility problems when distributing your program.

Having considered these factors, only you can decide when and if you should introduce machine and operating system dependencies into your programs.

5

INTERFACING WITH ASSEMBLY LANGUAGE ROUTINES

Although the subject of assembly language interfacing is covered in significant detail in the Turbo C user manual, it is such a difficult and confusing subject that it will be examined here from a different perspective.

As efficient and powerful as Turbo C is, there are times when you must write a routine using assembler. There are three reasons for this:

To increase speed and efficiency of the routine   Although Turbo C produces extremely fast, compact object code, no compiler will consistently create code that is as fast or compact as that written by an excellent programmer using assembler. In run-time–sensitive tasks, you will want to *hand optimize* various critical sections. You, the programmer, know what the code is actually doing, so you can often perform optimizations that the compiler cannot.

To perform some machine-specific function unavailable in Turbo C Certain instructions cannot be generated by the Turbo C compiler. For example, it is not possible to change data segments with a C instruction or perform an efficient rotate on a byte or word.

To use third-party routines Sometimes it is necessary to take purchased subroutine libraries (for things like graphics and floating point math) in object format because the developer will not sell the source code. Occasionally it is possible simply to link these routines with code compiled by your compiler; at other times you must write an interface module to correct any differences in the interface used by Turbo C and the routines you purchased.

A word of warning: The interfacing of Turbo C code with assembly code is definitely an advanced topic. This chapter is intended for readers who have some familiarity with assembly language programming. (This chapter will not teach you how to program in assembler; it assumes you know how.) If you are not in this category, you will still find the material interesting, but please do not try the examples! It is easy to do something slightly wrong and create a disaster, such as erasing your hard disk.

The examples in this chapter use the 8086/8088/80286 processor, assume a DOS environment, and require that you use the small (default) memory model. To try the examples in this chapter you must have a copy of Turbo Assembler (TASM) or Microsoft's MASM macro assembler program version 3.0 (or later).

There are two ways of combining assembly code routines with Turbo C. The first way involves the creation, assembly, and linkage of a separate assembly language routine with C functions. The second method uses the nonstandard extension called **asm**, which is added to Turbo C to embed inline assembly code instructions directly in C functions.

CALLING CONVENTIONS: AN OVERVIEW

Before beginning to work with assembly code routines you need to know something about the way Turbo C calls functions. A *calling convention* is the method that the implementers of a C compiler choose to pass information into functions and return values. The usual solutions use either the internal registers of the CPU or the system stack to pass information between functions. Generally C compilers use the stack to pass arguments to functions and registers to hold function return values. If an argument is one of the basic data types, the actual value is placed on the stack. If the argument is an array, its address is placed on the stack. When a C function begins execution, it retrieves its argument's values from the stack. Upon termination it passes back to the calling routine a return value in the register of the CPU. (Although in theory it could pass the return value on the stack, this is seldom done.)

In addition to defining the way to handle parameters and return values, the calling convention determines exactly what registers must be preserved and which ones you can use freely. Often a compiler produces object code that needs only a portion of the registers available in the processor. You must preserve the contents of the registers used by your compiler, generally by pushing their contents onto the stack before using them. Any other registers are generally free for your use.

When you write an assembly language module that must interface with code compiled by Turbo C, you must follow all the conventions that are defined and used by Turbo C. Otherwise you cannot hope to have assembly language routines correctly interfaced with your C code.

The Calling Conventions of Turbo C

In this section you will learn how Turbo C passes arguments to and returns values from a function. The section only examines the

default C parameter-passing method—not the optional **pascal**—
since the default method is by far the most common. Like most C
compilers, Turbo C passes arguments to functions on the stack.
The arguments are pushed onto the stack right to left. That is,
given the call

    func(*a*, *b*, *c*);

c is pushed first, then *b*, and finally *a*. Table 5-1 shows the number
of bytes occupied on the stack by each type.

    Upon entry into an assembly code procedure, you must save
the contents of the BP register on the stack and place the current
value of the stack pointer (SP) in BP. The only other registers that
you must preserve are SI and DI if your routine uses them.

    Your assembly language function must restore the value of BP,
SI, and DI and reset the stack pointer before returning.

Table 5-1.   The Number of Bytes on the Stack Required for Each
Data Type When Passed to a Function

Type	Number of Bytes
char	2
short	2
signed char	2
signed short	2
unsigned char	2
unsigned short	2
int	2
signed int	2
unsigned int	2
long	4
unsigned long	4
float	4
double	8
near pointer	2 (offset only)
far pointer	4 (segment and offset)

If your assembly language function returns a value, it is placed in the AX register if it is a 16-bit value. Otherwise it is returned according to Table 5-2.

CREATING AN ASSEMBLY CODE FUNCTION

The easiest way to learn to create assembly language functions is to see how Turbo C generates code by using the -S command-line compiler option. This option outputs an assembly language listing of the code that it generates. By examining this file you can learn a great deal, not only about how to interface to the compiler, but also about how Turbo C actually works.

Table 5-2.   Register Usage for Turbo C Return Values

Type	Register(s) and Meaning
char	AX
unsigned char	AX
short	AX
unsigned short	AX
int	AX
unsigned int	AX
long	Low-order word in AX High-order word in DX
unsigned long	Low-order word in AX High-order word in DX
float	Low-order word in AX High-order word in DX
double	Return on 8087 stack or at TOS in emulator
struct and union	Address to value
near pointer	AX
far pointer	Offset in AX, segment in DX

Remember that only the command-line version of Turbo C can produce an assembly code listing.

Let's begin with the following short program:

```
int add(int a, int b);

int sum;

main()
{
  sum = add(10, 20);
}

add(int a, int b)
{
  int t;

  t = a+b;
  return t;
}
```

The variable *sum* is intentionally declared as global so that you can see examples of both local and global data. If the program is called TEST, the following command line will create TEST.ASM:

     tcc -S test

The contents of TEST.ASM are shown here:

```
        ifndef  ??version
?debug  macro
        endm
        endif
        ?debug  S "test.c"
 _TEXT  segment byte public 'CODE'
 DGROUP group   _DATA,_BSS
        assume  cs:_TEXT,ds:DGROUP,ss:DGROUP
 _TEXT  ends
 _DATA  segment word public 'DATA'
 d@     label   byte
 d@w    label   word
 _DATA  ends
 _BSS   segment word public 'BSS'
 b@     label   byte
 b@w    label   word
        ?debug  C E909A32C1103792E63
 _BSS   ends
```

```
_TEXT      segment byte public 'CODE'
;          ?debug  L 6
_main      proc    near
;          ?debug  L 8
           mov     ax,20
           push    ax
           mov     ax,10
           push    ax
           call    near ptr _add
           pop     cx
           pop     cx
           mov     word ptr DGROUP:_sum,ax
@1:
;          ?debug  L 9
           ret
_main      endp
;          ?debug  L 11
_add       proc    near
           push    bp
           mov     bp,sp
           push    si
;          ?debug  L 15
           mov     si,word ptr [bp+4]
           add     si,word ptr [bp+6]
;          ?debug  L 16
           mov     ax,si
           jmp     short @2
@2:
;          ?debug  L 17
           pop     si
           pop     bp
           ret
_add       endp
_TEXT      ends
_BSS       segment word public 'BSS'
_sum       label   word
           db      2 dup (?)
_BSS       ends
           ?debug  C E9
_DATA      segment word public 'DATA'
s@         label   byte
_DATA      ends
_TEXT      segment byte public 'CODE'
_TEXT      ends
           public  _main
           public  _sum
           public  _add
           end
```

The program begins by establishing the various segments required by a Turbo C program. These will vary among the different memory models. (Remember that all examples in this chapter use the small memory model.) You can ignore the lines that begin with a question mark; these lines are for debugging purposes.

Notice that two bytes are allocated in the **_BSS** segment for the global variable *sum* near the end of the listing. The underscore in front of *sum* is added by the compiler to avoid confusion with any internal compiler names. It is added in front of all function and global variable names.

After the segments have been established, the program's code begins. In Turbo C the code segment is called **_TEXT**. The first thing that happens inside the **_main** procedure is that the two arguments to **_add** are pushed on the stack and **_add** is called as a **near** subroutine. It is **near** because you are using the small memory model. (For a large code model, the call would have to be **far**). Upon return from the **_add** function, the two **pop cx** instructions restore the stack to its original state. The next line moves the return value from **_add** into *sum*. Finally **_main** returns.

The function **_add** begins by saving SI and BP on the stack and then placing the value of SP into BP. At this point the stack looks like this:

a   Top of stack

b

BP

SI

The next three lines of code add the numbers together. Notice that Turbo C is using the register SI to hold the local variable *t*'s value. Even though the program did not specify that *t* should be a **register** type, Turbo C automatically made it one as part of its compiler optimizations. If the program had more than two register variables, space for them would be made on the stack. Finally the answer is placed in AX, BP and SI are popped, and **_add** returns. (The **jmp short** to label 2 is superfluous in this code and is generated as a side effect by Turbo C in this instance.)

You can assemble this assembly language file using TASM (or Microsoft's MASM), link it using the standard **tlink** utility, and run it. What is more interesting is that you can modify it to make it run faster but leave the C source code untouched. For example, you could remove the instructions that pushed and popped SI inside the **_add** function (because it is apparent that SI is not used elsewhere in the program), remove the unnecessary **jmp short** instruction, and then assemble the file. Doing this is called *hand optimization*.

Now that you have seen how Turbo C compiles functions, it is just a short step to writing your own assembly language functions. One of the easiest ways to do this is to let the compiler generate an assembly language skeleton for you. Once you have the skeleton, all you have to do is fill in the details. For example, let's say you need to create an assembly routine that multiplies two integers. To have the compiler generate a skeleton for this function, first create a file containing only this function:

```
mul(int a, int b)
{
}
```

Next compile it with the -S option to produce an assembly language file. The file will look like this:

```
          ifndef  ??version
?debug    macro
          endm
          endif
          ?debug  S "mul.c"
  _TEXT   segment byte public 'CODE'
DGROUP    group   _DATA, BSS
          assume  cs:_TEXT,ds:DGROUP,ss:DGROUP
  _TEXT   ends
  _DATA   segment word public 'DATA'
d@        label   byte
d@w       label   word
  _DATA   ends
```

```
_BSS        segment  word public 'BSS'
ba          label    byte
baw         label    word
            ?debug   C E986A32C110479312E63
_BSS        ends
_TEXT       segment  byte public 'CODE'
;           ?debug   L 2
_mul        proc     near
            push     bp
            mov      bp,sp
a1:
;           ?debug   L 4
            pop      bp
            ret
_mul        endp
_TEXT       ends
            ?debug   C E9
_DATA       segment  word public 'DATA'
sa          label    byte
_DATA       ends
_TEXT       segment  byte public 'CODE'
_TEXT       ends
            public   _mul
            end
```

In this skeleton the compiler has done all the work of defining the proper segments and setting up the stack and registers. All you have to do is fill in the details. The finished **mul( )** function is shown here:

```
            ifndef   ??version
?debug      macro
            endm
            endif
            ?debug   S "mul.c"
_TEXT       segment  byte public 'CODE'
DGROUP      group    _DATA,_BSS
            assume   cs:_TEXT,ds:DGROUP,ss:DGROUP
_TEXT       ends
_DATA       segment  word public 'DATA'
da          label    byte
daw         label    word
_DATA       ends
_BSS        segment  word public 'BSS'
ba          label    byte
baw         label    word
            ?debug   C E986A32C110479312E63
_BSS        ends
_TEXT       segment  byte public 'CODE'
;           ?debug   L 2
```

```
;  ******************************************
; this is added to let the C program know about _mul
        public  _mul
_mul    proc    near
        push    bp
        mov     bp,sp
;  ******************************************
; here is the code to multiply the numbers
        mov     ax,[bp+4]       ;a
        imul    word ptr [bp+6] ;b
;******************************************
a1:
;       ?debug  L 4
        pop     bp
        ret
_mul    endp
_TEXT   ends
        ?debug  C E9
_DATA   segment word public 'DATA'
sa      label   byte
_DATA   ends
_TEXT   segment byte public 'CODE'
_TEXT   ends
        public  _mul
        end
```

Once this file is assembled it can be linked to any C program that requires it. For example, this program will print the number 10 on the screen. (Remember to link in **mul( )**.)

```
#include <stdio.h>

main()
{
  printf("%d ", mul(2, 5));
}
```

An easy way to compile and link this program is to use the command-line version of Turbo C. Assuming the program is called TEST.C and the **_mul( )** function is in MUL.ASM, the following command line will compile TEST, assemble MUL, and link them together automatically. (For this to work, you must be using TASM.)

TCC TEST MUL.ASM

When you specify the .ASM extension, Turbo C automatically invokes TASM to assemble that file.

You should notice that a line has been added directly before the first instruction of the procedure _mul. It is the line **public _mul**. This statement tells the assembler that the identifier _mul should be made available to any routine that needs it. This enables the C program to call _mul. You have to do this with any function that you want to be able to call from a C program. If there is data that the C program must know about, it should also be made public. The rule is very simple. Place the names of procedures that you want public in the CODE segment and the names of variables in the DATA segment.

The opposite of **public** is **extrn**. You use **extrn** when you want to call a C function or access a variable defined in a C program from an assembly language function. In this case you must declare the objects your assembly language routine needs to be external using the **extrn** assembler command. The general form of the **extrn** statement is

extrn <*object*> : <*attribute*>

If *object* is a function, *attribute* can be either **near** or **far**. If you are using a small code model, use **near**; otherwise use **far**. For variables, *attribute* may be one of the following values:

Value	Size in Bytes
byte	1
word	2
dword	4
qword	8
tbyte	10

For example, if your assembler routine needed to access the global integer variable *count* and the function **search( )**, you would place these statements at the start of the assembly language file:

```
extrn _count : word
extrn _search : near
```

Remember that the name of any assembly language function or external data that will be called by a Turbo C program must have an underscore in front of it.

A slightly more challenging situation arises when pointers are passed to a function. In this case accessing and altering the value of the argument requires indirect addressing methods. For example, assume that you need to create an assembly language function that negates the integer pointed to by the argument to the function. Assuming that this function is called **neg( )**, the following fragment will print the number −10 on the screen:

```
x = 10;

neg(&x);

printf("%d", x);  /* prints -10 */
```

In C the function would look like this:

```
neg(int *a)
{
  *a = -*a;
}
```

Turbo C generates the following assembly code for the **neg( )** function. (Remember that this assumes you are using the small data model.)

```
            ifndef  ??version
?debug      macro
            endm
            endif
            ?debug  S "neg.c"
  _TEXT     segment byte public 'CODE'
DGROUP      group   _DATA, BSS
            assume  cs:_TEXT,ds:DGROUP,ss:DGROUP
  _TEXT     ends
  _DATA     segment word public 'DATA'
da          label   byte
```

```
d@w         label    word
_DATA       ends
_BSS        segment  word public 'BSS'
b@          label    byte
b@w         label    word
            ?debug   C E90CA42C110479332E63
_BSS        ends
_TEXT       segment  byte public 'CODE'
;           ?debug   L 2
_neg        proc     near
            push     bp
            mov      bp,sp
;           ?debug   L 4
            mov      bx,word ptr [bp+4]
            mov      ax,word ptr [bx]
            neg      ax
            mov      bx,word ptr [bp+4]
            mov      word ptr [bx],ax
@1:
;           ?debug   L 5
            pop      bp
            ret
_neg        endp
_TEXT       ends
            ?debug   C E9
_DATA       segment  word public 'DATA'
s@          label    byte
_DATA       ends
_TEXT       segment  byte public 'CODE'
_TEXT       ends
            public   _neg
            end
```

The key lines of code (with comments added by the author) are

```
mov     bx,word ptr [bp+4]   ; get the address
mov     ax,word ptr[bx]      ; load the arg
neg     ax                   ; negate it
mov     bx,word ptr [bp+4]   ; redundant
mov     word ptr [bx],ax     ; store it
```

First, the address of the argument is loaded from the stack. Next, the relative addressing mode of the 8086 is used to load the integer to be negated. The **neg** instruction reverses the sign. The next instruction, which reloads BX, is technically unnecessary because BX is unchanged in this short program. (You can remove this line as a hand optimization.) The last instruction places the value back at the location pointed to by BX.

The best way to learn more about interfacing assembly language code with your C programs is to write short functions in C that do something like what you want the assembly language version to do and to use the assembly language compiler option to create an assembly language file. Most of the time you simply have to hand optimize this code instead of actually creating an assembly language routine from the ground up. It is quite easy to use assembly language functions along with your Turbo C code if you follow the rules precisely.

USING asm

Although not supported by the proposed ANSI standard, Turbo C has added the keyword **asm**, which allows inline assembly code to be made part of a C program without using a completely separate assembly language module. There are two advantages to this:

1. You are not required to write and maintain all the interface code.
2. All the code is in "one place," making support a little easier.

There is one drawback, however: **asm** is supported only by the command-line version of Turbo C.

To put inline assembly code in a Turbo C function you simply place the keyword **asm** at the beginning of each line of assembly code and then enter the assembly language statement. All code that follows the **asm** must be correct assembly code for your computer. Turbo C simply passes this code untouched to the assembler phase of the compiler.

A very simple example of inline assembly code is shown here. It is used to output information to a port, presumably for initialization purposes.

```
init_port1()
{
  printf("Initializing Port\n");
asm       out 26,255
asm       out 26,0
}
```

Here Turbo C automatically provides the code to save registers and return from the function. Notice that **asm** statements are not terminated by a semicolon; an assembly language statement is terminated by the end of the line.

To compile a program that contains one or more **asm** statements you must use TASM (or MASM) to assemble the assembly code. You should also specify the -B compiler option, which tells Turbo C that the file contains assembly code. This option prevents having to restart the compilation.

You could use inline assembly code to create **mul( )** (see the previous section) without actually creating a separate assembly language file. Using this approach, the code for **mul( )** is

```
mul(int a, int b)
{
asm     mov ax,word ptr 4[bp]
asm     imul word ptr 6[bp]
}
```

Remember that Turbo C provides all customary support for setting up and returning from a function call. All you have to do is provide the body of the function and follow the calling conventions to access the arguments. Although the use of a nonstandard feature certainly reduces portability, the use of assembly code probably reduces it more. So the use of **asm** can be recommended, especially for short assembly code fragments.

If you wish to place comments in **asm** statements you *must use* the standard C /* and */ methods. Do not use the semicolon convention used by most assemblers; it would confuse Turbo C.

Assembly code statements found inside a function are placed in the CODE segment. Those found outside a function are placed in the DATA segment.

Remember that whatever method you use, you are creating machine dependencies that will make your program difficult to port to a new machine. For the demanding situations that require assembly code, however, it is usually worth the effort.

USING __emit__()

A feature new to version 2.00 of Turbo C is the __emit__() function, which is used to insert values directly into the object code at the point of the __emit__() function. It has the prototype

void __emit__(*value list*)

where *value list* is a comma-separated list of values to be put into the object code. The principal advantage of using __emit__() is that Turbo C does not check the validity of the values, so you can use it to embed anything you like into the object code. Moreover, it can be used in the integrated development environment and **asm** cannot. However, since **asm** is supported by the command-line version of Turbo C and Turbo C can link to assembly code modules, the use of __emit__() can be recommended in only the most unusual of circumstances. (Frankly, this is a fairly dangerous function to use unless you are really an expert at machine language programming.)

WHEN TO CODE IN ASSEMBLER

Because of the difficulty of coding in assembler most programmers do it only when absolutely necessary. The general rule is: Don't do it; it creates too many problems! With this warning in mind, there are two times when coding in assembler makes sense. The first is when there is absolutely no other way to do it—that is, when you have to interface directly with a hardware device that cannot be handled by using Turbo C (because it requires exact timing, for example) or you have to link third-party routines to your Turbo C code. The second time is when a C program's execution time must be reduced.

When it is necessary to speed up a program, you should carefully choose which functions to code in assembler. If you code the wrong ones, you will see very little speed increase. If you choose the right one, your program will fly! It is easy to determine which functions to recode by reviewing how your program runs. The functions used inside loops (such as floating point math packages) are generally the ones to program in assembler because they are executed repeatedly. Recoding a function used only once or twice will not speed up your program much, but recoding a function that is used several times will. For example, consider the following **main( )** function:

```
main()
{
  register int t;

  init();

  for(t=0; t<1000; ++t) {
    phase1();
    phase2();
    if(t==10) phase3();
  }

  byebye();
}
```

Clearly, recoding **init( )** and **byebye( )** will not measurably affect the speed of this program because they execute only once. However, both **phase1( )** and **phase2( )** are executed 1000 times and definitely have a major effect on the run time of this program. Because **phase3( )** is executed only once, it should not be recoded even though it is inside the loop.

With careful thought you can make major speed improvements to your program by recoding only a few functions in assembler. Remember that the greatest speed increases come from better algorithms, not hand-optimized assembly routines. You should consider assembly code only after you have optimized the underlying algorithm.

6

GRAPHICS

This chapter will explore several of the more advanced features of Turbo C's graphics package. Although the chapter briefly reviews the basic graphing commands, such as **line( )**, **circle( )**, and **rectangle( )**, you should already have a general understanding of Turbo C's approach to graphics.

One of the central themes of this chapter will be the creation of video adapter-independent graphics code. Because of the way Turbo C's graphics system operates, you can create graphics programs that will run correctly no matter what graphics adapter is in the system. The advantage of adapter-independent graphics routines is that you need only one version of your program, not one for each video adapter type.

A BRIEF REVIEW OF TURBO C'S CORE GRAPHICS FUNCTIONS

Before reviewing Turbo C's most basic graphics functions, it is important to understand that they operate through a *viewport*. The viewport is the area of the screen that receives graphics output. By default the entire screen is the active viewport, but your program can define other viewports. Most of the graphics functions operate relative to the viewport, not the screen. The upper left corner of a viewport is always location 0,0. The most common style of viewport clips output at its border, not allowing anything to be displayed beyond its boundary. Turbo C's graphics system does not consider clipped output an error.

It is important to remember that all of Turbo C's graphics functions are **far**. For this reason you must include the file **graphics.h** in any program that uses a graphics function.

Initializing the Graphics System

Before you can use any of the graphics functions you need to put the video adapter into one of the graphics modes by using the **initgraph( )** function, which has the prototype

```
void far initgraph(int far *driver, int far *mode,
                   char far *path);
```

The **initgraph( )** function loads into memory a graphics driver that corresponds to the number pointed to by *driver*. No graphics functions can operate without a graphics driver in memory. The *mode* parameter points to an integer that specifies the video mode used by the graphics functions. Finally, you can specify a path to the driver in the string pointed to by *path*. If you don't specify a path, the program searches the current working directory.

The graphics drivers are contained in .BGI files, which must be available on the system. To specify the driver, use its number or macroname (found in **graphics.h**). Valid *driver* values are

Macro	Equivalent
DETECT	0
CGA	1
MCGA	2
EGA	3
EGA64	4
EGAMONO	5
IBM8514	6

HERCMONO	7
ATT400	8
VGA	9
PC3270	10

When you use **DETECT**, **initgraph( )** automatically detects the type of video hardware present in the system, selects the video mode with the greatest resolution, and sets *driver* and *mode* to appropriate values.

If your program sets the *mode*, it must use one of the graphics modes shown in Table 6-1.

All the examples in this chapter use the autodetect feature. This allows the program to adjust automatically to any graphics environment.

To stop using a graphics video mode and return to a text mode, you use either **closegraph( )** or **restorecrtmode( )**. Their prototypes are

```
void far closegraph(void)
void far restorecrtmode(void)
```

You should use the **closegraph( )** function when your program is going to continue executing in text mode. This function frees memory used to hold fonts, drivers, and internal buffers and resets the video mode to what it was before the call to **initgraph( )**. If your program is going to switch between text and graphics modes, use **restorecrtmode( )**. It resets the video adapter to the mode it was in before the first call to **initgraph( )** but does not discard the fonts, drivers, or internal buffers. If your program is terminating, it really doesn't matter which function you use.

Determining the Graphics Environment

When you let Turbo C's graphics system set the video mode, your program needs some way to know about the environment. The **getviewsettings( )** function returns the viewport dimensions, and

Table 6-1.   The Turbo C Graphics Driver and Modes Macro

Driver	Mode	Value	Resolution
CGA	CGAC0	0	320×200
	CGAC1	1	320×200
	CGAC2	2	320×200
	CGAC3	3	320×200
	CGAHI	4	640×200
MCGA	MCGAC0	0	320×200
	MCGAC1	1	320×200
	MCGAC2	2	320×200
	MCGAC3	3	320×200
	MCGAMED	4	640×200
	MCGAHI	5	640×480
EGA	EGALO	0	640×200
	EGAHI	1	640×350
EGA64	EGA64LO	0	640×200
	EGA64HI	1	640×350
EGAMONO	EGAMONOHI	3	640×350
HERC	HERCMONOHI	0	720×348
ATT400	ATT400C0	0	320×200
	ATT400C1	1	320×200
	ATT400C2	2	320×200
	ATT400C3	3	320×200
	ATT400CMED	4	640×200
	ATT400CHI	5	640×400
VGA	VGALO	0	640×200
	VGAMED	1	640×350
	VGAHI	2	640×480
PC3270	PC3270HI	0	720×350
IBM8514	IBM8514LO	0	640×480
	IBM8514HI	1	1024×768

getmaxcolor( ) returns the number of colors allowed in the current video mode.

The prototype for **getviewsettings( )** is

void **far** getviewsettings(struct viewporttype far *info*)

The structure **viewporttype** is defined in **graphics.h** as shown here:

```
struct viewporttype {
  int left, top, right, bottom;
  int clipflag;
}
```

The fields **left, top, right,** and **bottom** hold the coordinates of the upper left and lower right corners of the viewport. When **clipflag** is 0, there is no clipping of output that overruns the viewport boundaries. When **clipflag** is other than 0, clipping is performed to prevent boundary overrun.

Different video modes allow a different number of colors. For example, CGA mode 4 allows four colors, but EGA/VGA mode 14 supports 16 colors. Your program must use **getmaxcolor()** to determine how many colors are available. Its prototype is

```
int far getmaxcolor(void);
```

The **getmaxcolor()** function returns the largest valid color value for the current video mode. In all modes the first color is 0, the second is 1, and so on to the limit supported by the current video mode. Knowing the maximum color number means that you know all the available colors.

A correctly written graphics program should use the values returned by **getviewsettings()** and **getmaxcolor()** to allow the program to adjust automatically to different video modes instead of hard-coding these values.

The Basic Plotting Functions

The most fundamental graphing functions are those that draw a point, a line, and a circle. In Turbo C these functions are called **putpixel()**, **line()**, and **circle()**, respectively. Their prototypes are as follows:

```
void far putpixel(int x, int y, int color);
void far line(int startx, int starty, int endx, int endy);
void far circle(int x, int y, int radius);
```

The **putpixel( )** function writes the specified color to the location determined by x and y.

The **line( )** function draws a line from the location specified by *startx*, *starty* to the location specified by *endx*, *endy* in the current drawing color. The default drawing color is white.

The **circle( )** function draws a circle of radius *radius* in the current drawing color with the center at the location specified by x, y.

If any of the coordinates are out of range, no action is taken.

Setting the Drawing Color

You can set the current drawing color by using **setcolor( )**, whose prototype is

```
void far setcolor(int color);
```

The value of *color* must be in the range valid for the current graphics mode. Once the color has been changed, subsequent write operations take place in the new color.

Filling an Area

You can fill any enclosed shape using the **floodfill( )** function. Its prototype is

```
void far floodfill(int x, int y, int bordercolor);
```

To use this function to fill an enclosed shape, call it with the coordinates of a point inside the shape and the color of the lines that make up the shape (its border). Make sure that the object you are filling is completely enclosed. If it isn't, area outside the shape will get filled as well. What the object is filled with is determined by the current fill pattern and fill color. By default, Turbo C uses the background color, but you can change the way objects are filled by using **setfillstyle( )**, whose prototype is

void far setfillstyle(int *pattern*, int *color*);

The values for *pattern* and their macro equivalents (defined in **graphics.h**) appear in Table 6-2.

Now that you have reviewed Turbo C's basic graphics functions, it is time to explore some of its more advanced ones.

CREATING PIE GRAPHS

One of Turbo C's most powerful graphics functions is **pieslice( )**, which displays a slice of a pie graph in the current fill color and style and has the prototype

void far pieslice(int x, int y, int *start*, int *end*,
int *radius*);

Table 6-2.   The Fill Patterns

Macro	Value	Meaning
EMPTY_FILL	0	Fill with background color
SOLID_FILL	1	Fill with solid color
LINE_FILL	2	Fill with lines
LTSLASH_FILL	3	Fill with light slashes
SLASH_FILL	4	Fill with slashes
BKSLASH_FILL	5	Fill with backslashes
LTBKSLASH_FILL	6	Fill with light backslashes
XHATCH_FILL	8	Fill with hatching
INTERLEAVE_FILL	9	Fill with interleaving
WIDEDOT_FILL	10	Fill with widely spaced dots
CLOSEDOT_FILL	11	Fill with closely spaced dots
USER_FILL	12	Fill with custom pattern

Here, x and y specify in pixels the center of an imaginary circle from which a pie slice is cut. The beginning and end of the slice's arc are defined by *start* and *end*, which are specified in degrees, with 0 degrees being on the right horizontal. The radius of the slice is specified in pixels by *radius*.

The following program demonstrates the **pieslice( )** function. It prompts the user for the number of slices and inputs the size of each slice as an integer. It then computes a normalization factor that is used to transform the raw data into a proportional slice of the circle. Finally, it draws the pie chart centered on the screen, computing the beginning and end of each arc from the normalized data. This program will work for any graphics video mode.

```c
/* Construct pie charts from user entered data. */
#include <graphics.h>
#include <conio.h>
#include <stdio.h>
#include <stdlib.h>

#define MAX 360

main()
{
  int driver, mode;
  int slice[MAX];
  int count, i, size, color;
  int start, end;
  float norm_factor;
  int maxcolor;
  struct viewporttype info;

  do {
    printf("How many slices (1-359): ");
    scanf("%d", &count);
  }while(count<1 || count>359);

  for(i=0; i<count; i++) {
    printf("enter value for slice %d: ", i+1);
    scanf("%d", &slice[i]);
  }

  /* computer normalization factor */
  size = 0;
  for(i=0; i<count; i++)  size += slice[i];
  norm_factor = 360.0 /(float) size;

  driver = DETECT;
  initgraph(&driver, &mode, "");
```

```
getviewsettings((struct viewporttype far *) &info);

maxcolor = getmaxcolor();

start = end = 0;
for(i=0, color = 1; i<count; i++, color++) {
  setfillstyle(SOLID_FILL, color);

  /* compute endpoint */
  end = end + (int) slice[i]*norm_factor;

  /* if last segment, make sure that last radian
     is at degree 360
  */
  if(i==count-1 && end!=360) end = 360;
  pieslice(info.right/2, info.bottom/2,
           start, end, info.bottom/4);

  start = end;

  if(i%2) end++; /* average the effects of truncation */

  /* recycle colors if necessary */
  if(color==maxcolor) color = 1;
 }

getch();
closegraph();
return 0;
}
```

CREATING BAR GRAPHS

Another powerful Turbo C graphics function creates bars that can
be used to create bar graphs. This function is called **bar( )**, and its
prototype is

    void far bar(int *left*, int *top*, int *right*, int *bottom*);

The **bar( )** function draws a rectangular bar that has its upper
left corner defined by *left*, *top* and its lower right corner defined
by *right*, *bottom*. The bar is filled with the current fill pattern and
color.

The following program illustrates the **bar( )** function. It first
prompts the user for the number of entries and then inputs the

information and computes a normalization factor. Finally, it displays a bar graph representation of the data by using vertical bars. The normalization factor does two jobs:

1. It makes certain that the largest bar fits on the screen.
2. It ensures that the entire screen height is used.

The **bar( )** function computes the normalization factor by finding the bar with the largest value and dividing the height of the screen by that value. In this way data with values larger than the height of the screen is automatically compressed, while data with very small values is expanded. In either case the relationships between the data are kept the same, only the scale is changed. The program also automatically computes the width and spacing between the bars.

```c
/* Construct bar charts from user entered data. */
#include <graphics.h>
#include <conio.h>
#include <stdio.h>
#include <stdlib.h>

#define MAX 100

main()
{
  int driver, mode;
  int bars[MAX];
  int count, i, size, color;
  float norm_factor;
  struct viewporttype info;
  int spacing;
  int maxcolor;

  do {
    printf("How many bars (1-99): ");
    scanf("%d", &count);
  } while(count<1 || count>99);

  for(i=0; i<count; i++) {
    printf("value for bar %d: ", i+1);
    scanf("%d", &bars[i]);
  }

  driver = DETECT;
  initgraph(&driver, &mode, "");
```

```
getviewsettings((struct viewporttype far *) &info);

maxcolor = getmaxcolor();

/* computer normalization factor */
size = 0;
/* find the largest bar */
for(i=0; i<count; i++)
  if(bars[i]>size) size = bars[i];
norm_factor = (float) info.bottom / (float) size;

/* determine how much distance between bars */
spacing = info.right / count;

for(i=0, color = 1; i<count; i++, color++) {
  setfillstyle(SOLID_FILL, color);
  bar(i*spacing, info.bottom - (int) norm_factor*bars[i],
      i*spacing+(spacing/2), info.bottom);
  /* recycle colors if necessary */
  if(color==maxcolor) color = 1;
  }

getch();
closegraph();
return 0;
}
```

You can create three-dimensional bar graphs using **bar3d( )**, which has the prototype

> void far bar3d(int *left*, int *top*, int *right*, int *bottom*,
>   int *depth*, int *topflag*);

The **bar3d( )** function is the same as **bar( )** except that it produces a three-dimensional bar of *depth* pixels. The bar is outlined in the current drawing color. If you want a two-dimensional, outlined bar, use **bar3d( )** with a *depth* of 0. If *topflag* is not 0, a top will be added to the bar; if it is 0, the bar will not have a top. If you enter the six values 30, 10, 20, 40, 30, and 50, the output of the bar program will look like Figure 6-1.

How deep a bar should be is somewhat subjective. The Turbo C manual recommends that a three-dimensional bar be one-quarter as deep as it is wide. Using this rule, try substituting this call to **bar3d( )** for the one to **bar( )** in the preceding program:

```
bar3d(i*spacing, info.bottom - (int) norm_factor*bars[i],
      i*spacing+(spacing/2), info.bottom,
      ((i*spacing+(spacing/2)) - i*spacing) / 4, 1);
```

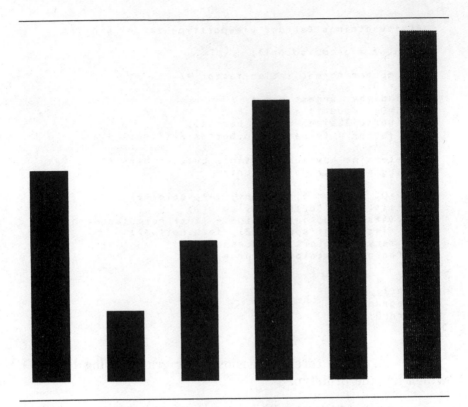

Figure 6-1.   Output from the bar graph program

USING getimage( ) AND putimage( )

The **getimage( )** function is used to copy a region of the graphics window into a buffer. The **putimage( )** function puts the contents of a buffer on the screen. They have the prototypes

```
void far getimage(int left, int top, int right, int bottom,
                    void far *buf);
void far putimage(int left, int top, void far *buf, int op);
```

The function **getimage( )** copies the contents of a rectangular portion of the screen defined by its upper left and lower right coordinates to the buffer pointed to by *buf*. To display a buffer of graphics data previously stored with **getimage( )**, use **putimage( )**. You need to specify the upper left corner coordinates of the area where you want the image displayed. The value of *op* determines exactly how the image is written to the screen. Its valid enumerated values (found in **graphics.h**) are

Name	Value	Meaning
COPY_PUT	0	Overwrite destination
XOR_PUT	1	Exclusive-OR with destination
OR_PUT	2	Inclusive-OR with destination
AND_PUT	3	AND with destination
NOT_PUT	4	Invert source image

The size of the buffer in bytes for a given region is returned by the **imagesize( )** function. You should use this function instead of trying manually to compute the space needed because **imagesize( )** returns the correct value no matter what video mode is in use. Its prototype is

```
unsigned far imagesize(int left, int top, int right,
                        int bottom);
```

The following program demonstrates the **getimage( )**, **imagesize( )**, and **putimage( )** functions. The program fills the entire screen with white; creates a box, fills it, and draws two diagonal lines; and then copies the box using **COPY_PUT** first and then **XOR_PUT**.

```
/* This program demonstrates how a graphics image can be
   moved using getimage(), imagesize(), and putimage().
*/
#include <graphics.h>
#include <stdlib.h>
#include <conio.h>

main()
{
  int driver, mode;
  int size;
  void *buf;
  struct viewporttype info;

  driver = DETECT;
  initgraph(&driver, &mode, "");

  getviewsettings((struct viewporttype far *) &info);

  setfillstyle(SOLID_FILL, WHITE);
  rectangle(0, 0, info.right, info.bottom);
  floodfill(1, 1, WHITE);

  setcolor(RED);
  rectangle(0, 0, info.right/4, info.bottom/4);

  /* create a box */
  setfillstyle(SOLID_FILL, GREEN);
  floodfill(1, 1, WHITE);
  setcolor(GREEN);
  line(0, 0, info.right/4, info.bottom/4);
  line(0, info.bottom/4, info.right/4, 0);
  getch();

  /* move the image */
  /* first, get the image's size */
  size = imagesize(0, 0, info.right/4, info.bottom/4);
  if(size !=-1) { /* alloc memory for the image */
    buf = malloc(size);
    if(buf) {
      getimage(0, 0, info.right/4, info.bottom/4, buf);
      putimage(info.right/3, info.bottom/3, buf, COPY_PUT);
      putimage((info.right/4)*3, (info.bottom/4)*3, buf, XOR_PUT);
    }
  }
  getch();
  closegraph();
  return 0;
}
```

TEXT OUTPUT IN GRAPHICS MODE

Although you can use Turbo C's standard text output functions, such as **printf()**, in most graphics modes, that is not the most flexible alternative. To take the greatest advantage of Turbo C's graphics environment you will want to use the graphics mode text output functions described in this section.

The graphics function that outputs text to the graphics viewport is **outtext( )**. Its prototype is

void far outtext(char *str);

This function outputs the string pointed to by *str* at the current position. (In graphics mode, there is no visible cursor, but the current position on the screen is maintained as if there were an invisible cursor.) In the *Turbo C User's Guide*, this position is called CP. The principle advantages of using **outtext( )** are its abilities to output text in different fonts, sizes, or directions and to clip output that would overrun the viewport. By contrast, **printf( )** cannot clip output.

To change the style, size, or direction of the text output by **outtext( )**, use **settextstyle( )**, whose prototype is

void far settextstyle(int *font*, int *direction*, int *charsize*);

The *font* parameter determines the type of font used. The default is an 8×8 bit-mapped font. You can give **font** one of these values. (The macros are defined in **graphics.h**.)

Font	Value	Meaning
DEFAULT_FONT	0	8×8 bit-mapped font
TRIPLEX_FONT	1	Stroked triplex font
SMALL_FONT	2	Small stroked font
SANS_SERIF_FONT	3	Stroked sans serif font
GOTHIC_FONT	4	Stroked gothic font

The direction in which the text will be displayed, left to right or bottom to top, is determined by the value of *direction*, which can be either **HORIZ_DIR** (0) or **VERT_DIR** (1).

The *charsize* parameter is a multiplier that increases the character size. It may have a value from 0 through 10.

The following program illustrates the use of the **settextstyle( )**

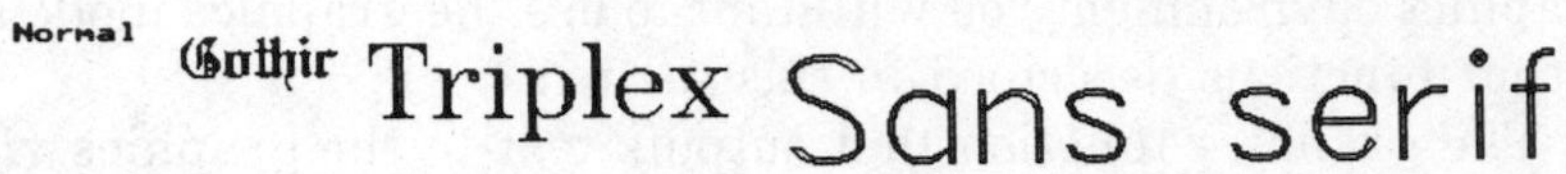

Normal   Gothic Triplex   Sans serif

Figure 6-2.   Turbo C's graphics fonts

function. It shows each font in various sizes. Its output is shown in
Figure 6-2.

```
/* Demonstrate some different text fonts and sizes. */
#include <graphics.h>
#include <conio.h>
#include <stdlib.h>

main()
{
  int driver, mode;

  driver = DETECT; /* autodetect */
  initgraph(&driver, &mode, "");

  outtext("Normal  ");

  /* Gothic font, three times normal size */
  settextstyle(GOTHIC_FONT, HORIZ_DIR, 3);
  outtext("Gothic ");

  /* Triplex font, five times normal size */
  settextstyle(TRIPLEX_FONT, HORIZ_DIR, 5);
  outtext("Triplex ");

  /* Sans serif font, seven times normal size*/
  settextstyle(SANS_SERIF_FONT, HORIZ_DIR, 7);
  outtext("Sans serif");

  getch();
  closegraph();
  return 0;
}
```

When you change the size of the 8×8 bit-mapped font, its
dimensions are simply multiplied by the value of *charsize*. That is,
if *charsize* is 2, the bit-mapped characters will be drawn in a

16×16–pixel square. The stroked fonts are proportionally spaced, however, which means that *i*, for example, will be narrower than an *m*. To determine the height and width of a stroked font character you use the **textheight( )** and **textwidth( )** functions, respectively. They have the prototypes

    int far textheight(char far *str*);
    int far textwidth(char far *str*);

These functions return the height and width in pixels of the strings pointed to by *str*.

One other important thing to understand about **outtext( )** is that it does not process newline characters. There is no way to make it perform a carriage return or linefeed operation.

To put text at a specific viewport location, use the **outtextxy( )** function, whose prototype is

    void far outtextxy(int *x*, int *y*, char *str*);

The string will be written at the specified viewport coordinates. If *x*, *y*, or both are out of range, no output will be displayed.

You can use the **outtextxy( )** function to create a banner program that displays a moving message in large letters on the screen. The message moves from right to left until a key is pressed. This program uses the bit-mapped font. The size of each character is nine times greater than its default; therefore, the height and width of each is 9*8, or 72, pixels.

```
/* BANNER: A program that scrolls a message from right to
   left using large normal font characters.
*/

#include <graphics.h>
#include <conio.h>
#include <stdio.h>
#include <alloc.h>
#include <stdlib.h>

#define MAX 1024

main()
{
```

```
int driver, mode;
int height, width;
char *p, s[2], mess[MAX];
struct viewporttype info;
int  size;
void *buf, *clearbuf;

printf("Enter your message (less than %d):\n", MAX);
gets(mess);

driver = DETECT; /* autodetect */
initgraph(&driver, &mode, "");

getviewsettings((struct viewporttype far *) &info);

settextstyle(DEFAULT_FONT, HORIZ_DIR, 9);
height = 9*8; /* default font is 8 pixels high */
width = 9*8;  /* default font is 8 pixels wide */

/* Allocate buffer to hold the part of the screen
   that contains the message less room for the character
   on the left.
*/
size = imagesize(width, (info.bottom/2)-(height/2),
                       info.right, (info.bottom/2)+(height/2));
buf = (void *) malloc(size);
if(!buf) {
  printf("allocation error");
  exit(1);
}

/* Allocate the buffer that will be used to clear the
   character position on the right that next character
   will be written to.
*/
size = imagesize(0, 0, width, height);
clearbuf = malloc(size);
if(!clearbuf) {
  printf("allocation error");
  exit(1);
}

/* get a character-sized piece of blank screen */
getimage(0, 0, width, height, clearbuf);

p = mess;
s[1] = '\0';
while(!kbhit()) {
  /* shift existing text to left */
  getimage(width, (info.bottom/2)-(height/2),
             info.right, (info.bottom/2)+(height/2), buf);
  putimage(0, (info.bottom/2)-(height/2), buf, COPY_PUT);
```

```
    /* get next character */
    *s = *p;

    /* clear the new character position */
    putimage(info.right-width, (info.bottom/2)-(height/2),
             clearbuf, COPY_PUT);

    /* output the character */
    outtextxy(info.right-width, (info.bottom/2)-(height/2),
             (char far *) s);
    p++;
    if(!*p) p = mess;   /* go back to start of message */
  }
  getch();
  closegraph();
  return 0;
}
```

CHANGING THE LINE STYLE

Turbo C allows you to change the way a line is drawn. All lines
are solid by default, but you can specify dotted, dashed, dot-
dashed, or custom-designed lines. To change the way lines are
drawn use **setlinestyle( )**, whose prototype is

> void far setlinestyle(int *style*, unsigned *pattern*,
>   int *width*);

The *style* element holds the style of the line. It will be one of the
following enumerated values (defined in **graphics.h**).

Value	Meaning
SOLID—LINE	Unbroken line
DOTTED—LINE	Dotted line
CENTER—LINE	Centered dot (dash-dot-dash) line
DASHED—LINE	Dashed line
USERBIT—LINE	User-defined line

If *style* is equal to **USERBIT—LINE**, the 16-bit pattern in *pattern* determines how the line appears. Each bit in the pattern cor-

responds to one pixel. If that bit is set, the pixel is turned on; otherwise it is turned off.

The *thickness* element will have one of the following values:

Value	Meaning
NORM_WIDTH	1 pixel wide
THICK_WIDTH	3 pixels wide

The value of the *pattern* parameter is important only if **USERBIT_LINE** is the value of *style*.

This program displays a line in each of Turbo C's built-in styles and in one custom style:

```
/* Line style demonstration. */
#include <graphics.h>
#include <conio.h>
#include <stdlib.h>

main()
{
  int driver, mode;
  struct viewporttype info;

  driver = DETECT;
  initgraph(&driver, &mode, "");

  getviewsettings((struct viewporttype far *) &info);

  /* default solid line */
  line(0, 0, info.right, 0);
  getch();

  setlinestyle(DOTTED_LINE, 0, NORM_WIDTH);
  line(0, 10, info.right, 10);
  getch();

  setlinestyle(CENTER_LINE, 0, NORM_WIDTH);
  line(0, 20, info.right, 20);
  getch();

  setlinestyle(DASHED_LINE, 0, NORM_WIDTH);
  line(0, 30, info.right, 30);
  getch();

  setlinestyle(USERBIT_LINE, 146, THICK_WIDTH);
  line(0, 40, info.right, 40);
  getch();
  closegraph();
  return 0;
}
```

CREATING A CUSTOM FILL PATTERN

Although Turbo C supplies a number of interesting fill patterns, including cross-hatching, it is sometimes useful to be able to define your own personal fill patterns. Custom fill patterns can give your graphics presentations a distinctive appearance. To create a custom fill pattern, use **setfillpattern( )**, whose prototype is

   void far setfillpattern(char far *pattern*, int *color*);

The **setfillpattern( )** function sets the fill pattern used by various functions, such as **floodfill( )**, to that pointed to by *pattern*. The array must be at least 8 bytes long. The pattern is arranged as an 8-bit by 8-byte pattern. When a bit is on, the color specified by *color* is displayed; otherwise the background color is used.

The easiest way to design a fill pattern is to draw an 8×8 matrix on a piece of paper and color in the appropriate squares. Beginning with the top row, translate each blank square as a 0 and each colored square as a 1. Convert the binary value for each row into a decimal or hexadecimal number and assign the values to the bytes in the buffer beginning with the top row.

Another way to create an interesting fill pattern is to generate it by using Turbo C's random number generator. The following program generates a new fill pattern each time it is run because the **randomize( )** function causes a new random sequence to be returned by **rand( )** each time the program executes. The patterns created by this approach are quite intriguing and, for the most part, pleasing. Notice that the output of **rand( )** is converted to the range 0 through 255, by using the modulus operator.

```
/* Generate fill random fill patterns. */
#include <graphics.h>
#include <stdlib.h>
#include <time.h>   /* used by randomize() */
#include <conio.h>

main()
{
  int driver, mode;
  struct viewporttype info;
  char fill_buf[8];
```

```
    int i;

    driver = DETECT; /* autodetect */
    initgraph(&driver, &mode, "");

    getviewsettings((struct viewporttype far *) &info);

    /* create a randomized fill pattern */
    randomize();
    for(i=0; i<8; i++)  fill_buf[i] = rand() % 256;

    setfillpattern(fill_buf, RED);
    setfillstyle(USER_FILL, RED);

    rectangle(0, 0, info.right/2, info.bottom/2);
    floodfill(1, 1, WHITE);

    getch();
    closegraph();
    return 0;
}
```

THE drawpoly() AND fillpoly() FUNCTIONS

You can draw any odd-shaped polygon using Turbo C's **drawpoly()** function, whose prototype is

> void far drawpoly(int *numpoints*, int far **points*)

The **drawpoly()** function draws a polygon using the current drawing color. The *numpoints* parameter specifies the number of end points in the polygon. Since each point consists of both x and y coordinates, the integer array pointed to by *points* must be at least twice as large as the number of points. Within this array, each point is defined by its x,y coordinate pairs with the x coordinate first. For example, to define the first endpoint as 10,20 you would use code like this:

```
int points[SIZE];

points[0] = 10;
points[1] = 20;
```

You can fill a polygon with the current fill color and pattern by using **fillpoly( )**, whose prototype is

void far fillpoly(int *numpoints*, int far **points*);

The **fillpoly( )** function fills the object defined by the array pointed to by *points* in the current drawing color. The number of endpoints must equal *numpoints*.

The following program provides an interesting demonstration of **drawpoly( )** and **fillpoly( )**. It loads an array with 500 randomly generated endpoints, draws the polygon defined by these points, and fills it. Each time you run the program it creates a new polygon. Some of the objects are quite fascinating.

```
/* drawpoly() and fillpoly() demonstration. */

#include <graphics.h>
#include <stdlib.h>
#include <conio.h>
#include <time.h>

#define MAX 500

main()
{
  int driver, mode;
  int poly[MAX];
  int i;
  struct viewporttype info;

  driver = DETECT;
  initgraph(&driver, &mode, "");

  getviewsettings((struct viewporttype far *) &info);

  randomize();
  for(i=0; i<MAX; i++)  {
    if(!(i%2))
      poly[i] = rand() % info.right;
    else
      poly[i] = rand() % info.bottom;
  }

  drawpoly(MAX/2, poly);

  setfillstyle(SOLID_FILL, BLUE);
  fillpoly(MAX/2, poly);
  getch();
  closegraph();
  return 0;
}
```

AN INTERESTING GRAPHICS PROGRAM

A short program closes this chapter on graphics. It uses Turbo C's
random number generator to create what appears to be a satellite
picture of a coastline. For the purposes of this discussion, consider
a coastline to be an irregular, random series of inlets, peninsulas,
and bays—in other words, a random collection of a variety of
geometric shapes. The program defines seven basic "shapes" and
with each loop selects one of these shapes at random. Each shape
consists of a transformation of a set of x,y coordinates. The point
at the new x,y position is turned on and the process repeats. You
will be surprised at how much the output of this program looks
like a distant view of a coastline. You might want to try experi-
menting with different shapes. The outcome of a sample run
appears in Figure 6-3.

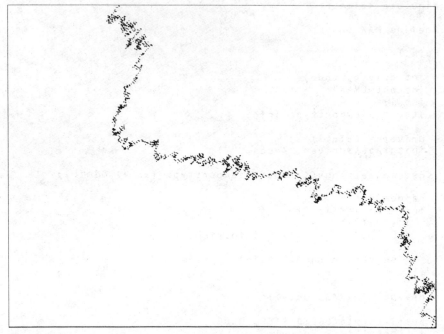

Figure 6-3.   A synthesized coastline created by the COASTLINE
program

```
/* COASTLINE: A program that uses the random number generator
   and graphics to synthesize a coastline.
*/
#include <graphics.h>
#include <stdlib.h>
#include <conio.h>
#include <time.h>  /* used by randomize() */

main()
{
  int driver, mode;
  struct viewporttype info;
  int x, y;

  driver = DETECT;
  initgraph(&driver, &mode, "");

  /* Get screen dimensions */
  getviewsettings((struct viewporttype far *) &info);
  rectangle(0, 0, info.right, info.bottom);

  x = y = 0;

  randomize();

  do {
    switch(rand()%7) {
      case 0:
        x--;
        y--;
        break;
      case 1:
        x++;
        y++;
        break;
      case 2:
        x+=3;
        y-=2;
        break;
      case 3:
        x-=2;
        y+=3;
        break;
      case 4:
        x++;
        break;
      case 5:
        y--;
        break;
      case 6:
        y += rand()%3;
        x -= rand()%3;
    }
    putpixel(x, y, WHITE);
  } while(!kbhit());

  closegraph();
  return 0;

}
```

7

STATISTICS

At some point everyone who owns or frequently uses a computer will need to perform some sort of statistical analysis. You can use statistics in a wide variety of situations—for example, to monitor or try to predict the movement of stock prices in a portfolio, to perform clinical testing to establish safe limits for a new drug, or to compile batting averages for a Little League team. The branch of mathematics that deals with the condensation, manipulation, and extrapolation of data is called *statistics*.

Statistical analysis is quite a young discipline. It had its birth in the 1700s as an outgrowth of studies on games of chance. Indeed, probability and statistics are closely related. Modern statistical analysis began around the turn of this century when it became possible to sample and handle large sets of data with some ease. The advent of the computer made it possible to correlate and manipulate rapidly even larger amounts of data and to convert this data easily into a form that we can readily use. Today, because of government's and media's drive for an ever-increasing amount of information, every aspect of our lives is permeated with statistical information. It is difficult to listen to the radio or TV news or to read a newspaper article without hearing or seeing a statistic.

Although Turbo C was not designed specifically for statistical programming, it works quite well and offers some flexibility not found in the more common business languages such as COBOL or

BASIC. Among its advantages are the speed and ease with which it can interface with its powerful graphics functions.

In this chapter you will study various statistics and procedures including

- Mean
- Median
- Standard deviation
- Regression equation (line of best fit)
- Coefficient of correlation

as well as some simple graphing techniques.

SAMPLES, POPULATIONS, DISTRIBUTIONS, AND VARIABLES

Before using statistics it is important to understand a few key concepts. Generally speaking statistical information is derived by taking a *sample* of specific data points and then drawing generalizations about them. Each sample comes from the universe of all possible outcomes for the situation under study, which is called the *population*. For example, if you wished to measure the output of a box factory over the period of a year by generalizing from the Wednesday output figures, the sample would consist of a year's worth of Wednesday figures, taken from the population of the output of each day in the year. If the sample is exhaustive, it can even equal the population. In the case of the box factory we could have the sample be equal to the population by using the actual output figures, five days a week, for the entire year. When the sample is less than the population, there is always room for error, and in many cases the probability for this error can be known. For this chapter you will be assuming that the sample is the same as the population and hence will not be concerned with the sample error problem.

Things like election projections and opinion polls use a sample to project information about the population as a whole. You might, for example, use statistical information about the Dow Jones stocks to make an inference about the stock market in general. Of course the validity of these conclusions varies widely. Other applications of statistics use a sample that equals or nearly equals the population to summarize a large set of numbers for easier handling. For example, a board of education will usually report on the *average* grade point for a class rather than enumerating each student's grade individually.

Statistics are affected by the way events are distributed in the population. Several distributions are common in nature, but the most important, and the only one we will be using, is the *normal distribution* or "bell-shaped curve," with which you are probably familiar (see Figure 7-1).

As is suggested by the graph, the elements in a normal distribution are found mostly in the middle. In fact, the curve is completely symmetrical around its peak, which is also the average for all the elements. The further you are from the middle, in either direction, the fewer elements there are. Many things in real life have a generally normal distribution.

In any statistical process there is always an *independent variable*, which is the number under study, and a *dependent variable*, which is the factor that determines the independent variable. This

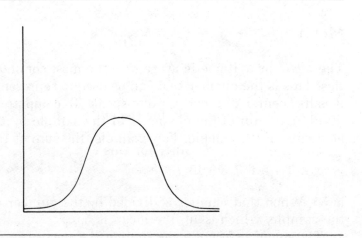

Figure 7-1.   The normal distribution curve

chapter will be using time for the dependent variable, that is, the stepwise incremental passage of events. For example, in watching a stock portfolio, you may wish to see the movement of the stock on a daily basis. Therefore you are concerned with the movement of stock prices over a given period, not with the actual calendar date of each price. (Of course, some advanced analysis might use the actual calendar dates to see if there is a correlation between calendar dates and stock prices.)

This chapter will develop the individual statistical functions that will be assembled into a menu-driven program at the end. You will be able to use this program both to perform a wide variety of statistical analyses and to plot information on the screen.

THE BASIC STATISTICS

Three important numbers form the basis of much statistical analysis and are useful in their own right. They are the *mean* (arithmetic average), the *median*, and the *mode*. Each of these is examined here.

Throughout this chapter the discussion refers to elements of a sample. For ease and convenience, those elements will be called D, and will be indexed from 1 to N, where N is the number of the last element.

Mean

The *mean* or arithmetic average is the most common of all statistics. This is the number that can be used to represent a set of data; it is its "center of gravity," so to speak. To compute the mean, you divide the sum of the elements in the sample by the number of elements in the sample. For example, the sum of the set

1 2 3 4 5 6 7 8 9 10

is 55. When that number is divided by the number of elements in the sample, which is 10, the mean is 5.5.

The general formula for finding the mean is

$$M = \frac{D_1+D_2+D_3+\ldots+D_N}{N}$$

or

$$M = \frac{1}{N} \sum_{i=1}^{N} D_1$$

Here the Σ symbol is used to indicate the summation of all elements between 1 and N.

The statistical functions in this chapter assume that all data elements are stored in an array of floating-point numbers and that the number of sample elements is known. The following function computes the mean of an array of *num* floating-point numbers. It returns the floating-point average.

```
/* Compute the average. */
float mean(float *data, int num)
{
  int t;
  float avg;

  avg = 0;
  for(t=0; t<num; ++t)
    avg += data[t];

  avg /= num;

  return avg;
}
```

For example, if you called **mean( )** with a ten-element array that contained the numbers 1 through 10, it would return the result 5.5.

Median

The median of a sample is the middle value based on order of magnitude. For example, in the sample set

1 2 3 4 5 6 7 8 9

5 is the median because it is in the middle. In the set

   1 2 3 4 5 6 7 8 9 10

either 5 or 6 could be used as the median. In a well-ordered sample that has a normal distribution, the median and the mean will be very similar. However, as the sample moves further from the standard normal distribution curve, the difference between the median and the mean increases. Calculating the mean of a sample is as simple as sorting the sample and selecting the middle element, which is indexed as $N/2$.

The function **median( )** shown here returns the value of the middle element in a sample. Because the data must be sorted to compute the median, the code uses a modified version of the quicksort developed in Chapter 1.

```c
/* Find the median. */
float median(float *data, int num)
{
  register int t;
  float dtemp[MAX];

  /* copy data for sorting */
  for(t=0; t<num; ++t) dtemp[t] = data[t];

  quick(dtemp, num);  /* sort data into ascending order */
  return dtemp[num/2];
}

/* Quicksort setup. */
void quick(float *item, int count)
{
  qs(item, 0, count-1);
}

/* Quicksort. */
void qs(float *item, int left, int right)
{
  register int i, j;
  float x, y;

  i = left; j = right;
  x = item[(left+right)/2];

  do {
    while(item[i]<x && i<right) i++;
    while(x<item[j] && j>left) j--;
```

```
      if(i<=j) {
        y = item[i];
        item[i] = item[j];
        item[j] = y;
        i++; j--;
      }
    } while(i<=j);

    if(left<j)  qs(item, left, j);
    if(i<right) qs(item, i, right);
}
```

Mode

The *mode* of a sample is the value of the most frequently occurring element. For example, given the set

   1 2 3 3 4 5 6 6 6 7 8 9

the mode would be 6 because it occurs three times. The mode need not be unique; for example, the sample

   10 20 30 30 40 50 60 60 70

has two modes—30 and 60—because they both occur twice.

The following function, called **find—mode( )**, returns the mode of a sample. If there is more than one mode, it returns the last one found.

```
/* Find the mode. */
float find_mode(float *data, int num)
{
  register int t, w;
  float md, oldmode;
  int count, oldcount;

  oldmode = 0; oldcount = 0;
  for(t=0; t<num; ++t) {
    /* First, check each value to see how many
       times it occurs in the array.
    */
    md = data[t];
    count = 1;
    for(w=t+1; w<num; ++w)
      if(md==data[w]) count++;
```

```
   /* If it occurs more times than the current
        mode, use it instead.
   */
   if(count>oldcount) {
     oldmode = md;
     oldcount = count;
   }
 }
 return oldmode;
}
```

Using the Mean, Median, and Mode

The purpose of the mean, median, and mode is to provide one number that is the condensation of all the numbers in the sample. However, each represents the sample in a different way. Generally, the mean is by far the most useful number. Because it uses the values of all the elements in its computation, it partially reflects all the elements in the sample. The main disadvantage of the mean is its sensitivity to one extreme value. Suppose, for example, that in Widget, Inc. the president's salary is $100,000 per year, and each of the nine employees' salaries is $10,000. The average wage at Widget is $19,000; but this figure does not fairly represent the actual situation.

In response to examples like the salary dispersion at Widget, the mode is sometimes used instead of the mean. Here the mode of the salaries at Widget is $10,000, a figure that more accurately reflects the actual situation. However, the mode can also be misleading. Consider a company that makes cars in five different colors. In a given week the company made

- 100 green
- 100 orange
- 150 blue
- 200 black
- 190 white

Here the mode of the sample is black, because 200 were made, more than any other color. But it would be misleading to suggest that the company makes mostly black cars.

The median is an interesting number because its validity is based on the hope that the sample will reflect a normal distribution. For example, if the sample is

1 2 3 4 5 6 7 8 9 10

the median is 5 (or 6) and the mean is 5.5. In this case the median and mean are similar, but in the sample

1 1 1 1 5 100 100 100 100

the median is still 5, but the mean is about 46.

The fact that in certain circumstances the mean, the mode, or the median cannot be counted on to give meaningful numbers by itself leads to one of the most important numbers in statistics, the variance.

Variance and Standard Deviation

Although the "one number" summary, such as the mean or median, is very convenient, it suffers from the fact that it can easily mislead rather than inform. If you give a little thought to this problem, you can see that the cause of the difficulty is not in the number itself, but in the fact that it does not convey any information about the variations of the data. For example, given the following sample

1 1 1 1 9 9 9 9

the mean is 5, but there is no element in the sample that is even close to 5. What you would like to know is *how close each element in the sample is to the mean.* Knowing how variable the data is will help you interpret the mean, median, and mode better. You can find the variability of a sample by computing its *variance* and *standard deviation.*

The variance—and its square root, the standard deviation— are numbers that tell us the average deviation from the sample mean. Of the two, the standard deviation is the most important because it can be thought of as the average of the distances each element is from the mean of the sample. The variance is computed as shown here:

$$V = \frac{1}{N} \sum_{i=1}^{N} (D_i - M)^2$$

Here N is the number of elements in the sample, and M is the sample mean. It is necessary to square the difference of the mean and each element to produce only positive numbers. If the numbers were not squared, they would always sum to 0.

Of course the variance, V, produced by the above formula is of limited value to you because it is difficult to understand. Its square root, called the standard deviation, is the number you are really looking for. The standard deviation is derived by finding the variance and then taking its square root as shown here:

$$std = \sqrt{\frac{1}{N} \sum_{i=1}^{N} (D_i - M)^2}$$

Again N is the number of elements in the sample, and M is the sample mean.

Consider the following sample:

11 20 40 30 99 30 50

Compute the variance as follows:

D	$D-M$	$(D-M)^2$
11	−29	841
20	−20	400
40	0	0
30	−10	100

	D	D−M	(D−M)²
	99	59	3481
	30	−10	100
	50	10	100
Sum	280	0	5022
Mean(M)	40	0	717.42

Here the average of the squared differences is 717.42. To derive the standard deviation, simply take the square root of that number; the result is approximately 26.78. To interpret the standard deviation, remember that it is the *average distance the elements in the sample are from the mean of the sample.*

The standard deviation aids us by allowing us to know how representative the mean is of the entire sample. For example, if you owned a candy bar factory and your plant foreman reported that daily output averaged 2500 bars last month, but that the standard deviation was 2000, you would have a pretty good idea that the production line needed better supervision.

An important rule of thumb is that, assuming your sample follows a standard normal distribution, about 68% of the sample will be within one standard deviation from the mean and about 95% will be within two standard deviations.

The following function will compute and return the standard deviation of a given sample:

```c
/* Compute the standard deviation. */
float std_dev(float *data, int num)
{
  register int t;
  float std, avg;

  avg = mean(data, num);   /* get average */
  std = 0;
  for(t=0; t<num; ++t)
    std+=((data[t]-avg)*(data[t]-avg));

  std /= num;
  std = (float) sqrt((double) std);
  return std;
}
```

SIMPLE PLOTTING ON
THE SCREEN

Before going on to more advanced statistics, let's digress a bit by discussing how to represent data in graphic form. The advantage of using graphs in conjunction with statistics is that they convey the meaning more clearly and accurately to others. A graph also shows at a glance how the sample is actually distributed and how variable the data is. The routines developed here will be limited to two-dimensional graphs, that is, graphs that use the x,y coordinate system. (The creation of three-dimensional graphs is a unique discipline and beyond the scope of this book.)

There are two basic forms of two-dimensional graphs: the bar graph and the scatter graph. As you saw in Chapter 6, the bar graph uses solid bars to represent the magnitude of each element, while the scatter graph uses only single points located at x,y coordinates. An example of each is shown in Figure 7-2. The bar chart is generally used with a relatively small set of information, such as the gross national product for the last ten years, or the percentage output of a factory on a monthly basis. The scatter graph is generally used to display a large number of data points, such as the daily stock price of a company over a year. A modification of the scatter graph produces a solid line connecting the data points, which is useful for plotting projections.

This section develops two functions called **barplot( )** and **scatterplot( )**, which will automatically scale and plot an array of floating-point values. The functions will be written so that they automatically work with any type of graphics adapter.

To make the plotting routine handle arbitrarily sized units, we need to *normalize* the data before plotting it and alter the scale used if necessary. You saw a simple example of normalization in Chapter 6. Let's examine it more fully here. The process of normalization involves finding a ratio between the actual range of the data and the physical range of the screen and multiplying each data element by this ratio to produce a number within the range of the screen. The formula to do this for the y axis is

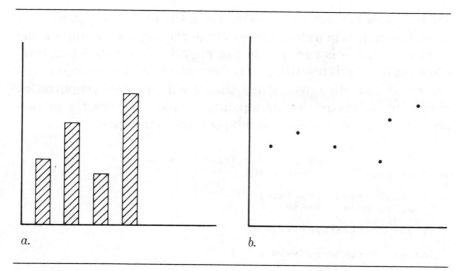

Figure 7-2.   Samples of a bar graph (*a*) and a scattergraph (*b*)

$$Y' = Y * \frac{horizontal\ dimension}{(max-min)}$$

where Y' is the value used to call the plotting function. To make the screen appear full, it is common to spread the scale when the data is in only a small portion of the screen's range.

The general procedure for normalizing is to find the difference between the greatest and smallest values in the sample. This number is used to divide the vertical resolution of the screen. The ratio is then used to convert the sample data into the proper scale.

The function **barplot( )** scales the x and y axes and plots a bar graph. The maximum number of bars that can be graphed depends on the number of pixels in the horizontal dimension of the graphics mode being used. The x axis is assumed to be time and is in increments of one unit.

The **barplot( )** function is shown here. Notice that it uses

Turbo C's autodetect ability to initialize the graphics system. This gives the program automatic access to the highest resolution the computer that it is running on can provide. Also notice that **barplot( )** calls **getviewsettings( )** to determine the dimensions of the screen. These dimensions are then used by the normalization procedure to ensure that data points are plotted correctly no matter what graphics mode and adapter are being used.

```
/* Display a bar chart of num items of data. */
void barplot(float *data, int num)
{
  int y, t, max, min, incr;
  float a, norm, spread;
  char s[80];
  struct viewporttype status;

  initgraph(&driver, &mode, "");

  /* find the dimensions of the screen */
  getviewsettings(&status);

  /* first find max value to enable normalization */
  max = getmax(data, num);
  min = getmin(data, num);
  if(min>0) min = 0;
  spread = max-min;
  norm = status.bottom/spread; /* absolute increment/spread */
  sprintf(s, "%d", min);
  outtextxy(0, status.bottom-10, s);
  sprintf(s, "%d", max);
  outtextxy(0, 0, s);
  for(t=10; t<status.bottom-10; t+=10)
    outtextxy(0, t, "-");

  setcolor(RED);
  for(t=0; t<num; ++t) {
    a = data[t];
    a = a-min;
    a *= norm; /* normalize */
    y = a; /* type conversion */
    incr = status.bottom/num;
    line(((t*incr)+20), status.bottom-y,
        ((t*incr)+20), status.bottom);
    line(((t*incr)+21), status.bottom-y,
        ((t*incr)+21), status.bottom);
  }
  getch();
  restorecrtmode();
}
```

The **barplot( )** function uses Turbo C's **line( )** function to construct the bar. As the function is shown, it displays a double line because on high-resolution adapters, such as the VGA, a single line is very thin. (You can change this to a single line if you like.) The code uses **line( )** instead of Turbo C's **bar( )** function because **line( )** is easier to use in this situation and **bar( )** is better suited to plotting relatively few bars. The **barplot( )** function is designed to plot up to several hundred bars. Notice that this version also prints hash marks every ten pixels along the left side of the screen for reference.

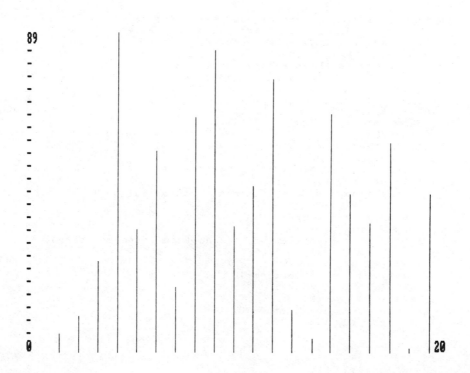

Figure 7-3.   A sample bar graph produced by **barplot( )**

Figure 7-3 gives a sample of the output of **barplot( )** with twenty elements. Although **barplot( )** by no means provides all the features you may desire, it will do a good job of displaying a single sample.

You need to make only a slight modification to **barplot( )** to make a function that plots a scatter graph. The main alteration is to change the **line( )** function to **putpixel( )** so that only one point is plotted. However, on high-resolution adapters, a single point is quite faint. So **scatterplot( )** actually plots five points, creating a very small star. If your system has only low-resolution capabilities, you should delete all but the first call to **putpixel( )**. The function **scatterplot( )** is shown here:

```c
/* Display scatter chart of num items of data.
   Call with minimum value for Y and max values
   for Y and X.  Also specify color.
*/
void scatterplot(float *data, int num,
                 int ymin, int ymax, int xmax,
                 int color)
{
  int y, t, incr;
  float norm, a, spread;
  char s[80];
  struct viewporttype status;

  /* find the dimensions of the screen */
  getviewsettings(&status);
  /* first find max value to enable normalization */

  if(ymin>0) ymin = 0;
  spread = ymax-ymin;
  norm = status.right/spread; /* absolute increment/spread */

  sprintf(s, "%d", ymin);
  outtextxy(0, status.bottom-10, s);
  sprintf(s, "%d", ymax);
  outtextxy(0, 0, s);
  for(t=10; t<status.bottom-10; t+=10)
    outtextxy(0, t, "-");

  incr = status.bottom/xmax;
  for(t=0; t<num; ++t) {
    a = data[t];
    a = a-ymin;
```

```
a *= norm; /* normalize */
y = a; /* type conversion */
putpixel((((t*incr)+20), status.bottom-y, color);
putpixel((((t*incr)+21), status.bottom-y, color);
putpixel((((t*incr)+19), status.bottom-y, color);
putpixel((((t*incr)+20), status.bottom-y-1, color);
putpixel((((t*incr)+20), status.bottom-y+1, color);
  }

}
```

Notice that in **scatterplot( )** the minimum and maximum values of the data are passed into the function instead of being computed by the function as was the case in **barplot( )**. This allows the plotting of multiple data sets on the same screen without changing the scale. Also, **scatterplot( )** includes a color argument so that different data can be plotted in different colors. Figure 7-4 shows a sample scatter graph of 30 data elements produced by this function.

PROJECTIONS AND THE REGRESSION EQUATION

One of the most common uses of statistical information is to make "informed guesses" about the future, even though everyone knows that the past does not necessarily predict the future and there are exceptions to every rule. We like to study past events because trends often do continue into the future, and in case they do we would like to know specific values at future points in time. This process is called making a *projection* or *trend analysis*.

For example, consider a ten-year study of life spans that collected the following (fictitious) data:

Year	Lifespan
1980	69
1981	70
1982	72

Year	Lifespan
1983	68
1984	73
1985	71
1986	75
1987	74
1988	78
1989	77

You might ask (1) is there a trend here at all; (2) if there is, which

Figure 7-4.   A sample scatter graph produced by **scatterplot( )**

way is it going; and (3) if there is a trend, what is the likely life expectancy in, say, 1995?

First, simply make a bar graph of this data; it is shown in Figure 7-5.

These graphs give the distinct impression that life spans are generally getting longer. Also, if you laid a ruler down on the graphs in a way that basically fit the data and drew a line that extended all the way into 1995, you could project that the life span

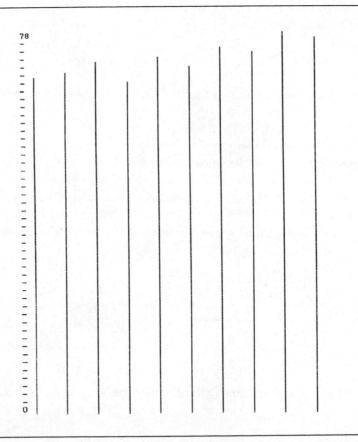

Figure 7-5.   Bar graph of life expectancy

in 1995 would be about 82 years. Although this intuitive analysis is fairly good, a more formal method would be even better.

Given a set of historical data, one way to make projections is to find the *line of best fit* relative to the data. This is what you did with the ruler by hand. A line of best fit is one that most closely represents each point of the data and its trend. This means that although some, or even all, of the actual data points may not be on the line, this line best represents them. The validity of the line is based on how closely the sample data points come to being on the line.

You should recall that a line in two-dimensional space has the basic equation:

$$Y = a + bX$$

where X is the dependent variable and Y is the independent variable, a is Y-intercept and b is the slope of the line. Therefore, to find a line that best fits a sample, you must determine a and b.

Although any number of methods can be used to determine the values of a and b, the most common and generally considered best, is called the *method of least squares*. The general idea behind it is to minimize the distance between the actual data points and the line. It involves two steps. In the first step, you compute b, the slope of the line, and in the second you find the Y-intercept a. To find b you use the formula

$$b = \frac{\sum_{i=1}^{N} (X_i - M_x)(Y_i - M_y)}{\sum_{i=1}^{N} (X_i - M_x)^2}$$

where M_x is the mean of the X coordinate and M_y is the mean of the Y coordinate. The derivation of this formula is beyond the scope of this book, but having found b, you can use it to compute the Y-intercept a, as shown here:

$$a = M_y - bM_x$$

Given this equation it is possible to plug in any number for X and find the value of Y. For example, if you use the life expectancy data, you will find that the regression equation looks like this:

$$Y = 67.46 + 0.95 * X$$

Therefore, to find the life expectancy in 1995, which is the 15th year from 1980, solve the equation

$$\text{Life Expectancy} = 67.46 + 0.95 * 15 = {\sim}82$$

At this point it is important to determine how well the line of best fit for the data actually correlates with it. If the line and data have only a slight correlation, the regression line is of little interest or use. If the line fits the data well, however, it is a much more valid indicator. The most common way to determine and represent the correlation of the data to the regression line is to compute the *correlation coefficient*, which is a number between 0 and 1. The correlation coefficient is essentially a percentage that represents the amount of deviation from the mean explained by the line. This may sound confusing, but it really isn't. In loose terms, it is related to the distance each data point in the sample is from the line. If the correlation coefficient is 1, the data corresponds perfectly to the line. A coefficient of 0 means that there is no correlation between the line and the points; in fact any line would be as good as (or better than) the one used. The formula to find the correlation coefficient is

$$Cor = \cfrac{\cfrac{1}{N} \sum\limits_{i=1}^{N} (X_i - M_x)(Y_i - M_y)}{\sqrt{\cfrac{1}{N} \sum\limits_{i=1}^{N} (X_i - M_x)^2} \; \sqrt{\cfrac{1}{N} \sum\limits_{i=1}^{N} (Y_i - M_y)^2}}$$

where M_x is the mean of X and M_y is the mean of Y. Generally, a value of 0.81 is considered a strong correlation. It means that about 66% of the data fits the regression line. To convert any correlation coefficient into a percentage, simply square it.

The function **regress( )**, which uses the methods described to find the regression equation and the coefficient of correlation and optionally to scatter plot both the sample data and the regression line, is shown here:

```
/* Compute the regression equation. */
void regress(float *data, int num)
{
  float a, b, x_avg, y_avg, temp, temp2;
  float data2[580], cor;
  int t, min, max;
  char s[80];

  /* find mean of y */
  y_avg = 0;
  for(t=0; t<num; ++t) y_avg += data[t];
  y_avg /= num;

  /* find mean of x */
  x_avg = 0;
  for(t=1; t<=num; ++t) x_avg += t;
  x_avg /= num;

  /* now find b */
  temp = 0; temp2 = 0;
  for(t=1; t<=num; ++t) {
  temp += (data[t-1]-y_avg)*(t-x_avg);
  temp2 += (t-x_avg) * (t-x_avg);
}
```

```
    b = temp/temp2;

    /* now find a */
    a = y_avg-(b*x_avg);

    /* now compute coefficient of correlation */
    for(t=0; t<num; ++t) data2[t] = t+1; /* load x axis */
    cor = temp/(num);
    cor = cor/(std_dev(data, num) * std_dev(data2, num));

    printf("regression equation is: Y = %f + %f * X\n", a, b);
    printf("Correlation Coefficient: %f\n", cor);
    printf("plot data points and regression line? (y/n) ");
    gets(s);
    if(toupper(*s)=='N') return;

    initgraph(&driver, &mode, "");

    /* now do scatter graph and regression line */
    for(t=0; t<num*2; ++t)  /* create plot regression line */
      data2[t] = a+(b*(t+1));

    min = getmin(data, num)*2;
    max = getmax(data, num)*2;
    scatterplot(data, num, min, max, num*2, GREEN);
    scatterplot(data2, num*2, min, max, num*2, RED);
    getch();
    restorecrtmode();
}
```

Figure 7-6 shows a scatter plot of both the sample data and the regression line. Notice that the graph dimensions are twice as big as the original data. This allows the regression line space to show its projections. The key to using projections like this is to remember that the past does not necessarily predict the future; if it did, life would be no fun!

MAKING A COMPLETE STATISTICS PROGRAM

So far in this chapter you have developed several functions that perform statistics on one variable. Now you will put them together

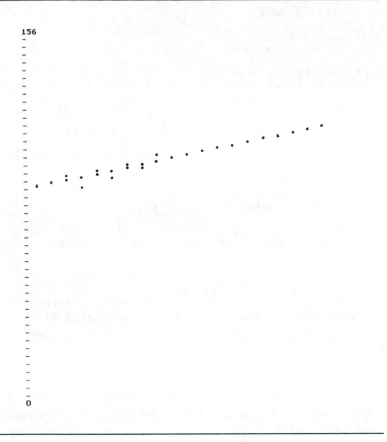

Figure 7-6.   Regression line for life expectancy

to form a complete program that you can use to analyze data, print bar charts or scatter plots, and do projections. Before you can develop the complete program, you must define a data structure to hold the data and create a few support routines.

First the program needs an array to hold the sample information. You can use a single-dimension floating-point array called *data* of size *MAX*, with *MAX* being defined to fit the largest sample needed. Here 100 is chosen arbitrarily. The **main( )** function and the menu selection function **menu( )** are shown here:

```
#define MAX 100

main()  /* stats driver */
{
  char ch;
  float data[MAX];  /* this array will hold data */
  float a, m, md, std;
  int num=0; /* number of data items */

  for(;;) {
    ch = menu();
    switch(ch) {
      case 'E': num = enter_data(data);
        break;
      case 'B':a = mean(data, num);
        std = std_dev(data, num);
        m = median(data, num);
        md = find_mode(data, num);
        printf("Average: %f\n", a);
        printf("Standard Deviation: %f\n", std);
        printf("Median: %f\n", m);
        printf("Mode: %f\n", md);
        break;
      case 'R': regress(data, num);
        break;
      case 'D': display(data, num);
        break;
      case 'L': num = load(data);
        break;
      case 'S': save(data, num);
        break;
      case 'P': barplot(data, num);
        break;
      case 'Q': return 0;
    }
  }

}

/* Get user selection. */
menu(void)
{
  char ch;
  do {
    printf("\nEnter data\n");
    printf("Basic statistics \n");
    printf("Regression line and scatter plot\n");
    printf("Plot a bar graph\n");
    printf("Save\n");
    printf("Load\n");
    printf("Display data\n");
    printf("Quit\n\n");
    printf("choose one (E, B, R, P, S, L, D, Q): ");
```

```
    ch = toupper(getche());
  } while(!strchr("BESLQDPR", ch));
  printf("\n");
  return ch;
}
```

The function **strchr( )** in **menu( )** returns a pointer to the first character in the string that matches the character in its second argument. If no match is found, it returns a null pointer. It is used to ensure that only a valid selection is returned to **main( )**.

Aside from the statistical functions developed already you will need routines to save and load data. The **save** routine must also store the number of data elements and the **load** routine must read back that number. These functions are shown here:

```
/* Save the data file. */
void save(float *data, int num)
{
  FILE *fp;
  int t;
  char s[80];

  printf("enter filename: ");
  gets(s);

  if((fp=fopen(s, "w"))==NULL) {
    printf("cannot open file\n");
    exit(1);
  }
  putw(num, fp);   /* write out count */

  for(t=0; t<num; ++t) fprintf(fp, "%f ", data[t]);

  fclose(fp);
}

/* Load the data file. */
load(float *data)
{
  FILE *fp;
  int t, num;
  char s[80];

  printf("enter filename: ");
  gets(s);
```

```
  if((fp=fopen(s, "r"))==NULL) {
    printf("cannot open file\n");
    exit(1);
  }

  num = getw(fp);
  for(t=0; t<num; ++t) fscanf(fp, "%f", &data[t]);

  fclose(fp);
  return num;
}
```

For your convenience, the entire program is listed here:

```
/* A simple statistics program. */

#include <stdio.h>
#include <dos.h>
#include <ctype.h>
#include <string.h>
#include <stdlib.h>
#include <graphics.h>
#include <conio.h>
#include <math.h>

#define MAX 100

float mean(float *, int), std_dev(float *, int);
float median(float *, int), find_mode(float*, int);
void save(float *, int), display(float *, int);
void regress(float *, int), barplot(float *, int);
void scatterplot(float *, int, int, int, int, int);
void quick(float *, int), qs(float *, int, int);
int menu(void), enter_data(float *);
int getmax(float *, int), getmin(float *, int);
int load(float *);

int driver = DETECT, mode = EGAHI;

main()  /* stats driver */
{
  char ch;
  float data[MAX];  /* this array will hold data */
  float a, m, md, std;
  int num=0; /* number of data items */

  for(;;) {
    ch = menu();
```

```c
      switch(ch) {
          case 'E': num = enter_data(data);
            break;
          case 'B':a = mean(data, num);
            std = std_dev(data, num);
            m = median(data, num);
            md = find_mode(data, num);
            printf("Average: %f\n", a);
            printf("Standard Deviation: %f\n", std);
            printf("Median: %f\n", m);
            printf("Mode: %f\n", md);
            break;
          case 'R': regress(data, num);
            break;
          case 'D': display(data, num);
            break;
          case 'L': num = load(data);
            break;
          case 'S': save(data, num);
            break;
          case 'P': barplot(data, num);
            break;
          case 'Q': return 0;
      }
    }

}

/* Get user selection. */
menu(void)
{
  char ch;
  do {
    printf("\nEnter data\n");
    printf("Basic statistics \n");
    printf("Regression line and scatter plot\n");
    printf("Plot a bar graph\n");
    printf("Save\n");
    printf("Load\n");
    printf("Display data\n");
    printf("Quit\n\n");
    printf("choose one (E, B, R, P, S, L, D, Q): ");
    ch = toupper(getche());
  } while(!strchr("BESLQDPR", ch));
  printf("\n");
  return ch;
}

/* Display the data. */
void display(float *data, int num)
{
  int t;
```

```c
   for(t=0; t<num; ++t)
     printf("item %d; %f\n", t+1, data[t]);

   printf("\n");
}

/* Input the data. */
enter_data(float *data)
{

  int t, num;

  printf("number of items?: ");
  scanf("%d%*c", &num);

  for(t=0; t<num; ++t) {
    printf("enter item %d: ", t+1);
    scanf("%f%*c", &data[t]);
  }
  return num;
}

/* Compute the average. */
float mean(float *data, int num)
{
  int t;
  float avg;

  avg = 0;
  for(t=0; t<num; ++t)
    avg += data[t];

  avg/=num;

  return avg;
}


/* Compute the standard deviation. */
float std_dev(float *data, int num)
{
  register int t;
  float std, avg;

  avg = mean(data, num);  /* get average */
  std = 0;
  for(t=0; t<num; ++t)
    std+=((data[t]-avg)*(data[t]-avg));

    std /= num;
    std = (float) sqrt((double) std);
    return std;
  }
```

```
/* Find the median. */
float median(float *data, int num)
{
  register int t;
  float dtemp[MAX];

  /* copy data for sorting */
  for(t=0; t<num; ++t) dtemp[t] = data[t];

  quick(dtemp, num);  /* sort data into ascending order */

  return dtemp[num/2];
}

/* Find the mode. */
float find_mode(float *data, int num)
{
  register int t, w;
  float md, oldmode;
  int count, oldcount;

  oldmode = 0; oldcount = 0;
  for(t=0; t<num; ++t) {
    /* First, check each value to see how many
       times it occurs in the array.
    */
    md = data[t];
    count = 1;
    for(w=t+1; w<num; ++w)
      if(md==data[w]) count++;

    /* If it occurs more times than the current
       mode, use it instead.
    */
    if(count>oldcount) {
      oldmode = md;
      oldcount = count;
    }
  }
  return oldmode;
}

/* Compute the regression equation. */
void regress(float *data, int num)
{
  float a, b, x_avg, y_avg, temp, temp2;
  float data2[580], cor;
  int t, min, max;
  char s[80];

  /* find mean of y */
  y_avg = 0;
```

```
   for(t=0; t<num; ++t) y_avg += data[t];
   y_avg /= num;

   /* find mean of x */
   x_avg = 0;
   for(t=1; t<=num; ++t) x_avg += t;
   x_avg /= num;

   /* now find b */
   temp = 0; temp2 = 0;
   for(t=1; t<=num; ++t) {
     temp += (data[t-1]-y_avg)*(t-x_avg);
     temp2 += (t-x_avg) * (t-x_avg);
   }

   b = temp/temp2;

   /* now find a */
   a = y_avg-(b*x_avg);

   /* now compute coefficient of correlation */
   for(t=0; t<num; ++t) data2[t] = t+1; /* load x axis */
   cor = temp/(num);
   cor = cor/(std_dev(data, num) * std_dev(data2, num));

   printf("regression equation is:Y = %f + %f * X\n", a, b);
   printf("Correlation Coefficient: %f\n", cor);
   printf("plot data points and regression line? (y/n) ");
   gets(s);
   if(toupper(*s)=='N') return;

   initgraph(&driver, &mode, "");

   /* now do scatter graph and regression line */
   for(t=0; t<num*2; ++t)  /* create plot regression line */
     data2[t] = a+(b*(t+1));

   min = getmin(data, num)*2;
   max = getmax(data, num)*2;
   scatterplot(data, num, min, max, num*2, GREEN);
   scatterplot(data2, num*2, min, max, num*2, RED);
   getch();
   restorecrtmode();
}

/* Display a bar chart of num items of data. */
void barplot(float *data, int num)
{
   int y, t, max, min, incr;
   float a, norm, spread;
   char s[80];
```

```
      struct viewporttype status;

      initgraph(&driver, &mode, "");

      /* find the dimensions of the screen */
      getviewsettings(&status);

      /* first find max value to enable normalization */
      max = getmax(data, num);
      min = getmin(data, num);
      if(min>0) min = 0;
      spread = max-min;
      norm = status.bottom/spread; /* absolute increment/spread */
      sprintf(s, "%d", min);
      outtextxy(0, status.bottom-10, s);
      sprintf(s, "%d", max);
      outtextxy(0, 0, s);
      for(t=10; t<status.bottom-10; t+=10)
        outtextxy(0, t, "-");

      setcolor(RED);
      for(t=0; t<num; ++t) {
        a = data[t];
        a = a-min;
        a *= norm; /* normalize */
        y = a; /* type conversion */
        incr = status.bottom/num;
        line(((t*incr)+20), status.bottom-y,
            ((t*incr)+20), status.bottom);
        line(((t*incr)+21), status.bottom-y,
            ((t*incr)+21), status.bottom);
      }
      getch();
      restorecrtmode();
}

/* Display scatter chart of num items of data.
   Call with minimum value for Y and max values
   for Y and X.  Also specify color.
*/
void scatterplot(float *data, int num,
                 int ymin, int ymax, int xmax,
                 int color)
{
      int y, t, incr;
      float norm, a, spread;
      char s[80];
      struct viewporttype status;

      /* find the dimensions of the screen */
      getviewsettings(&status);
      /* first find max value to enable normalization */
```

```
    if(ymin>0) ymin = 0;
    spread = ymax-ymin;
    norm = status.right/spread; /* absolute increment/spread */

    sprintf(s, "%d", ymin);
    outtextxy(0, status.bottom-10, s);
    sprintf(s, "%d", ymax);
    outtextxy(0, 0, s);
    for(t=10; t<status.bottom-10; t+=10)
      outtextxy(0, t, "-");

    incr = status.bottom/xmax;
    for(t=0; t<num; ++t) {
      a = data[t];
      a = a-ymin;
      a *= norm; /* normalize */
      y = a; /* type conversion */
      putpixel(((t*incr)+20), status.bottom-y, color);
      putpixel(((t*incr)+21), status.bottom-y, color);
      putpixel(((t*incr)+19), status.bottom-y, color);
      putpixel(((t*incr)+20), status.bottom-y-1, color);
      putpixel(((t*incr)+20), status.bottom-y+1, color);
    }

}

/* Returns the maximum value of the data. */
getmax(float *data, int num)
{
  int t, max;

  for(max=data[0],t=1; t<num; ++t)
    if(data[t]>max) max=data[t];
  return max;
}

/* Returns the minimum value of the data. */
getmin(float *data, int num)
{
  int t, min;

  for(min=data[0],t=1; t<num; ++t)
    if(data[t]<min) min=data[t];
  return min;
}

/* Save the data file. */
void save(float *data, int num)
{
  FILE *fp;
  int t;
  char s[80];
```

```
    printf("enter filename: ");
    gets(s);

    if((fp=fopen(s, "w"))==NULL) {
    printf("cannot open file\n");
    exit(1);
  }
  putw(num, fp);  /* write out count */

  for(t=0; t<num; ++t) fprintf(fp, "%f ", data[t]);

  fclose(fp);
}

/* Load the data file. */
load(float *data)
{
  FILE *fp;
  int t, num;
  char s[80];

  printf("enter filename: ");
  gets(s);
  if((fp=fopen(s, "r"))==NULL) {
    printf("cannot open file\n");
    exit(1);
  }

  num = getw(fp);
  for(t=0; t<num; ++t) fscanf(fp, "%f", &data[t]);

  fclose(fp);
  return num;
}

/* Quicksort setup. */
void quick(float *item, int count)
{
  qs(item, 0, count-1);
}

/* Quicksort. */
void qs(float *item, int left, int right)
{
  register int i, j;
  float x, y;

  i = left; j = right;
  x = item[(left+right)/2];

  do {
```

```
   while(item[i]<x && i<right) i++;
   while(x<item[j] && j>left) j--;

   if(i<=j) {
     y = item[i];
     item[i] = item[j];
     item[j] = y;
     i++; j--;
   }
 } while(i<=j);
 if(left<j)  qs(item, left, j);
 if(i<right) qs(item, i, right);
}
```

USING THE STATISTICS
PROGRAM

To give you an idea of how you might use the statistics program developed in this chapter, you will now develop a simple stock market analysis example using Widget, Inc. You will be trying to decide whether it is a good time to invest in Widget by buying stock or selling "short" (selling shares you do not have and hoping for a rapid price drop so that you can buy them later at a cheaper price), or to invest elsewhere.

For the past 24 months, Widget's stock price has been

Month	Stock Price
1	$10
2	10
3	11
4	9
5	8
6	8
7	9
8	10
9	10
10	13

Month	Stock Price
11	$11
12	11
13	11
14	11
15	12
16	13
17	14
18	16
19	17
20	15
21	15
22	16
23	14
24	16

First determine if Widget's stock price has established a trend. After entering the figures you find the following basic statistics:

Mean	$12.08
Standard deviation	2.68
Median	11
Mode	11

Next, plot a bar graph of the stock price as shown in Figure 7-7.

It looks like there may be a trend, but it is best to perform a formal regression analysis. The regression equation is

$$y = 7.90 + 0.33 * x$$

with a correlation coefficient of 0.86, or about 74%. This is quite good; in fact a definite trend is clear. Printing a scatter graph, as shown in Figure 7-8, makes this strong growth readily apparent

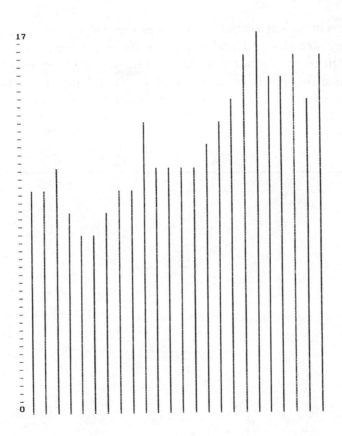

Figure 7-7.   Bar chart of Widget's stock price

and could cause an investor to throw caution to the wind and buy
1000 shares as quickly as possible!

FINAL THOUGHTS ON STATISTICS

The correct use of statistics requires a general understanding of
how they are derived and what the numbers really mean. It is
important to remember that past events do not necessarily predict
the future (except in some general way, perhaps) and that blind
reliance on statistical evidence can cause some very disturbing
results.

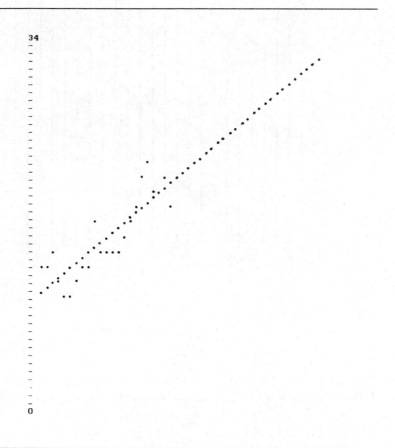

Figure 7-8.   Scatter graph of Widget's stock with regression line

8

CODES AND DATA COMPRESSION

For some reason, there seems to be a high correlation between people who like computers and programming and those who like to play with codes and ciphers. Perhaps it is because all codes involve algorithms, just as programs do. Or maybe it is just an affinity for cryptic things that most people cannot understand. Many programmers feel a great deal of satisfaction when a non-programmer looks at a program listing and says something like "That sure looks complicated!" After all, we do call the act of writing a program "coding."

Cryptography goes hand in hand with data compression, which is the compaction of information into a smaller space than is usually used. Data compaction is included in this chapter because it can play a role in encryption and uses many of the same principles.

Computer-based crytography is important for two main reasons:

1. There is a need to keep sensitive data on shared systems secure. Although password protection is adequate for many situations, truly important, confidential files are routinely coded to provide a higher level of protection.

2. Computer-based codes are needed for secure data transmission—for example, by governments or by private broadcasters to protect their sky-to-earth station transmissions.

Because these types of coding procedures are so complex, they are usually handled by a digital computer.

In addition to the coded nature of compacted data, data compression is commonly used to increase the storage capacity of various storage devices. Although the cost of storage devices has fallen sharply in the past few years, it may still be necessary to fit more information into smaller areas.

A SHORT HISTORY OF CRYPTOGRAPHY

Although no one knows when secret writing began, one of the earliest known examples is found on a cuneiform tablet made around 1500 B.C. that contains a coded formula for making pottery glaze. The Greeks used codes as early as 475 B.C., and the upper classes in Rome frequently used simple ciphers during the reign of Julius Caesar. Like so many other intellectual pursuits, cryptography waned during the Dark Ages except for occasional use by monks. With the birth of the Italian Renaissance the art of cryptography once again began to flourish, and during the reign of Louis XIV of France, for example, government messages used a code based on 587 randomly selected keys.

In the 1800s two events helped move cryptography forward:

1. Edgar Allan Poe published stories featuring coded messages, such as the "Gold Bug," which excited the imagination of many.

2. Samuel F.B. Morse invented the telegraph and the Morse code. The Morse code is important because it was the first binary (dots and dashes) representation of the alphabet to receive wide use.

By World War I several nations had constructed "code machines" that permitted the easy encoding and decoding of text by using sophisticated ciphers. These mechanical devices were able to use ciphers of significant complexity. At this point the story of cryptography changes slightly, to the story of code breaking.

Before mechanical devices were used to encode and decode messages, complex ciphers were used infrequently because of the time and effort required both for encoding and decoding. Hence, most codes could be broken within a relatively short period of time. However, the art of code breaking became much more difficult when code machines were used. Although the use of modern computers would have made breaking even those codes fairly easy, they do not dwarf the incredible talent of Herbert Yardley, still considered the grand master code breaker of all time. In 1915 he broke the U.S. diplomatic code (in his spare time) and then went on to his greatest accomplishment: the breaking of the Japanese diplomatic code in 1922, without knowing Japanese! He did this by using frequency tables of the Japanese language. It is sad that by the time World War II came around, the major method used to break codes was to steal the enemy's code machine and thereby forego the tedious but intellectually satisfying process of code breaking. In fact, it is commonly accepted that the Allies' possession of a German code machine (unknown to the Germans) contributed greatly to the outcome of the war.

With the advent of computers, especially multiuser computers, secure and unbreakable codes have become even more necessary. Not only do computer users occasionally need to keep their files secret, but also they must manage and regulate access to the computer itself. Users have developed numerous methods of encrypting data files, and the DES (Data Encryption Standard) algorithm, accepted by the National Bureau of Standards, has traditionally been considered secure from code-breaking efforts. However, rumors persist that DES is breakable and may not be suitable for all situations.

The Basic Types of Ciphers

There are two basic types of the more traditional coding methods:

1. *Transposition ciphers* essentially scramble the characters of a message according to some rule.

2. *Substitution ciphers* replace one character with another, but leave the message in the proper order.

These codes can be carried to whatever level of complexity is desired and can even be mixed. The digital computer adds a third basic encryption technique, called *bit manipulation*, that alters the computerized representation of data by some algorithm.

All three methods can make use of a *key* if desired. A key is generally some string of characters that is needed to decode a message. Do not confuse the key with the encryption method, however, because the key itself is never sufficient to decode; the encryption algorithm must also be known. What the key does is "personalize" a coded message so that only the people who know the key can decode it—at least easily—even though the method used to encode the message may be generally accessible.

You should become familiar with two terms: *plain text* and *cipher text*. The plain text of a message is the one anybody can read; the cipher text is the encoded version.

This chapter will look at various computerized methods of coding text files by using each of the three basic methods described above. It explores several short programs that encode and decode text files. Remember that with one exception all these programs have both a **code( )** and a **decode( )** function. The **decode( )** function always reverses the **code( )** process used to create the cipher text.

SUBSTITUTION CIPHERS

A substitution cipher is a method of encrypting a message by regularly substituting one character for another. One of the simplest forms of substitution cipher involves offsetting the alphabet by a specified amount. For example, if each letter is offset by three,

abcdefghijklmnopqrstuvwxyz

becomes

defghijklmnopqrstuvwxyzabc

Therefore an *a* becomes a *d*, a *b* becomes an *e*, and so on. You should notice that the letters *abc* were shifted from the front to the end. To encode a message using this method, you simply substitute the shifted alphabet for the real one. For example, the message

meet me at sunset

becomes

phhw ph dw vxqvhw

The program shown here enables you to code any text message with any offset by specifying which letter begins the alphabet:

```
/* Simple substitution cipher. */

#include <ctype.h>
#include <stdio.h>
#include <stdlib.h>

void code(char *input, char *output, char start);
void decode(char *input, char *output, char start);

main(int argc, char *argv[])
{
  if(argc!=5) {
    printf("usage: input output encode/decode offset\n");
    exit(1);
  }
```

```
    if(!isalpha(*argv[4])){
      printf("start letter must be alphabetical character\n");
      exit(1);
    }

    if(toupper(*argv[3])=='E')code(argv[1], argv[2], *argv[4]);
    else decode(argv[1], argv[2], *argv[4]);
    return 0;
}

void code(char *input, char *output, char start)
{
  int ch;
  FILE *fp1, *fp2;

  if((fp1=fopen(input, "r"))==NULL) {
    printf("cannot open input file\n");
    exit(1);
  }

  if((fp2=fopen(output, "w"))==NULL) {
    printf("cannot open output file\n");
    exit(1);
  }

  start = tolower(start);
  start = start-'a';
  do {
    ch = getc(fp1);
    ch = tolower(ch);
    if(isalpha(ch)) {
      ch += start; /* shift the letter */
      if(ch>'z') ch -= 26; /* wrap around */
    }
    putc(ch, fp2);
    if(feof(fp1)) break;

  } while(!ferror(fp1) && !ferror(fp2));
  fclose(fp1); fclose(fp2);
}

void decode(char *input, char *output, char start)
{
  int ch;
  FILE *fp1, *fp2;

  if((fp1=fopen(input, "r"))==NULL) {
    printf("cannot open input file\n");
    exit(1);
  }

  if((fp2=fopen(output, "w"))==NULL) {
    printf("cannot open output file\n");
    exit(1);
  }
```

```
start = tolower(start);
start = start-'a';
do {
  ch = getc(fp1);
  ch = tolower(ch);
  if(isalpha(ch)) {
    ch -= start; /* shift letter back to original */
    if(ch<'a') ch += 26;   /* wrap around */
  }
  putc(ch, fp2);
  if(feof(fp1)) break;
} while(!ferror(fp1) && !ferror(fp2));
fclose(fp1); fclose(fp2);
}
```

For example, to use this program to code a file called "message" by putting the coded version into a file called "cmess," and offsetting the alphabet two places, you would type from the command line

>code message cmess encode c

To decode you would type

>code cmess message decode c

Although a substitution cipher based on a constant offset may fool schoolchildren, it is generally not suitable because it is too easy to crack. There are, after all, only 26 possible offsets, and you could try all of them in a short time. A better version of the substitution cipher uses a scrambled alphabet instead of a simple offset. A second failing of the simple substitution cipher is that it preserves the spaces between words. This would make it doubly easy for a code breaker to crack. A better version would require that spaces also be encoded. (Actually, all punctuation should be encoded, but for simplicity's sake the examples here will not do this.) For example, you could map the following randomized string containing every letter of the alphabet and the space onto the alphabet as shown here:

qazwsxedcrfvtgbyhnujm ikolp
abcdefghijklmnopqrstuvwxyz<space>

You may be wondering if there is a significant improvement in the security of a message encoded using a randomized version of the alphabet versus the simple offset version. The answer is yes because there are 26! (26 factorial) ways to arrange the alphabet, and with the space that number becomes 27! ways. Remember that the factorial of a number is that number times every whole number smaller than it down to 1. That is, 6! is 6*5*4*3*2*1 = 54. Therefore 26! is a very large number.

The program shown here is an improved substitution cipher that uses the randomized alphabet shown above. If you encoded the message

meet me at sunset

in the improved substitution cipher program, it would look like this:

tssjptspqjpumgusj

This is, obviously, a harder code to break.

```c
/* Improved substitution cipher. */
#include <ctype.h>
#include <stdio.h>
#include <stdlib.h>

void code(char *input, char *output);
void decode(char *input, char *output);
int find(char *s, char ch);

char sub[28]=    "qazwsxedcrfvtgbyhnujm ikolp";
char alphabet[28]="abcdefghijklmnopqrstuvwxyz ";

main(int argc, char *argv[])
{
  if(argc!=4) {
    printf("usage: input output encode/decode\n");
    exit(1);
  }
  if(toupper(*argv[3])=='E') code(argv[1], argv[2]);
  else decode(argv[1], argv[2]);
  return 0;
}
```

```
void code(char *input, char *output)
{
  int ch;
  FILE *fp1, *fp2;

  if((fp1=fopen(input, "r"))==NULL) {
    printf("cannot open input file\n");
    exit(1);
  }

  if((fp2=fopen(output, "w"))==NULL) {
    printf("cannot open output file\n");
    exit(1);
  }

  do {
    ch = getc(fp1);
    ch = tolower(ch);
    if(isalpha(ch) || ch==' ')
      ch = sub[find(alphabet, ch)];
    putc(ch, fp2);
    if(feof(fp1)) break;
  } while(!ferror(fp1) && !ferror(fp2));
  fclose(fp1); fclose(fp2);
}

void decode(char *input, char *output)
{
  int ch;
  FILE *fp1, *fp2;

  if((fp1=fopen(input, "r"))==NULL) {
    printf("cannot open input file\n");
    exit(1);
  }

  if((fp2=fopen(output, "w"))==NULL) {
    printf("cannot open output file\n");
    exit(1);
  }

  do {
    ch = getc(fp1);
    ch = tolower(ch);
    if(isalpha(ch) || ch==' ')
      ch = alphabet[find(sub, ch)];
    putc(ch, fp2);
    if(feof(fp1)) break;
  } while(!ferror(fp1) && !ferror(fp2));

  fclose(fp1); fclose(fp2);
}

/* Find the correct index. */
```

```
find(char *s, char ch)
{
  register int t;
  for(t=0; t<28; t++) if(ch==s[t]) return t;
  return -1;
}
```

Although you will examine code breaking a little later in this chapter, it should be pointed out that even this improved substitution code can still be easily broken by using a frequency table of the English language, which records statistical information about the use of each letter of the alphabet. (You can see this type of substitution used in the "cryptograms" next to the crossword puzzle in many newspapers.) If you look at the coded message, you can readily see that s almost certainly has to be e, the most common letter in the English language, and p must be a space. The rest of the message can be decoded with a little effort. Futhermore, the larger the coded message is, the easier it is to crack with a frequency table.

To impede the progress of a code breaker applying frequency tables to a coded message, you can use a *multiple substitution cipher*. In this case, the same letters in the plain text message will not necessarily be represented by the same letter in the coded form. You can accomplish this easily by adding a second randomized alphabet and switching between it and the first alphabet each time a space is encountered. Suppose the second alphabet is

poi uytrewqasdfghjklmnbvcxz

The program shown here will switch randomized alphabets after a space is encountered. Hence spaces will not be encoded. Using it to code the message

meet me at sunset

produces the coded form

tssj su qj kmdkul

To see how this works, let's set up the ordered alphabet and the two randomized alphabets (called R1 and R2) over one another.

```
alphabet: abcdefghijklmnopqrstuvwxyz<space>
R1:       qazwsxedcrfvtgbyhnujm ikolp
R2:       poi uytrewqasdfghjklmnbvcxz
```

Here is how the program operates. At the start the first random alphabet is used. This randomized alphabet is used for the word *meet* and produces the cipher text *tssj*. The space following *meet* causes the second randomized alphabet to be used for the word *me*. This produces the cipher text *su*. Next the space causes the first randomized alphabet to be selected. This process of alternating alphabets continues until the message ends.

The use of multiple substitution ciphers makes it much harder to break a code by using frequency tables because different letters stand for the same thing at different times. If you think about it, it would be possible to use several different randomized alphabets and a somewhat more complex switching routine toward the goal of having all the letters in the coded text occur equally often. This would make a frequency table useless in breaking the code. The multiple substitution cipher shown here will work only with the letters of the alphabet:

```
/* Multiple substitution cipher. */

#include <ctype.h>
#include <stdio.h>
#include <stdlib.h>

void code(char *input, char *output);
void decode(char *input, char *output);
int find(char *s, char ch);

char sub[28]=    "qazwsxedcrfvtgbyhnujm ikolp";
char sub2[28]=   "poi uytrewqasdfghjklmnbvcxz";
char alphabet[28]="abcdefghijklmnopqrstuvwxyz ";

main(int argc, char *argv[])
{
  if(argc!=4) {
    printf("usage: input output encode/decode\n");
```

```
      exit(1);
   }
   if(toupper(*argv[3])=='E') code(argv[1],argv[2]);
.  else decode(argv[1],argv[2]);
   return 0;
}

void code(char *input, char *output)
{
   int ch, change;
   FILE *fp1, *fp2;

   if((fp1=fopen(input,"r"))==NULL) {
      printf("cannot open input file\n");
      exit(1);
   }

   if((fp2=fopen(output,"w"))==NULL) {
      printf("cannot open output file\n");
      exit(1);
   }

   change = 1;
   do {
      ch = getc(fp1);
      ch = tolower(ch);
      if(isalpha(ch))
         if(change)
            ch = sub[find(alphabet, ch)];
         else
            ch = sub2[find(alphabet, ch)];
      putc(ch, fp2);
      if(feof(fp1)) break;
      if(ch==' ') change = !change;
   } while(!ferror(fp1) && !ferror(fp2));
   fclose(fp1); fclose(fp2);
}

void decode(char *input, char *output)
{
   int ch,change;
   FILE *fp1, *fp2;

   if((fp1=fopen(input,"r"))==NULL) {
      printf("cannot open input file\n");
      exit(1);
   }

   if((fp2=fopen(output,"w"))==NULL) {
      printf("cannot open output file\n");
      exit(1);
   }
```

```
    change = 1;
    do {
      ch = getc(fp1);
      ch = tolower(ch);
      if(isalpha(ch))
      if(change)
        ch = alphabet[find(sub, ch)];
      else
        ch = alphabet[find(sub2, ch)];
    putc(ch, fp2);
    if(feof(fp1)) break;
    if(ch==' ')   change=!change;
  } while(!ferror(fp1) && !ferror(fp2));
  fclose(fp1); fclose(fp2);
}

/* Find an element */
find(char *s, char ch)
{
  register int t;

  for(t=0; t<28; t++) if(ch==s[t]) return t;
  return -1;
}
```

TRANSPOSITION CIPHERS

A transposition cipher is one in which the actual characters of the message are rearranged according to some algorithm to conceal the content of the text. In one of the earliest known uses of a transposition code the Spartans used a device called a "skytale" around 475 B.C. A skytale is basically a message written crossways on a strap wrapped around a cylinder. The strap is unwound and delivered to the recipient of the message, who wraps it around a cylinder of the same size to read the message. In actual practice this method leaves something to be desired because it is possible to keep trying different-sized cylinders until the message begins to make sense.

You can create a computerized version of a skytale by placing a message into an array one way and writing it out a different way. For example, if you have the following **union**,

```
union message {
  char s[100];
  char s2[20][5];
} skytale;
```

which is initialized to nulls, by placing the message

    meet me at sunset

into the one-dimensional array *skytale.s* but viewing it as the two-dimensional array *skytale.s2*, it would look like

m	e	e	t	
m	e		a	t
	s	u	n	s
e	t	0	0	0
0	0	0	0	0

Then if you wrote the array out a column at a time, the message would look like

    mm e...eest...e u...tan... ts...

where the periods indicate the null padding. To decode the message, you fill the columns in *skytale.s2*. Then the array *skytale.s* is displayed in normal order. The array *skytale.s* can be printed as a string because the message is null terminated. The following program uses this method to code and decode messages:

```c
/* Skytale cipher */

#include <ctype.h>
#include <stdio.h>
#include <stdlib.h>

union message {
  char s[100];
  char s2[20][5];
} skytale;

void code(char *input, char *output);
void decode(char *input, char *output);

main(int argc, char *argv[])
{
  int t;

  for(t=0; t<100; ++t) skytale.s[t]='\0';  /* load array */

  if(argc!=4) {
    printf("usage: input output encode/decode\n");
    exit(1);
  }

  if(toupper(*argv[3])=='E') code(argv[1], argv[2]);
  else decode(argv[1], argv[2]);
  return 0;
}

void code(char *input, char *output)
{
  int t, t2;
  FILE *fp1, *fp2;

  if((fp1=fopen(input, "r"))==NULL) {
    printf("cannot open input file\n");
    exit(1);
  }

  if((fp2=fopen(output, "w"))==NULL) {
    printf("cannot open output file\n");
    exit(1);
  }

  for(t=0;  t<100;  ++t) {
    skytale.s[t] = getc(fp1);
    if(feof(fp1))  break;
  }

  for(t=0;  t<5;  ++t)
```

```
      for(t2=0;  t2<20;  ++t2)
        putc(skytale.s2[t2][t], fp2);

    fclose(fp1);  fclose(fp2);
}

void decode(char *input, char *output)
{
  int t, t2;
  FILE *fp1, *fp2;

  if((fp1=fopen(input, "r"))==NULL) {
    printf("cannot open input file\n");
    exit(1);
  }

  if((fp2=fopen(output, "w"))==NULL) {
    printf("cannot open output file\n");
    exit(1);
  }

  for(t=0;  t<5 && !feof(fp1);  ++t)
    for(t2=0;  t2<20 && !feof(fp1);  ++t2)
      skytale.s2[t2][t] = getc(fp1);

  for(t=0;  t<100;  ++t)
    putc(skytale.s[t], fp2);

  fclose(fp1);  fclose(fp2);
}
```

Of course, there are other methods of obtaining transposed messages. One method particularly suited for use by computer involves swapping letters within the message as defined by some algorithm. For example, you can employ an algorithm that transposes letters up to a specified distance, starting from the front of the array and alternating its exchange with the end of the array, as shown here:

```
/* A transposition cipher. */

#include <ctype.h>
#include <stdio.h>
#include <stdlib.h>

void code(char *input, char *output, int dist);
void decode(char *input, char *output, int dist);

main(int argc, char *argv[])
{
  int dist;
```

```
      if(argc!=5) {
          printf("usage: input output encode/decode distance\n");
          exit(1);
      }

      dist=atoi(argv[4]);
      if(toupper(*argv[3])=='E') code(argv[1], argv[2], dist);
      else decode(argv[1], argv[2], dist);
      return 0;
  }

void code(char *input, char *output, int dist)
{
    char done, temp;
    int t;
    char s[256];
    FILE *fp1, *fp2;

    if((fp1=fopen(input, "r"))==0) {
      printf("cannot open input file\n");
      exit(1);
    }

    if((fp2=fopen(output, "w"))==0) {
      printf("cannot open output file\n");
      exit(1);
    }

    done = 0;
    do {
      for(t=0; t<(dist*2); ++t) {
        s[t] = getc(fp1);
        if(feof(fp1)) {
          s[t] = '\0';   /* if eof then null */
          done = 1;
        }
      }
      for(t=0; t<dist; t++) {
        temp = s[t];
        s[t] = s[t+dist];
        s[t+dist] = temp;
        t++;
        temp = s[t];
        s[t] = s[dist*2-t];
        s[dist*2-t] = temp;
      }
      for(t=0; t<dist*2; t++) putc(s[t], fp2);
    } while(!done);
    fclose(fp1);  fclose(fp2);
}

void decode(char *input, char *output, int dist)
{
    char done, temp;
    int t;
```

```
   char s[256];
   FILE *fp1, *fp2;

   if((fp1=fopen(input, "r"))==0) {
     printf("cannot open input file\n");
     exit(1);
   }

   if((fp2=fopen(output, "w"))==0) {
     printf("cannot open output file\n");
     exit(1);
   }

   done=0;
   do {
     for(t=0; t<(dist*2); ++t) {
       s[t] = getc(fp1);
       if(feof(fp1)) {
         s[t] = '\0';  /* if eof then null */
         done = 1;
       }
     }
     for(t=0; t<dist; t++) {
       t++;
       temp = s[t];
       s[t] = s[dist*2-t];
       s[dist*2-t] = temp;
       t--;
       temp = s[t];
       s[t] = s[t+dist];
       s[t+dist] = temp;
       t++;
     }
     for(t=0; t<dist*2; t++) putc(s[t], fp2);
   } while(!done);
   fclose(fp1);  fclose(fp2);
}
```

Using this method, with a distance of ten, the message

meet me at sunset

will look something like

    <space>usetn smte metae

Used by themselves, transposition ciphers suffer from the fact
that the transposition process often accidentally creates clues. In

the above text the partial words *set* and *me* are somewhat suggestive.

BIT MANIPULATION CIPHERS

The digital computer has given rise to a new method of encoding by manipulating the bits that compose the actual characters of the plain text. This method of encryption is called a *bit manipulation cipher*. Although the purists among you will claim that bit manipulation (or *alteration*, as it is sometimes called) is really just a variation on the substitution cipher, the concepts, methods, and options differ so significantly that it must be considered a cipher method in its own right.

There are two reasons for the popularity of bit manipulation ciphers:

1. They are well suited for use on a computer because they employ operations easily performed by the system.
2. The cipher text tends to look completely unintelligible, which adds to the security of the message by making the data look like unused or crashed files.

Bit manipulation ciphers are generally applicable only to computer-based files and cannot be used to create a hard copy message because the bit manipulations tend to produce nonprinting characters. For this reason, you can assume that any file coded by bit manipulation methods will remain in a computer file.

To convert plain text into cipher text bit manipulation ciphers, alter the actual bit pattern of each character by using one or more of the following logical operators:

AND
OR
XOR
1's complement

C is perhaps the best language for creating bit manipulation ciphers because it supports the following bitwise operators:

Operator	Meaning
¦	OR
&	AND
^	XOR
~	1's complement

The simplest and least secure bit manipulation cipher uses only the 1's complement operator, ~. Remember that the 1's complement operator causes each bit within a byte to be inverted. That is, a 1 becomes a 0, and a 0 becomes a 1. Therefore a byte complemented twice is the same as the original. The following program codes any text file. Notice that it must open the output file of the encode operation and the input file of the decode operation as binary files because the 1's complement operation tends to produce non-ASCII characters.

```
/* 1's complement cipher */
#include <stdio.h>
#include <stdlib.h>
#include <ctype.h>

void code(char *input, char *output);
void decode(char *input, char *output);

main(int argc, char *argv[])
{
  if(argc!=4) {
    printf("usage: input output encode/decode\n");
    exit(1);
  }
  if(toupper(*argv[3])=='E') code(argv[1], argv[2]);
  else decode(argv[1], argv[2]);
  return 0;
}

void code(char *input, char *output)
{
  int ch;
  FILE *fp1, *fp2;

  if((fp1=fopen(input, "r"))==NULL) {
```

```
      printf("cannot open input file\n");
      exit(1);
}

if((fp2=fopen(output, "wb"))==NULL) {
   printf("cannot open output file\n");
   exit(1);
   }

   do {
      ch = getc(fp1);
      ch = ~ch;
      putc(ch, fp2);
      if(feof(fp1)) break;
   } while(!ferror(fp1) && !ferror(fp2));
   fclose(fp1); fclose(fp2);
}

void decode(char *input, char *output)
{
   int ch;
   FILE *fp1, *fp2;

   if((fp1=fopen(input, "rb"))==NULL) {
      printf("cannot open input file\n");
      exit(1);
   }

   if((fp2=fopen(output, "w"))==NULL) {
      printf("cannot open output file\n");
      exit(1);
   }

   do {
      ch = getc(fp1);
      ch = ~ch;
      if(feof(fp1)) break;
      putc(ch, fp2);
   } while(!ferror(fp1) && !ferror(fp2));
   fclose(fp1); fclose(fp2);
}
```

It is not easy to show what the cipher text of a message would look like because the bit manipulation used here generally creates nonprinting characters. Try it on your computer and examine the file—it will look quite cryptic, indeed.

There are really two problems with this simple coding scheme:

1. The encryption program does not use a key to decode, so anyone with access to the program can decode an encoded file.

2. Perhaps more important, this method would be easily spotted by any experienced computer programmer.

An improved method of bit manipulation coding uses the XOR operator, ^. The XOR operator has the following truth table:

```
^ | 0 | 1
—|—|—
0 | 0 | 1
—|—|—
1 | 1 | 0
```

or, in words, the outcome of the XOR operation is true if—and only if—one operand is true and the other is false. This gives the XOR a unique property; if you XOR a byte with another byte, called the "key," and then take the outcome of that operation and XOR it again with the key, you will get the original byte back. For example:

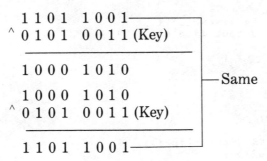

This process could be used to code a file and it solves the two problems with the simple 1's complement version:

1. Because it uses a key, the encryption program alone cannot decode a file.

2. Because the use of a key makes each file unique, it is not obvious to someone schooled only in computer science just what has been done to the file.

The key need not be only one byte long; in fact, you could use a key of several characters and alternate the characters through the file. This example, however, uses a single character key to keep the program uncluttered.

```c
/*   XOR cipher. */

#include <stdio.h>
#include <stdlib.h>
#include <ctype.h>

void code(char *input, char *output, char key);
void decode(char *input, char *output, char key);

main(int argc, char *argv[])
{
  if(argc!=5) {
    printf("usage: input output decode/encode key\n");
    exit(1);
  }
  if(toupper(*argv[3])=='E')
    code(argv[1], argv[2], *argv[4]);
  else
    decode(argv[1], argv[2], *argv[4]);
  return 0;
}

void code(char *input, char *output, char key)
{
  int ch;
  FILE *fp1, *fp2;

  if((fp1=fopen(input, "r"))==NULL) {
    printf("cannot open input file\n");
    exit(1);
  }

  if((fp2=fopen(output, "wb"))==NULL) {
    printf("cannot open output file\n");
    exit(1);
  }

  do {
    ch = getc(fp1);
    ch = ch^key;
    putc(ch, fp2);
    if(feof(fp1)) break;
  } while(!ferror(fp1) && !ferror(fp2));
  fclose(fp1);  fclose(fp2);
}
```

```
void decode(char *input, char *output, char key)
{
  int ch;
  FILE *fp1, *fp2;

  if((fp1=fopen(input, "rb"))==NULL) {
    printf("cannot open input file\n");
    exit(1);
  }

  if((fp2=fopen(output, "w"))==NULL) {
    printf("cannot open output file\n");
    exit(1);
  }

  do {
    ch = getc(fp1);
    ch = ch^key;
    if(feof(fp1)) break;
    putc(ch, fp2);
  } while(!ferror(fp1) && !ferror(fp2));
  fclose(fp1);  fclose(fp2);
}
```

Notice that the output file of the encode operation and the input file of the decode operation must be opened as binary files.

Try this program. You will see that not only is the file unintelligible, but also it can only be decoded by using the key.

DATA COMPRESSION

Data compression is essentially making the same amount of information fit into a smaller space. It is not limited to computers; consider microfilm, for example. However, it is often used in computer systems to increase the storage of the system, save transfer time (especially over phone lines), and provide a level of security. Although many data compression schemes are available, this section looks at only two of them: (1) bit compression, in which more than one character fits into a single byte, and (2) character deletion, in which actual characters from the file are deleted.

Eight into Seven

Although all computers must have bytes that are an even power of two (because of the binary representation of data in the machine), the uppercase and lowercase letters and punctuation require only about 63 different codes, which need only a 6-bit byte. (A 6-bit byte could have values of 0 through 63.) However, most computers use an 8-bit byte; hence, 25% of the byte's storage is wasted. You could actually compact four characters into three if you could use the last two bits in each byte. The only problem is the way the ASCII codes are organized: there are more than 63 different ASCII character codes, and the uppercase and lowercase alphabet falls more or less in the middle. This means that some of the characters needed will require at least seven bits. It is possible to use a non-ASCII representation (which is done on rare occasions), but it is not generally advisable. An easier option is to compact eight characters into seven by making use of the fact that no letter or common punctuation mark uses the eighth bit of a byte. Therefore, you can use the eighth bit of each of the seven bytes to store the eighth character. You should realize that many computers, the IBM PC included, use 8-bit characters to represent special or graphics characters, and some word processors use the eighth bit for text-processing instructions. Using this type of data compaction will work only on "straight" ASCII files, which do not use the eighth bit for anything.

To visualize how this would work, consider the following eight characters represented as 8-bit bytes:

```
byte 1: 0 1 1 1   0 1 0 1
byte 2: 0 1 1 1   1 1 0 1
byte 3: 0 0 1 0   0 0 1 1
byte 4: 0 1 0 1   0 1 1 0
byte 5: 0 0 0 1   0 0 0 0
byte 6: 0 1 1 0   1 1 0 1
byte 7: 0 0 1 0   1 0 1 0
byte 8: 0 1 1 1   1 0 0 1
```

As you can see, the eighth bit is always 0. This is always the case unless it is used for parity checking. The easiest way to compress eight characters into seven is to distribute the seven significant bits of byte 1 into the seven unused eighth bit positions of bytes 2 through 8. If this is done, the seven remaining bytes will look like this:

```
                 ┌──────byte 1─read down
byte 2: 1 1 1 1  1 1 0 1
byte 3: 1 0 1 0  0 0 1 1
byte 4: 1 1 0 1  0 1 1 0
byte 5: 0 0 0 1  0 0 0 0
byte 6: 1 1 1 0  1 1 0 1
byte 7: 0 0 1 0  1 0 1 0
byte 8: 1 1 1 1  1 0 0 1
```

To reconstruct byte 1, you need only put it back together by taking the eighth bit off each of the seven bytes.

The compression technique described here will compress any text file by 12.5%. This is a fairly substantial saving. For example, if you were transmitting the source code for your favorite program to a friend over long-distance phone lines, you would be saving 12.5% of the transmission expense. (Remember that the object code, or executable version of the program, will need the full 8 bits.)

The program shown here compresses a text file as described earlier. Be aware that in order for the algorithm to work correctly at the end of the file, up to seven extra bytes may be appended to the output file. Thus, on extremely short files (less that 56 bytes) the compressed file may be longer than the noncompressed file. However, these bytes are insignificant in longer files. You might find it interesting to try to alter the algorithm so this is not the case. (It's not as easy as you may think.)

```
/* Bit-compression */

#include <stdio.h>
#include <stdlib.h>
#include <ctype.h>
```

```
void compress(char *input, char *output);
void decompress(char *input, char *output);

main(int argc, char *argv[])
{
  if(argc!=4) {
    printf("usage: input output compress/decompress\n");
    exit(1);
  }
  if(toupper(*argv[3])=='C')
    compress(argv[1], argv[2]);
  else
    decompress(argv[1], argv[2]);
  return 0;
}

void compress(char *input, char *output)
{
  char ch, ch2, done, t;
  FILE *fp1, *fp2;

  if((fp1=fopen(input, "r"))==NULL) {
    printf("cannot open input file\n");
    exit(1);
  }

  if((fp2=fopen(output, "w"))==NULL) {
    printf("cannot open output file\n");
    exit(1);
  }

  done = 0;
  do {
      /* get first byte, the one that will
         be distributed into the next 7 bytes
      */
      ch = getc(fp1);
      ch = ch << 1;   /* shift off top bit */

      /* distribute remaining 7 bits into next
         7 bytes
      */
      for(t=0; t<7; ++t) {
        ch2 = getc(fp1);
        if(feof(fp1)) {
          ch2 = 0;
          done = 1;
        }
        ch2 = ch2 & 127; /* turn off top bit of next byte */
```

```
            /* now, OR in next bit from the first byte */
            ch2 = ch2 | ((ch<<t) & 128);
            putc(ch2, fp2);
        }
        if(feof(fp1)) break;
    } while(!done && !ferror(fp1) && !ferror(fp2));
    fclose(fp1);  fclose(fp2);
}

void decompress(char *input, char *output)
{
    unsigned char ch, ch2, t;
    char s[7], temp;
    FILE *fp1, *fp2;

    if((fp1=fopen(input, "r"))==NULL) {
        printf("cannot open input file\n");
        exit(1);
    }

    if((fp2=fopen(output, "w"))==NULL) {
        printf("cannot open output file\n");
        exit(1);
    }

    do {
        ch = 0;
        /* reconstruct the first byte */
        for(t=0;  t<7;  ++t) {
            temp = getc(fp1);
            ch2 = temp;   /* type conversion */
            s[t] = ch2 & 127;   /* turn off top bit */
            ch2 = ch2 & 128;    /* turn off all but top bit */
            ch2 = ch2 >> (t+1);  /* shift over existing bits */
            ch = ch | ch2;       /* OR in the next bit */
        }

        putc(ch, fp2);  /* write out the first byte */

        /* write out the remaining 7 */
        for(t=0; t<7; ++t) putc(s[t], fp2);

        if(feof(fp1)) break;
    } while(!ferror(fp1) && !ferror(fp2));
    fclose(fp1);  fclose(fp2);
}
```

This code is fairly complex because the bits that form the first byte must be shifted into their proper positions. However, you should try to follow it through until you are confident that you understand the **compress( )** and **decompress( )** operations.

The 16-Character Language

Although not suitable for most situations, a very interesting method of data compression involves the deletion of unnecessary letters from words—essentially making most words abbreviations. The data compression is achieved because the unused characters are not stored. If you think about it, the saving of space by using abbreviations is very common; that is the reason for using *Mr.* instead of *Mister*, for example. Instead of using actual abbreviations, the approach here will automatically remove certain letters from a message. To do this requires a *minimal alphabet*. A minimal alphabet is one in which several seldom-used letters have been removed, leaving only those necessary to form most words or avoid ambiguity. Any character not in the minimal alphabet will be extracted from any word in which it appears. Exactly how many characters there are in a minimal alphabet is open to discussion, but the following program will use the 14 most common letters plus spaces and newlines. The next few paragraphs explain why.

In order to automate the abbreviation process, you need to know which are the most frequently used letters in the alphabet to create a minimal alphabet. Although you could, in theory, count the letters in each word in the dictionary, different writers use a different frequency mix than others, so a frequency chart based only on the words that make up the English language may not reflect the actual usage frequency of letters. (It would also take a *long* time to do.) As an alternative, let's count the usage frequency of the letters in this chapter and use them as a basis for a minimal alphabet. First, you need a program to do this. It is quite simple and is shown here:

```
/* Character frequency program. */
#include <stdio.h>
#include <ctype.h>
#include <stdlib.h>

main(int argc, char *argv[])
{
  FILE *fp1;
  int alpha[26], t;
  int space=0, period=0, comma=0;
  char ch;
```

```
if(argc!=2) {
  printf("Please specify text file.\n");
  exit(1);
}

if((fp1=fopen(argv[1], "r"))==NULL) {
  printf("cannot open input file\n");
  exit(1);
}

for(t=0; t<26; t++) alpha[t]=0;

do {
  ch = getc(fp1);
  if(isalpha(ch))
    alpha[toupper(ch)-'A']++;
  else switch(ch) {
    case ' ': space++;
      break;
    case '.': period++;
       break;
    case ', ': comma++;
       break;
  }
} while(!feof(fp1));

for(t=0; t<26; ++t)
  printf("%c: %d\n", 'A'+t, alpha[t]);

printf("period: %d\n", period);
printf("space: %d\n", space);
printf("comma: %d\n", comma);
fclose(fp1);
}
```

The program skips all punctuation except periods, commas, and spaces. By running this program on the text of this chapter, you get the following frequency:

A: 2525
B: 532
C: 838
D: 1145
E: 3326
F: 828
G: 529
H: 1086
I: 2242

```
J:  39
K:  94
L:  1103
M:  1140
N:  2164
O:  1767
P:  697
Q:  62
R:  1656
S:  1672
T:  3082
U:  869
V:  376
W:  370
X:  178
Y:  356
Z:  20
SPACE:  5710
PERIOD:  234
COMMA:  513
```

The frequency of letters in this chapter compares well with the standard English mix and is offset only slightly by the repeated use of the C keywords in the programs.

To achieve significant data compression, you need to cut the alphabet substantially, especially because you will be removing the least frequently used letters. Although there are many different ideas about exactly what a workable minimum alphabet is, the 14 most common letters, plus the space, comprise around 85% of all characters used in this chapter. Because the newline character is necessary to preserve word breaks, it must also be included. Therefore, the minimal "alphabet" (consisting of 14 characters, a space, and a newline) based on letter frequency in this chapter is

A C D E H I L M N O R S T U <space> <newline>

The program shown here will remove all characters except the 16 selected:

```
/* Character deletion program. */
#include <stdio.h>
#include <stdlib.h>
#include <string.h>
#include <ctype.h>

void comp2(char *input, char *output);

main(int argc, char *argv[])
{
  if(argc!=3) {
    printf("usage: input output\n");
    exit(1);
  }
  comp2(argv[1],argv[2]);
  return 0;
}

void comp2(char *input, char *output)
{
  char ch;
  FILE *fp1,*fp2;

  if((fp1=fopen(input,"r"))==NULL) {
    printf("cannot open input file\n");
    exit(1);
  }

  if((fp2=fopen(output,"w"))==NULL) {
    printf("cannot open output file\n");
    exit(1);
  }

  do {
    ch = getc(fp1);
    if(feof(fp1)) break;
    if(strchr("ACDEJILMNORSTU '\n'", toupper(ch))) {
      if(ch=='\n') putc('\r',fp2);
      putc(ch,fp2);
    }
  } while(!ferror(fp1) && !ferror(fp2));
  fclose(fp1); fclose(fp2);
}
```

If you use this program on the message

```
Attention High Command:

      Attack successful. Please send additional supplies and
      fresh troops.  This is essential to maintain our
      foothold.

      General Frashier
```

the compressed message would look like this:

```
Attention i Command
        Attac successul  lease send additional sulies and
        res troos    Tis is essential to maintain our
        ootold

        eneral rasier
```

As you can see, although the message is largely readable, there is some ambiguity, which is the chief drawback of this method of data compression. However, if you knew the vocabulary of the originator of the message, you could probably select a better minimal alphabet that would help remove some of this ambiguity. In spite of the potential for ambiguity, you saved quite a bit of space. The original message was 168 bytes long, and the compacted message was 142 bytes long, a saving of about 16%.

It is interesting to note that if both character deletion and bit compression were applied to the message, about 28% less storage would be needed. The ability to do this could be very important. For example, if you were a submarine captain and wanted to send a message to HQ but did not want to give away your position, you might want to compress the message using both methods to make the transmission as short as possible.

Both the bit compression and character deletion methods of data compression have uses in encryption. Bit compression further encrypts the information and makes decoding harder. The character deletion method has one wonderful advantage: If it is used before encryption, it disguises the character frequency of the source language.

CODE BREAKING

No chapter on encryption methods is complete without at least a brief look at code breaking. The art of code breaking is essentially one of trial and error. A digital computer makes it relatively easy to break ciphers by exhaustive trial and error. However, the more complex codes either cannot be broken or require techniques and

resources not commonly available. This section will stick to breaking the more straightforward codes.

If you wish to break a message that was ciphered using the
simple substitution method with an offset alphabet, all you need to
do is try all 26 possible offsets to see which one fits. A program to
do this is shown here:

```
/* Code breaker from simple substitution ciphers. */

#include <ctype.h>
#include <stdio.h>
#include <stdlib.h>

void bc(char *input);

main(int argc, char *argv[])
{
  if(argc!=2) {
    printf("usage: input\n");
    exit(1);
  }
  bc(argv[1]);
  return 0;
}

/* Try to break a simple substitution cipher. */
void bc(char *input)

{
  register int t, t2;
  char ch, s[1000], q[10];
  FILE *fp1;

  if((fp1=fopen(input, "r"))==NULL) {
    printf("cannot open input file\n");
    exit(1);
  }

  /* read in message */
  for(t=0; t<1000; ++t) {
    s[t] = getc(fp1);
    if(s[t]==EOF) break;
  }
  s[t] = '\0';
  fclose(fp1);

  /* try different substitutions */
  for(t=0; t<26; ++t) {
    for(t2=0; s[t2]; t2++) {
      ch = s[t2];
      if(isalpha(ch)) {
```

```
      ch = tolower(ch)-t;
      if(ch<'a') ch += 26;
    }
    printf("%c", ch);
  }
  printf("\n");
  printf("decoded? (y/n): ");
  gets(q);
  if(*q=='y') break;
}
printf("\noffset is: %d", t);

}
```

With only a slight variation you could use the same program to break ciphers using a random alphabet. In this case, you would substitute manually entered alphabets as shown in the program here:

```
/* Code breaker for random substitution ciphers. */

#include <ctype.h>
#include <stdio.h>
#include <stdlib.h>

char sub[28];
char alphabet[28]="abcdefghijklmnopqrstuvwxyz ";

void bc2(char *input);
int find(char *s, char ch);

main(int argc, char *argv[])
{
  char s[80];

  if(argc!=2) {
    printf("usage: input");
    exit(1);
  }

  do {
    printf("enter test alphabet:\n");
    gets(sub);
    bc2(argv[1]);
    printf("\nIs this right?: (y/n) ");
    gets(s);
  } while(tolower(*s)!='y');
  return 0;
}
```

```
/* Break a random substitution cipher. */
void bc2(char *input)
{
  char ch;
  FILE *fp1;

  if((fp1=fopen(input, "r"))==NULL) {
    printf("cannot open input file\n");
    exit(1);
  }

  do {
    ch = getc(fp1);
    if(feof(fp1)) break;
    if(isalpha(ch) || ch==' ') {
      printf("%c", alphabet[find(sub, ch)]);
    }
  } while(!ferror(fp1));
  fclose(fp1);
}

/* Find the corresponding character. */
find(char *s, char ch)
{
  register int t;

  for(t=0; t<28; t++) if(ch==s[t]) return t;
}
```

One improvment you could try is to let the computer automatically generate different random alphabets.

Unlike the substitution ciphers, the transposition and bit manipulation ciphers are harder to break using the trial-and-error methods shown here. If you have to break such complex codes, good luck!

Oh, and by the way: hsaovbno wlymljapvu pz haahpuhisl, pa vjjbyz vusf hz hu hjjpklua.

9

RANDOM NUMBER GENERATORS AND SIMULATIONS

Sequences of random numbers are used in a variety of programming situations, ranging from simulations (the most common) to games and other recreational software. The ANSI standard defines the **rand( )** function, which returns a pseudorandom integer between 0 and 32,767, and it is part of Turbo C's standard library. Although this function is quite good, sometimes you will want to create your own random number generating functions. For example, you may want to use multiple random number generators to allow independent control of various facets of your program. Or you may want a generator that skews its random numbers about some value when you are working with abnormal distributions. Whatever the case, the study and creation of random number generators has captivated programmers since the dawn of computers.

In this chapter you will learn how various random number generating functions are written and how to evaluate them. You will look at two interesting simulations that use the random number generators developed in the chapter. The first is a grocery store checkout simulation, and the second is a "random walk" stock portfolio manager.

RANDOM NUMBER GENERATORS

Technically, the term *random number generator* is absurd because numbers are not random! What is really meant by random number generator is something that creates a sequence of numbers that appears to be randomly ordered. Of course, this raises the more complex question of what is a random sequence of numbers. The only truly correct answer is that a random sequence of numbers is one in which all elements are completely unrelated. This leads to the paradox that any sequence can be both random and nonrandom depending on the way the sequence was obtained. For example, the following list of numbers

    1 2 3 4 5 6 7 8 9 0

was created by typing the top keys on the keyboard in order, so it certainly cannot be construed as random. But what if the same sequence was obtained by using a barrel full of numbered Ping-Pong balls and selecting each ball by some arbitrary method? That would definitely make it a random sequence! The point is that the randomness of a sequence depends on the way it was generated, not on what the actual sequence is.

Remember that sequences of numbers generated by a computer are always deterministic; that is, each number other than the first depends on the number that precedes it. Technically, this means that computers can create only quasi-random sequences of numbers. However, this is usually good enough for most problems, and this book will simply call them random sequences. (It's not clear that any sequence of numbers can be proven to be random or nonrandom anyway!)

Generally, a random sequence should be uniform, that is, one in which all numbers are equally likely to occur. Do not confuse this with the normal distribution or bell-shaped curve. In a uniform distribution all events are equally probable, so a graph of a uniform distribution is a flat line rather than a curve. As mentioned earlier, you might need a random sequence that is skewed about some value, but this would be a special case, not the norm.

Before the widespread use of computers, when random numbers were needed they were produced either by throwing dice or by pulling numbered balls from a barrel. In 1955 the RAND Corporation published a table of one million random digits obtained with help from a computerlike machine. In the early days of computer science many methods were devised to generate random numbers, but most were discarded. One particularly interesting method that almost worked was developed by none other than John Von Neumann, the father of the modern computer. It is often called the middle-square method, and it works as follows: Square the previous random number and extract the middle digits. For example, if you were creating three-digit numbers and the previous value was 121, you would square it, making 14,641, and extract the middle three digits, making the next number 464. The problem with this method is that it leads to a very short repeating pattern called a *cycle*, especially once a zero has entered the pattern. So this method is not used today.

The most common way to generate random numbers is by using the following equation:

$$R_{n+1} = (aR_n+c) \bmod m$$

where

$R >= 0$
$a >= 0$
$c >= 0$
$m > R_0$ $m>a$ $m>c$

This is sometimes called the *linear congruential method*.

At this point you are probably thinking this random number generating is a piece of cake, and it really does seem simple. There is a catch, though, because how well the above equation performs depends very heavily on the values of *a*, *c*, and *m*, and choosing those values is sometimes more an art than a science. Some very complex rules can help you choose those values, but this discussion is confined to a few simple rules and experimentation.

The modulus, *m*, should be fairly large because it determines the range of the random numbers. You should remember that the modulus operation yields the remainder of a division done with the same operands. Hence, $10 \div 4$ is 2 because 4 goes into 10 twice with a remainder of 2. Therefore, if the modulus is, say, 12, the randomizing equation can produce only the numbers 0 through 11, whereas with a modulus of 21,425 it can generate the numbers 0 through 21,424. The choice of the multiplier, *a*, and the increment, *c*, is much harder. Usually the increment is fairly small and the multiplier can be fairly large. A lot of testing is needed to confirm that a good generator has been created.

As a first example, look at one of the more common random number generators. The equation shown in **ran1( )** has been used as the basis for the random number generator in a number of popular languages.

```
float ran1(void)
{
  static long int a=100001;

  a = (a*125) % 2796203;
  return (float) a/2796203;
}
```

You should notice three very important things about this function:

■ The random number is actually an integer—**long int** in this case—even though the function returns a **float** because integers are necessary for the linear congruential method. But by convention, random number generators are expected to return a number between 0 and 1, and that requires a floating point.

- The "seed" or starting value is hard-coded into this function by using the **static long int a**. In this way, it can provide a seed value to the next call. Although for most situations this is fine, you could let the user specify the initial value in the hope of making the sequence a little more random. If you specified a user-specified seed value, the function would be

```
float ran1(float seed)
{
   static long int a;
   static char once=1;

   if(once){
     a = seed*1000;   /* get a first value */
     once = 0;
   }

   a = (a*125) % 2796203;
   return (float) a/2796203;
}
```

For the rest of this chapter, however, the functions will have their initial value hard-coded for simplicity.

- The random number is divided by the modulus before the return to obtain a number between 0 and 1. Although the random number generator **rand()** specified by ANSI and used by Turbo C returns a number between 0 and 32,767, traditionally random number generators have returned values between 0 and 1. (This is the format followed by BASIC, Turbo Pascal, FORTRAN, and other languages.) This is because random numbers are frequently used in probabilistic simulations that require values in this range. For the sake of tradition, this chapter will also create generators that return the values 0 through 1. If you give it a little thought, you will see that the value of a before the return line must be a value between 0 and 2,796,202. Therefore, when that number is divided by 2,796,203, the result is a number equal to or greater than 0 but less than 1. By the same reasoning, you can convert the output of the **rand( )** function to a value between 0 and 1 by dividing it by 32,767.

Many random number generators are not good because they produce nonuniform distributions; short, repeating sequences; or both. A secondary problem is that using the same random number generator over and over again can produce biased results based on these problems, even if they are very slight. The solution is to create several different generators and use them either individually or jointly to obtain more random numbers.

A second generator that produces a good distribution is called **ran2( )** and is shown here:

```
float ran2()
{
  static long int a=1;

  a = (a*32719+3) % 32749;
  return (float) a / 32749;
}
```

DETERMINING THE QUALITY OF A GENERATOR

All three of the random number generators discussed will produce a fairly good sequence of random numbers, yet the question remains: How does one know how random the numbers really are? That is, how good are these generators?

A number of different tests can be applied to a sequence of numbers to determine their randomness. None of these tests will tell you if a sequence is random; they tell you only if it is not. That is, the tests can identify a nonrandom sequence, but just because a specific test does not find a problem does not imply that a given sequence is indeed random. It does, however, raise one's confidence in the random number generator that produced the sequence. Most of these tests are either too complicated or time consuming in their most rigorous form for most applications. However, let's look briefly at some of the ways a sequence can be tested and how it can fail.

First, it is important to know how closely the distribution of the numbers in a sequence conforms to what you expect a random distribution to be. For example, suppose you are attempting to generate random sequences of the digits 0 through 9. The probability of each digit's occurring is 1/10 because there are ten possibilities for each number in the sequence, all of which are equally likely. Now assume that the sequence

9 1 8 2 4 6 3 7 5 8 2 9 0 4 2 4 7 8 6 2

is generated. Counting the number of times each digit occurs, you find

Digit	Occurrences
0	1
1	1
2	4
3	1
4	3
5	1
6	2
7	2
8	3
9	2

What you want to know is whether this distribution of the digits is sufficiently similar to the expected distribution.

A bit of a paradox is at hand here: If a random number generator is good, it will generate sequences randomly; and in a truly random state, all sequences are possible. This implies that any sequence generated should qualify as a valid random sequence. So how can you tell if the above sequence is random? In fact, how could any sequence of the ten digits be nonrandom, since any sequence is possible? The answer is that some sequences are less likely to be random than others. You can determine the probability that a given sequence will be random by using the *chi-square* test. The chi-square test basically takes the observed number of occurrences, subtracts the expected number of occurrences from it for all possible outcomes, and produces a number, generally called *V.* You can take this number and look it up in a table of chi-square values to find the likelihood that the sequence is random in distribution. (Figure 9-1 presents a small table; you can find complete tables in most statistics books.)

The formula to obtain *V* is

$$V = \sum_{1 \leq i \leq N} \frac{(O_i - E_i)^2}{E_i}$$

where

O_i is the number of observed occurrences
E_i is the expected number of occurrences
N is the number of discrete elements

	p=99%	p=95%	p=75%	p=50%	p=25%	p=5%
n=5	0.5543	1.1455	2.675	4.351	6.626	11.07
n=10	2.558	3.940	6.737	9.342	12.55	18.31
n=15	5.229	7.261	11.04	14.34	18.25	25.00
n=20	8.260	10.85	15.45	19.34	23.83	31.41
n=30	14.95	18.49	24.48	29.34	34.80	43.77

Figure 9-1.   Selected chi-square values

The value for E_i is determined by multiplying the probablity of that element's occurring by the number of observations. Because in this case each digit is expected to occur 1/10th of the time, and 20 samples were taken, the value for E will be 2 for all digits. The value of N is 10 because there are 10 possible elements, the digits 0-9. Therefore, the value for V is

$$V = \frac{(1-2)^2}{2} + \frac{(1-2)^2}{2} + \frac{(4-2)^2}{2} + \frac{(1-2)^2}{2} + \frac{(3-2)^2}{2} + \frac{(1-2)^2}{2} +$$

$$\frac{(2-2)^2}{2} + \frac{(2-2)^2}{2} + \frac{(3-2)^2}{2} + \frac{(2-2)^2}{2} = 5$$

To determine the likelihood that the sequence is not random, you find the row in the table that equals the number of observations; in this case it is the fourth row, where n equals 20. Then read across until you find a number that is greater than V. In this case it is in column 1. This means that there is a 99% likelihood that a sample of 20 elements will have V greater than 8.260. Therefore, there is only a 1% probability that it is a random sequence. To "pass" the chi-square test, it is necessary for V to be between 75% and 25% probable. (This range is derived by using mathematics beyond the scope of this book.)

But you might counter that conclusion with the following argument. Since all sequences are possible, how can you say that this sequence has only a 1% chance of being legitimate? The answer is that it is just a probability; the chi-square "test" is actually not a test at all, only a confidence builder. In fact, if you use the chi-square test, you ought to obtain several different sequences and average the results to avoid rejecting a good random number generator. In essence, any single sequence might be rejected, but several sequences, averaged together, should pass the test.

It must be pointed out, however, that a sequence could pass the chi-square test and still not be random. For example,

1 3 5 7 9 7 5 3 1

would pass the chi-square test but does not appear very random. Each group of four digits on either side of the 9 is in strictly ascending or descending order, so the sequence is not random; it is a *run*. A run is a strictly ascending or descending sequence of numbers at evenly spaced intervals. Runs can also be separated by "noise" digits. That is, the digits that make up the run may be spaced out in an otherwise random sequence. It is possible to design a test for this, but this chapter will not do so.

Another thing to test for is the length of the *period;* that is, how many numbers can be generated before the sequence begins to repeat, or worse, degenerate into a short cycle. All computer-based random number generators eventually repeat a sequence. The longer the period, however, the better the generator. Even though the frequency of the numbers within the period is uniformly distributed, the numbers do not constitute a random series because a truly random series does not repeat itself consistently. A period of several thousand numbers is generally sufficient for most applications. Again, there is a test for this, but it is not developed here.

Several other tests can be applied to determine the quality of a random number generator. In fact, more code has probably been written to test random number generators than to construct them. In spite of this, let's develop yet another test that will "visually" test random number generators by displaying graphically how the sequence is generated. Here's how the "test" will work.

Ideally, we want a graph based on the frequency of each number, but this is impractical because random number generators can produce thousands of different numbers. Instead, the program groups the output from the various generators by the tenths digit of each number; that is, the number 0.9365783 will be grouped under 9, and 0.34523445 will be grouped under 3. This means that the graphic representation of the output of the generator will have ten lines, each line representing the number of times a number in that group occurs. The program will also print the mean of each sequence, which can be used to detect a bias in the numbers. Like the other graphic programs in this chapter, this program makes use of Turbo C's graphics functions and requires a CGA compatible graphics adapter.

```c
/* Random number generator display program. */

#include <dos.h>
#include <graphics.h>
#include <stdio.h>
#include <stdlib.h>

int freq1[10]={0, 0, 0, 0, 0, 0, 0, 0, 0, 0};
int freq2[10]={0, 0, 0, 0, 0, 0, 0, 0, 0, 0};
int freq3[10]={0, 0, 0, 0, 0, 0, 0, 0, 0, 0};

float ran1(void), ran2(void);
void display(void);
int driver, mode;

main()
{

  int x, y;
  float f, f2, f3, r, r2, r3;
  char s[128];

  driver = CGA;
  mode = CGACO;

  initgraph(&driver, &mode, "");

  f=0; f2=0; f3=0;

  outtextxy(50, 0, "Comparison of Random Number");
  outtextxy(120, 20, "Generators");
  line(0, 180, 90, 180);
  line(110, 180, 200, 180);
  line(220, 180, 310, 180);
  outtextxy(25, 190, "ran1()          ran2()          rand()");

  for(x=0; x<1000; ++x) {
    r = ran1();
    f += r;
    y = r*10;
    freq1[y]++;

    r2 = ran2();
    f2 += r2;
    y = r2*10;
    freq2[y]++;
```

```
      /* normalize the rand() function */
      r3 = (float) rand() / 32767;
      f3 += r3;
      y = r3*10;
      freq3[y]++;

      display();
   }
   gets(s);
   closegraph();
   printf("mean of rand1() function 1: %f\n", f/1000);
   printf("mean of rand2() function 2: %f\n", f2/1000);
   printf("mean of rand() function .3: %f\n", f3/1000);
   return 0;
}

/* display the graph of the random numbers */
void display(void)
{
   register int t;
   for(t=0; t<10; ++t) {
     line(t*10, 180, t*10, 180-freq1[t]);
     line(t*10+110, 180, t*10+110, 180-freq2[t]);
     line(t*10+220, 180, t*10+220, 180-freq3[t]);
   }
}

float ran1(void)
{
   static long int a=100001L;

   a = (a*125) % 2796203L;
   return (float) a/2796203L;
}

float ran2(void)
{
   static long int a=1;

   a = (a * 32719+3) % 32749;
   return (float) a/32749;
}
```

The functions **ran1( )**, **ran2( )**, and **rand( )** are tested to create
a side-by-side comparison. Each function generates 1000 numbers
and updates the appropriate frequency array based on the digit in
the 1/10th position. Notice that the output of the **rand( )** function
is manually converted into a number between 0 and 1. The function **display( )** plots all three frequency arrays on the screen. This

is done each time through the loop, so you can actually watch the display grow. Figure 9-2 shows the output from each of the random number generators at the end of the 1000 numbers.

The mean for **ran1( )** is 0.496960, for **ran2( )** it is 0.490550, and for **rand( )** it is 0.500417. These are all quite acceptable. To use the display program effectively, you must watch both the shape of the graph and the way it grows, keeping an eye out for any short, repeating cycles.

This test is, of course, not conclusive, but it does provide insight into the way a generator produces its numbers, and it can

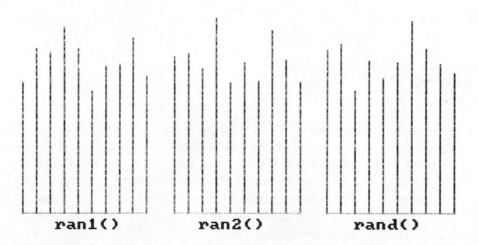

Figure 9-2.   Output from the random number generator display program

speed up the testing process by helping you reject obviously poor generators quickly. (It also makes a great program to run when someone asks you to show them your computer!)

USING MULTIPLE GENERATORS

You can improve the randomness of the sequences produced by the three generators by combining them under the control of one master function that selects between two of them based on the result of the third. The advantage of this method is that very long periods can be obtained and the effects of any cycle are diminished.

The **multiran()** function shown here combines **ran1()**, **ran2()**, and **rand()**:

```
float multiran()   /* random selection of generators */
{
   float f;

   f=(float) rand() /32767;

   if(f>.5) return ran1();
   else return ran2();
}
```

As you can see, the result of **rand()** is used to decide whether **ran1()** or **ran2()** becomes the value of the master function **multiran()**. Feel free to alter the mix between them by changing the constant in the **if** to obtain the exact distribution you require. A program to display the graph of **multiran()** and its mean is shown here. Figure 9-3 shows the final graph after 1000 random numbers have been computed.

```
/* Using multiple random number generators. */

#include <dos.h>
#include <graphics.h>
#include <stdio.h>
#include <stdlib.h>
```

```
int freq1[10]={0,0,0,0,0,0,0,0,0,0};

float ran1(void), ran2(void), multiran(void);
void  display(void);

int driver, mode;

main()
{
  int x, y;
  float  f=0.0, r;
  char s[128];

  driver = CGA;
  mode = CGACO;

  initgraph(&driver, &mode, "");

  outtextxy(50, 0, "Output Obtained by Combining");
  outtextxy(40, 20, "Three Random Number Generators");
  line(110, 180, 200, 180);

  for(x=0; x<1000; ++x) {
    r = multiran();
    f += r;
    y = r*10;
    freq1[y]++;
    display();
  }
  gets(s);
  closegraph();
  printf("mean of multiran(): %f\n", f/1000);
  return 0;
}

void display(void)
{
  register int t;

  for(t=0; t<10; ++t)
    line(t*10+110, 180, t*10+110, 180-freq1[t]);
}

/* This function combines the three random number
   generators.
*/
float multiran(void)
{
  float f;

  f=(float) rand() /32767;

  if(f>.5) return ran1();
  else return ran2();
}
```

```
float ran1(void)
{
  static long int a=100001;

  a = (a*125) % 2796203;
  return (float) a/2796203;
}

float ran2(void)
{
  static long int a=1;

  a = (a * 32719+3) % 32749;
  return (float) a/32749;
}
```

The mean of **multiran( )** is 0.495913.

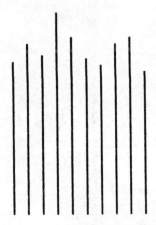

Figure 9-3. The final graph of **multiran()**

SIMULATIONS

For the remainder of this chapter you will be looking at two uses of random number generators as they apply to simulations. A simulation is a computerized model of some real-world situation. Quite literally, anything can be simulated, and the success of the simulation is based mostly on how well the programmer understands and is sensitive to the event being simulated. Because real-world situations often have thousands of variables, many things are difficult to simulate meaningfully. But several events do lend themselves to simulation.

Simulations are important for two reasons:

- You can alter the parameters of a situation to observe the results, even though in real life such experimentation might be too costly or dangerous. For example, a simulation of a nuclear power plant can be used to test the effects of certain types of failures.

- You can create situations that cannot occur in the real world. For example, a psychologist might want to study the effects of increasing the intelligence of a mouse gradually to that of a human to see at what point the mouse runs a maze the fastest. Although this can obviously not be done, a simulation may provide some insight into the nature of intelligence versus instinct.

Simulating a Checkout Line

The first simulation you will look at is of a checkout line in a grocery store. The store is open for ten hours a day with peak hours being from 12 to 1 P.M. and from 5 to 6 P.M., with the 12 to 1 P.M. slot being twice as busy as normal and the 5 to 6 P.M. slot being three times as busy. The simulation uses one random number generator to "create" customers, another to determine how long it will take to check out each customer, and a third to decide which of the open lines the customers will go to. The goal of the simulation is to help management find the minimum number of checkout lines that should be available over a typical shopping day. The only constraint is that the number of people in a line at any time is limited to 10.

The key to this type of simulation is the creation of multiple processes. Although C does not support simultaneous processing, you can simulate it by having each function used inside the main program loop do some work and return—in essence, by using manual time slicing. For example, the function that simulated the checkout will check out only part of each customer's order each time it is called. In this way, each function inside the main loop will continue to execute. The **main( )** function of the checkout program, along with its global data, is shown here:

```
/* Grocery store checkout line simulation. */
#include <dos.h>
#include <graphics.h>
#include <stdio.h>
#include <stdlib.h>
#include <conio.h>
#include <time.h>

float ran1(void), ran2(void);
void  display(void), add_cust(void);
void check_out(void), add_queue(void);
int allfull(void);

char queues[10];
char qopen[10];
int  cust;   /* total number of customers */
int sim_time=0;
int driver, mode;

main()
{

  char s[128];
  int x;

  driver = CGA;
  mode = CGAC0;

  initgraph(&driver, &mode, "");

  randomize();
```

```
for(x=0; x<10; ++x) {
  queues[x] = 0;
  qopen[x] = 0;   /* all closed at start of day */
}
outtextxy(160, 190, "1            10");
outtextxy(30, 190, "Check-out lines:");
qopen[0] = 1;  /* open up number 1 */
do {
  add_cust();  /* add customers */
  add_queue(); /* add another check out line */
  display();    /* show state of system */
  check_out(); /* check the customer out */
  display();
  if(sim_time>30 && sim_time<50) add_cust();
  if(sim_time>70 && sim_time < 80) {
      add_cust();
      add_cust();
  }
  sim_time++;
} while (!kbhit() && sim_time<100);
gets(s);
closegraph();
return 0;
}
```

The main loop is used to drive the entire simulation:

```
do {
  add_cust();  /* add customers */
  add_queue(); /* add another check out line */
  display();    /* show state of system */
  check_out(); /* check the customer out */
  display();
  if(sim_time>30 && sim_time<50) add_cust();
  if(sim_time>70 && sim_time < 80) {
      add_cust();
      add_cust();
  }
  sim_time++;
} while (!kbhit() && sim_time<100);
```

The function **add_cust( )** uses either **ran1( )** or **rand( )** to generate the number of customers arriving at the checkout lines at each request. The **add_queue( )** function is used both to place the customers in an open checkout line, based on the results of **ran2( )**, and to open a new line if all currently open lines are full. The **display( )** function shows a graphic representation of the simula-

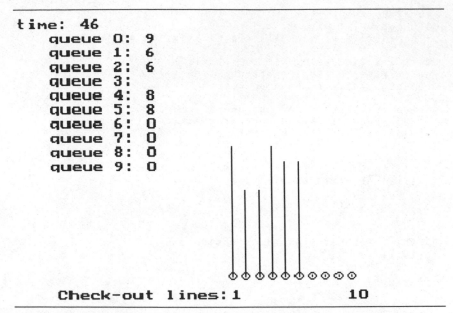

```
time: 46
    queue 0: 9
    queue 1: 6
    queue 2: 6
    queue 3:
    queue 4: 8
    queue 5: 8
    queue 6: 0
    queue 7: 0
    queue 8: 0
    queue 9: 0
```

Check-out lines:1   10

Figure 9-4.   Sample output from the checkout simulation

tion. The **checkout( )** function uses **ran2( )** to assign each customer a checkout count, and each call decrements that count by 1. When a customer's count is 0, the customer leaves the checkout line.

The *sim—time* variable is used to alter the rate at which customers are generated to match the peak hours of the store. In essence, each pass through the loop is a tenth of an hour.

Several variables in the program are under your direct control. First, it is possible to alter the number of customers and the way they arrive. You could also change **add—cust( )** to return gradually more or fewer customers as the peak hours approach and wane. The program makes the assumption that customers will randomly choose which line to stand in. Although this will be true of some customers, others will obviously choose the shortest line. This could be added to the simulation by altering the

add—queue( ) function so that it sometimes puts a customer into the shortest line and sometimes places customers randomly. A last point: The simulation does not account for the occasional accident, such as a dropped ketchup bottle or an unruly customer, that would cause a line to stall temporarily.

The entire program is shown here for your convenience. Sample output is shown in Figure 9-4.

```c
/* Grocery store checkout line simulation. */
#include <dos.h>
#include <graphics.h>
#include <stdio.h>
#include <stdlib.h>
#include <conio.h>
#include <time.h>

float ran1(void), ran2(void);
void  display(void), add_cust(void);
void check_out(void), add_queue(void);
int allfull(void);

char queues[10];
char qopen[10];
int  cust;   /* total number of customers */
int sim_time=0;

int driver, mode;

main()
{

  char s[128];
  int x;

  driver = CGA;
  mode = CGACO;

  initgraph(&driver, &mode, "");

  randomize();

  for(x=0; x<10; ++x) {
    queues[x] = 0;
    qopen[x] = 0;    /* all closed at start of day */
  }
  outtextxy(160, 190, "1            10");
  outtextxy(30, 190, "Check-out lines:");
  qopen[0] = 1;   /* open up number 1 */
```

```
      do {
         add_cust();  /* add customers */
         add_queue(); /* add another check out line */
         display();   /* show state of system */
         check_out(); /* check the customer out */
         display();
         if(sim_time>30 && sim_time<50) add_cust();
         if(sim_time>70 && sim_time < 80) {
            add_cust();
            add_cust();
         }
         sim_time++;
      } while (!kbhit() && sim_time<100);
      gets(s);
      closegraph();
      return 0;
   }

/* Add a customer to a line. */
void add_cust(void)
{

   float f;
   static char swap=0;

   /* use two different number generators */
   if(swap) f = ran1();    /* to get a random number */
   else f = (float) rand() / 32767;
   swap = !swap;

   if(f<.3) return;    /* no customers */
   else if(f<.6) {
      cust++;   /* add one customer */
      return;
   }
   else if(f<.7) {
      cust += 2;   /* add two customers */
      return;
   }
   else if(f<.8) {
      cust += 3;   /* add three customers */
      return;
   }
   else cust += 4; /* add four customers */
}

/* Check out the customer. */
void check_out(void)
{
   static char count[10]={0, 0, 0, 0, 0, 0, 0, 0, 0, 0};
   register int t;
```

```
  for(t=0; t<10; ++t) {
    if(queues[t]) {
      /* get check out time */
      while(count[t]==0) count[t] = ran2()*5;
      count[t]--;
      if(count[t]==0) queues[t]--;
    }
    if(!queues[t]) qopen[t] = 0;    /* close the line */
  }
}

/* Add another checkout line. */
void add_queue(void)
{
  register int t;
  int line;

  while(cust) {
    if(allfull())
      for(t=0; t<10; t++) if(!qopen[t]) {
        qopen[t] = 1;
        break;
      }

    /* randomly assign customers to open lines */
    line = ((float) rand()/32767)*10;
    if(qopen[line] && queues[line]<10) {
      queues[line]++;
      cust--;
    }
    if(t==10) return;    /* all queues full */
  }
}

/* Return 1 if all lines are full; 0 otherwise. */
int allfull(void)
{
  register int t;

  for(t=0; t<10; t++) if(queues[t]<10 && qopen[t]) return 0;
  return 1;
}

/* Show the current state of the system. */
void display(void)
{
  register int t, i;
  char s[128];

  setcolor(0);
  sprintf(s, "time: %d", sim_time-1);
```

```
outtextxy(0, 0, s);
setcolor(2);
sprintf(s, "time: %d", sim_time);
outtextxy(0, 0, s);
for(t=0; t<10; ++t) {
  /* first, erase the old line by printing in no color */
  setcolor(0);
  line((t*10)+160, 180, (t*10)+160, 80);
  setcolor(1);
  /* now, draw the circle */
  circle((t*10)+160, 180, 3);
  setcolor(2);
  /* now draw current state of the queue */
  line((t*10)+160, 180, (t*10)+160, 180-queues[t]*10);
  sprintf(s,"queue %d: %d  ", t+1, queues[t]);

  /* first, erase old value */
  setcolor(0);
  for(i=0; i<10; i++) {
    sprintf(s, "%c%c", 0+i, 0+i);
    outtextxy(96, (t+1)*10, s);
  }

  /* now, display the state of the queue */
  setcolor(2);
  sprintf(s, "queue %d: %d", t, queues[t]);
  outtextxy(25, (t+1)*10, s);
  }
}

float ran1(void)
{
  static long int a=100001L;

  a = (a*125) % 2796203L;
  return (float) a/2796203L;
}

float ran2(void)
{
  static long int a=1;

  a = (a * 32719+3) % 32749;
  return (float) a/32749;
}
```

Random Walk Portfolio Management

The art (or "science," if you prefer) of stock portfolio management is based on various theories and assumptions about a multitude of factors, including stock prices, PE ratios, the price of gold, the GNP, or even the phases of the moon. The computer scientist's revenge is to use the computer to simulate the free marketplace, that is, the stock exchange, and be free of all the theoretical worry.

You might be thinking that the stock exchange is simply too hard to simulate, that it has too many variables, too many unknowns—that it swings widely at times and at others coasts smoothly. Well, the problem itself is the solution! Because the marketplace is so complex, it can be thought of as randomly occurring events. This means that you can simulate the stock exchange as a series of disconnected random occurrences. This is affectionately called the *random walk* method of portfolio management. The term is derived from the classic thought experiment involving a drunk wandering a street, going from lamppost to lamppost in a random fashion. The essence of random walk theory is that you let chance be your guide...because it is as good as any other method!

Before continuing, be cautioned that the random walk method is generally discredited by professional money managers and is presented here for fun and enjoyment, not for actual investing.

The way to implement the random walk method is first to select ten companies by some chance method, such as throwing darts at *The Wall Street Journal*. Once you have selected ten companies, feed their names into the random walk simulation program, and it will tell you what to do with them.

There are basically five things the program can tell you to do with each company's stock:

- Sell
- Buy
- Sell short
- Buy on margin
- Hold (that is, do nothing)

The operations of buying, selling, and holding stock are obvious. When you sell short, you sell stock that you do not own in the hope that you will be able to buy it cheaper in the near future and deliver it to the person to whom you sold it. Selling short is a way to make money when the market is going down. When you buy on margin, you use, for a small fee, the money of the brokerage house to fund part of the cost of the stock that you purchase. If the stock increases enough, you make a lot more money than you could if you bought a smaller amount of stock with cash. This strategy makes money only in a "bull" market.

The random walk program is shown here. Notice that the program waits until you strike a key. In this way you can start using the sequence produced by the random number generator at a random point. Otherwise you would always get the same advice.

```
/* Random walk stock portfolio simulation. */
#include <stdio.h>
#include <time.h>
#include <stdlib.h>
#include <ctype.h>

char stock[10][30];   /* holds the company names */
float ran1(void);
char *action(void);
void enter(void);

main()
{
  register int t;
  char s[128];
```

```
    printf("Wait awhile, then press any key...");
    do {
      ran1();
    } while(!kbhit());

    enter();

    do {
      for(t=0; t<10; t++)
        printf("%30s: %s\n", stock[t], action());
      printf("Again? (y/n)");
      gets(s);
    } while(toupper(*s)=='Y' || *s=='\0');
    return 0;
}

void enter(void)
{
  register int t;

  for(t=0; t<10; t++) {
    printf("enter company name: ");
    gets(stock[t]);
  }
}

/* Return advice. */
char *action(void)
{
  register int x;
  float f;

  f = ran1();
  x = f*10;

  switch(x) {
    case 0: return "sell";
    case 1: return "buy";
    case 3: return "sell short";
    case 4: return "buy on margin";
    default: return "hold";
  }
}

float ran1(void)
{
  static long int a=100001L;

  a = (a*125) % 2796203L;
  return (float) a/2796203L;
}
```

Using the program requires following the instructions given subject to this interpretation.

Instruction	Meaning
Buy	Buy as much of the specified stock as you can afford without borrowing.
Sell	Sell all of the stock if any is owned, and randomly select a new company to take its place.
Sell short	Sell 100 shares of the specified company even though you don't own it in the hope that you can buy it cheaper in the future.
Buy on margin	Borrow money to buy shares of the specified stock.
Hold	Do nothing.

For example, if you ran this program using the fictitious company names of Com1 through Com10, the first day's advice might look like this:

Com1: sell
Com2: buy
Com3: buy on margin
Com4: sell short
Com5: hold
Com6: hold
Com7: hold
Com8: buy
Com9: hold
Com10: sell short

The second day's advice might be

Com1: hold
Com2: hold
Com3: sell
Com4: sell short
Com5: hold
Com6: hold

Com7: buy
Com8: buy on margin
Com9: hold
Com10: sell

You can run the program weekly instead of daily, if you prefer.

Feel free to alter the program in any way and perhaps have the program give you amounts to buy and sell as well. Again, remember that this program is for fun only and is not recommended as an actual investment strategy. But it is interesting to create a portfolio on paper and track its performance.

10

EXPRESSION PARSING
AND EVALUATION

How do you write a program that will accept as input a string containing a numeric expression, such as **(10−5)*3**, and compute the proper answer, in this case 15? If there is a "high priesthood" among programmers, it must be those few who know how to do this. Almost everyone who uses a computer is mystified by the way a high-level language converts complex expressions, such as **10*3−(4+*count*)/12**, into instructions that a computer can execute. This procedure is called *expression parsing*, and it is the backbone of all language compilers and interpreters, spreadsheet programs, and anything else that needs to convert numeric expressions written in human form into a context that can be used by the computer. Very few programmers know how to write an expression parser, and this realm of programming is generally considered off-limits except to those enlightened few. In reality, such is not the case.

Expression parsing is actually a very straightforward task like other programming tasks. (In some ways it is even easier because it works with the very strict rules of algebra.) This chapter will develop what is commonly called a *recursive descent parser* and all necessary support routines to enable a computer to evaluate complex numeric expressions. Once you have mastered its operation, you will be able to enhance and modify it to suit your needs, and other programmers will definitely think that you have entered the "high priesthood" of programmers!

EXPRESSIONS

Although expressions can be composed of all types of information, this chapter deals only with *numeric expressions*, which can be the following items:

- Numbers
- The operators $+ - / * ^ \% =$
- Parentheses
- Variables

The $^$ is used to indicate exponentiation, as in BASIC, and the $=$ is used as the assignment operator. These items can be combined in expressions according to the rules of algebra. Here are some examples:

$$10 - 8$$
$$(100 - 5) * 14/6$$
$$a + b - c$$
$$10 ^ 5$$
$$a = 10 - b$$

Assume this precedence for each operator:

$$
\begin{array}{ll}
\text{highest:} & ^ \\
& * \ / \ \% \\
& + - \\
\text{lowest:} & =
\end{array}
$$

Operators of equal precedence evaluate from left to right.

For the examples in this chapter, the following assumptions will be made:

- All variables are single letters; this means that 26 variables, the letters A through Z, are available for use.

- The variables will not be case sensitive; a and A will be treated as the same variable.

- All numbers are **float**, although you could easily write the routines to handle other types of numbers. Only a minimal amount of error checking is included in the routines to keep the important logic clear and easy to understand.

In case you have not thought about the problem of expression parsing, take a look at this sample expression and try to evaluate it:

$10 - 2 * 3$

You know that this expression has the value 4. Although you could very easily create a program that would compute that specific expression, the question is how to create a computer program that will give the correct answer for any arbitrary expression. At first you might think of a routine something like this:

```
a = get first operand
while(operands present) {
        op = get operator
        b = get second operand
        a = a op b
}
```

This routine attempts to work by getting the first operand, the operator, and the second operand; performing that operation; getting the next operator and operand, if any, and performing that operation; and so on. If you used this basic approach, the expression **10−2*3** would evaluate to 24 (that is, **8*3**), instead of the correct answer of 4, because this procedure neglects the precedence of the operators. You cannot simply take the operands and operators in order from left to right, because the multiplication must be done before the subtraction. Some beginners think that this could easily be overcome—and in some very restricted cases, it can—but the problem gets worse when parentheses, exponentiation, variables, function calls, and the like are added.

Although there are a few ways to write a routine that will evaluate expressions of this sort, the one developed here is the most easily written by a human and also the most common. (Some of the other methods used to write parsers employ complex tables that must be generated by another computer program. These are sometimes called *table-driven parsers*.) The method used here is called a *recursive descent parser*, and in the course of this chapter you will see how it got its name.

DISSECTING AN EXPRESSION

Before you can develop a parser to evaluate expressions, you need to be able to break an expression into its components. For example, the expression

$$A * B - (W + 10)$$

has the components A, $*$, B, $-$, $($, W, $+$, 10, and $)$. Each component represents an indivisible unit of the expression. In general, you need a routine that will return each item in the expression individually. The routine must also be able to skip spaces and tabs, and know when it has reached the end of the expression.

Each component of an expression is called a *token*. Therefore, the function that returns the next token in the expression is often called **get_token()**. You need a global character pointer to point to the expression string. In the version of **get_token()** shown here this is called **prog**. The **prog** pointer is global because it must maintain its value between calls to **get_token()** and allow other functions to access it. Each token will actually be returned in a global character array called *token*. Besides returning a token, you will also need to know what type of token is being returned. For the parser developed in this chapter you will need only three types: VARIABLE, NUMBER, and DELIMITER, where DELIMITER is used for both operators and parentheses. The type of each token is assigned to the global variable called *tok_type*. Here is **get_token( )** along with its necessary globals, **#define** statements, and support function:

```
#define DELIMITER  1
#define VARIABLE   2
#define NUMBER     3
extern char *prog;  /* holds expression to be analyzed */
char token[80];
char tok_type;

/* Return the next token. */
void get_token(void)
{

  register char *temp;

  tok_type = 0;
  temp = token;

  while(isspace(*prog)) ++prog;  /* skip over white space */

  if(strchr("+-*/%^=()", *prog)){
    tok_type = DELIMITER;
    /* advance to next char */
    *temp++ = *prog++;
  }
  else if(isalpha(*prog)) {
    while(!isdelim(*prog)) *temp++ = *prog++;
    tok_type = VARIABLE;
  }
  else if(isdigit(*prog)) {
    while(!isdelim(*prog)) *temp++ = *prog++;
    tok_type = NUMBER;
  }

  *temp = '\0';

}

/* Return true if c is a delimiter. */
isdelim(char c)
```

```
{
  if(strchr(" +-/*%^=()", c) || c==9 || c=='\r' || c==0)
    return 1;
  return 0;
}
```

Look closely at this function. Because people like to put spaces into expressions to add clarity but not meaning, leading spaces are skipped by using the library function **isspace()**, which returns true if its argument is any of the white-space characters. Once the spaces have been skipped, **prog** will be pointing to either a number, a variable, an operator, or a null if trailing spaces end the expression. If the next character is an operator, it is returned as a string in the global variable *token* and the type of DELIM-ITER is placed in *tok—type*. If the next character is a letter, it is assumed to be a variable, it is returned as a string in *token*, and *tok—type* is assigned the type VARIABLE. If the next character is a digit, the entire number is read and placed in *token* with a type of NUMBER. If it is none of the above, it is assumed that the end of the expression has been reached and *token* is null, signaling the end of the expression.

As stated earlier, to keep the code to this function clean, a certain amount of error checking has been omitted and some assumptions have been made. For example, any unrecognized character ends an expression, and variables can be any length but only the first letter is significant. You can fill in these and other details as your specific application dictates. It will be easy for you to modify or enhance **get—token()** to enable it to return character strings, other types of numbers, and so on from an input string a token at a time.

To understand how **get—token()** works, study what it returns for each token and type for the following expression:

$A + 100 - (B * C) /2$

Token	Token Type
A	VARIABLE
+	DELIMITER

100	NUMBER
–	DELIMITER
(	DELIMITER
B	VARIABLE
*	DELIMITER
C	VARIABLE
)	DELIMITER
/	DELIMITER
2	NUMBER
null	null

Remember that *token* always holds a null-terminated string, even if it contains only a single character.

EXPRESSION PARSING

There are a number of possible ways to parse and evaluate an expression. For use with a recursive descent parser, you should think of expressions as *recursive data structures*, that is, expressions that are defined in terms of themselves. If, for the moment, expressions can use only +, –, *, /, (, and), all expressions can be defined by using the following rules:

expression $\Rightarrow$ *term* [+ *term*] [– *term*]
term $\Rightarrow$ *factor* [* *factor*] [/ *factor*]
factor $\Rightarrow$ *variable, number* or (*expression*)

Any part of the above can be null.

Here the square brackets mean "optional" and the $\Rightarrow$ means "produces." In fact, these rules are usually called the *production rules* of the expression. You could define *term* as "*term* produces *factor* times *factor* or *factor* divided by *factor*." Notice that the precedence of the operators is implicit in the way an expression is defined.

The expression

10 + 5 * B

has two terms: 10 and 5*B. It has three factors: 10, 5, and *B*. These factors consist of two numbers and one variable.

On the other hand, the expression

14 * (7 − *C*)

has two terms, 14 and (7−*C*), consisting of one number and one parenthesized expression. The parenthesized expression evaluates to one number and one variable.

This process forms the basis for a recursive descent parser. A recursive descent parser is basically a set of mutually recursive functions that work in a chainlike fashion. At each appropriate step the parser performs the specified operations in the algebraically correct sequence. To see how this process works, parse the following expression and perform the arithmetic operations at the right time.

input expression: 9/3 − (100 + 56)

Step 1: Get first *term*: 9/3.

Step 2: Get each *factor* and divide integers. That value is 3.

Step 3: Get second *term*: (100 + 56). At this point, recursively start analyzing the second expression.

Step 4: Get each *factor* and add. That value is 156.

Step 5: Return from recursive call and subtract 156 from 3, yielding the answer −153.

If you are a little confused at this point, don't feel bad! This is a fairly complex concept that takes some getting used to. There are two basic things to remember about this recursive view of expressions:

1. The precedence of the operators is implicit in the way the production rules are defined.

2. This method of parsing and evaluating expressions is very similar to the way humans do the same thing.

A SIMPLE EXPRESSION PARSER

The remainder of this chapter develops two parsers. The first parses and evaluates only constant expressions, that is, expressions with no variables. This will show you the parser in its simplest form. The second parser includes the 26 variables *A* through *Z*.

Here is the entire simple version of the recursive descent parser for floating-point expressions:

```c
/* This module contains a simple expression parser
   that does not recognize variables.
*/

#include <stdlib.h>
#include <ctype.h>
#include <stdio.h>
#include <string.h>

#define DELIMITER  1
#define VARIABLE   2
#define NUMBER     3

extern char *prog;  /* holds expression to be analyzed */
char token[80];
char tok_type;

void get_exp(float *result), level2(float *result);
void level3(float *result), level4(float *result);
void level5(float *result);
void level6(float *result), primitive(float *result);
void get_token(void), putback(void);
void unary(char o, float *r);
void arith(char o, float *r, float *h);
void serror(int error);
int isdelim(char c);

/* Parser entry point. */
void get_exp(float *result)
{
  get_token();
  if(!*token) {
    serror(2);
    return;
  }
  level2(result);

}
```

```
/* Add or subtract two terms. */
void level2(float *result)
{
  register char  op;
  float hold;

  level3(result);
  while((op = *token) == '+' || op == '-') {
    get_token();
    level3(&hold);
    arith(op, result, &hold);
  }
}

/* Multiply or divide two factors. */
void level3(float *result)
{
  register char  op;
  float hold;

  level4(result);
  while((op = *token) == '*' || op == '/' || op == '%') {
    get_token();
    level4(&hold);
    arith(op, result, &hold);
  }
}

/* Process an exponent */
void level4(float *result)
{
  float hold;

  level5(result);
  if(*token== '^') {
    get_token();
    level4(&hold);
    arith('^', result, &hold);
  }
}

/* Evaluate a unary + or -. */
void level5(float *result)
{
  register char  op;

  op = 0;
  if((tok_type == DELIMITER) && *token=='+' || *token == '-') {
    op = *token;
    get_token();
  }
```

```
    level6(result);
    if(op)
      unary(op, result);
}

/* Process a parenthesized expression. */
void level6(float *result)
{
  if((*token == '(') && (tok_type == DELIMITER)) {
    get_token();
    level2(result);
    if(*token != ')')
      serror(1);
    get_token();
  }
  else
    primitive(result);
}

/* Get the actual value of a number. */
void primitive(float *result)
{

  if(tok_type==NUMBER) {
    *result = atof(token);
    get_token();
    return;
  }
  serror(0);  /* otherwise syntax error in expression */
}

/* Perform the indicated arithmetic. */
void arith(char o, float *r, float *h)
{
  register float t, ex;

  switch(o) {
    case '-':
      *r = *r-*h;
      break;
    case '+':
      *r = *r+*h;
      break;
    case '*':
      *r = *r * *h;
      break;
    case '/':
      *r = (*r)/(*h);
      break;
    case '%':
      t = (*r)/(*h);
```

```
        *r = *r-(t*(*h));
        break;
      case '^':
        ex = *r;
        if(*h==0) {
          *r = 1;
          break;
        }
        for(t=*h-1; t>0; --t) *r=(*r) * ex;
        break;
    }
}

/* Process a unary operator. */
void unary(char o, float *r)
{
  if(o=='-') *r = -(*r);
}

/* Return a token to its resting place. */
void putback(void)
{
  char *t;
  t = token;
  for(; *t; t++) prog--;
}

/* Display a syntax error. */
void serror(int error)
{
  static char *e[]= {
      "syntax error",
      "unbalanced parentheses",
      "no expression present"
       };
  printf("%s\n", e[error]);
}

/* Return the next token. */
void get_token(void)
{

  register char *temp;

  tok_type = 0;
  temp = token;

  while(isspace(*prog)) ++prog;  /* skip over white space */

  if(strchr("+-*/%^=()", *prog)){
    tok_type = DELIMITER;
    /* advance to next char */
    *temp++ = *prog++;
  }
```

```
  else if(isalpha(*prog)) {
    while(!isdelim(*prog)) *temp++ = *prog++;
    tok_type = VARIABLE;
  }
  else if(isdigit(*prog)) {
    while(!isdelim(*prog)) *temp++ = *prog++;
    tok_type = NUMBER;
  }

  *temp = '\0';

}

/* Return true if c is a delimiter. */
isdelim(char c)
{
  if(strchr(" +-/*%^=()", c) || c==9 || c=='\r' || c==0)
    return 1;
  return 0;
}
```

This parser can handle the following operators: +, −, *, /, %, integer exponentiation ($^\wedge$), and the unary minus. It can also deal with parentheses correctly. Notice that it has six levels as well as the **primitive( )** function, which returns the value of any number. It also includes routines for performing the various arithmetic operations, **arith( )** and **unary( )**, and the **get_token( )** code. The two global variables, *token* and *tok_type*, are used to return the next token and its type from the expression string. The **extern prog** is a pointer to the string that holds the expression.

The following simple **main( )** function demonstrates the use of the parser:

```
#include <stdio.h>
#include <alloc.h>
#include <stdlib.h>

char *prog;
void get_exp(void);

main()  /* Parser driver program */
{
  float answer;
  char *p;

  p = malloc(100);
  if(!p) {
```

```
    printf("allocation failure\n");
    exit(1);
  }

  /* Process expressions until a blank line
     is entered.
  */
  do {
    prog = p;
    printf("enter expression: ");
    gets(prog);
    if(!*prog) break;
    get_exp(&answer);
    printf("answer is: %.2f\n", answer);
  } while(*p);
  return 0;
}
```

To understand exactly how the parser evaluates an expression, work through the following expression, which is assumed to be pointed to by **prog**:

$$10 - 3 * 2$$

When **get—exp( )**, the entry routine into the parser, is called, it gets the first token and, if it is null, prints the message "no expression present" and returns. If there is a token present, **level2( )** is called. (The **level1( )** function is used when the assignment operator is added and is not needed here.) At this point in the example the token contains the number 10. Then **level2( )** calls **level3( )**, and **level3( )** calls **level4( )**, which in turn calls **level5( )**. If when **level5( )** checks to see if the token is a unary + or −, it is not, **level5( )** calls **level6( )**. Then **level6( )** either recursively calls **level2( )**, in the case of a parenthesized expression, or calls **primitive( )** to find the value of the integer. Finally **primitive( )** is executed and **result** contains the number 10, another token is retrieved, and the functions begin to return up the chain.

The token is now the operator − and the functions return to **level2( )**. What happens here is very important. Because the token is −, it is saved, the parser gets the new token, 3, and the descent down the chain begins again. Again **primitive( )** is entered, the integer 3 is returned in **result**, and the token, *, is read. This causes a return back up the chain to **level3( )**, where the final token, 2, is read. At this point the first arithmetic operation occurs with the multiplication of 2 and 3. This result is returned to **level2( )**, and the subtraction is performed, yielding an answer of 4. Although the process may at first seem complicated, you should work through some other examples to verify in your own mind that it functions correctly every time.

This parser would be suitable for use as a desktop calculator, as is illustrated by the sample driver program. It could also be useful in a limited database. Before you could use it in a language or a sophisticated calculator, however, you would have to add the ability to handle variables, which is the subject of the next section.

ADDING VARIABLES TO THE PARSER

All programming languages, many calculators, and many spreadsheets use variables to store values for later use. The simple parser in the preceding section needs to be expanded to include variables before it can be used for this. To include variables, you need to add several things to the parser. First, of course, are the variables themselves. As stated earlier, the parser developed here recognizes only the variables *A* through *Z*, although you can expand that if you like. Each variable uses one array location in a 26-element array of **float**s. The parser uses this array to hold the value of the variables.

```
float vars[26]= {      /* 26 user variables, A-Z */
  0.0, 0.0, 0.0, 0.0, 0.0, 0.0, 0.0, 0.0, 0.0, 0.0,
  0.0, 0.0, 0.0, 0.0, 0.0, 0.0, 0.0, 0.0, 0.0, 0.0,
  0.0, 0.0, 0.0, 0.0, 0.0, 0.0
};
```

As you can see, the variables are initialized to 0 as a courtesy to the user.

You also need a routine to look up the value of a given variable. Because the variable names are the letters *A* through *Z*, they can easily be used to index the array *vars* by subtracting the ASCII value for *A* from the variable name. The function **find—var( )** is shown here:

```
float find_var(char *s)
{
  if(!isalpha(*s)){
    serror(1);
    return 0;
  }
  return vars[toupper(*token)-'A'];
}
```

As this function is written, it actually accepts long variable names, but only the first letter is significant. You may modify this to fit your needs.

You must also modify the **primitive( )** function to handle both numbers and variables. The new version is shown here:

```
void primitive(float *result)
{

  switch(tok_type) {
    case VARIABLE:
      *result = find_var(token);
      get_token();
      return;
    case NUMBER:
      *result = atof(token);
      get_token();
      return;
    default:
      serror(0);
  }
}
```

Technically, this is all that is needed for the parser to use variables correctly; however, there is no way for these variables to be assigned a value. Often this is done outside the parser, but you can treat the equal sign as an assignment operator and make it part of the parser. There are various ways to do this. One method is to add a **level1( )** to the parser as shown next.

```
/* Process an assignment. */
void level1(float *result)
{
  int slot, ttok_type;
  char temp_token[80];

  if(tok_type==VARIABLE) {
    /* save old token */
    strcpy(temp_token, token);
    ttok_type = tok_type;

    /* compute the index of the variable */
    slot = toupper(*token)-'A';
    get_token();
    if(*token != '=') {
      putback(); /* return current token */
      /* restore old token - not assignment */
      strcpy(token, temp_token);
      tok_type = ttok_type;
    }
    else {
      get_token(); /* get next part of exp */
      level2(result);
      vars[slot] = *result;
      return;
    }
  }

  level2(result);
}
```

As you can see, the function needs to look ahead to determine whether an assignment is actually being made because a variable name always precedes an assignment but not every variable name implies an assignment expression. That is, the parser will accept *A=100* as an assignment but is also smart enough to know that *A/10* is an expression.

Here is the entire enhanced parser:

```
/* Recursive descent parser for floating point expressions
   which may include variables.
*/
#include <math.h>
#include <ctype.h>
#include <stdlib.h>
#include <stdio.h>
#include <string.h>
```

```
#define DELIMITER  1
#define VARIABLE   2
#define NUMBER     3

extern char *prog;   /* holds expression to be analyzed */
char token[80];
char tok_type;

float vars[26]= {      /* 26 user variables,  A-Z */
  0.0, 0.0, 0.0, 0.0, 0.0, 0.0, 0.0, 0.0, 0.0, 0.0,
  0.0, 0.0, 0.0, 0.0, 0.0, 0.0, 0.0, 0.0, 0.0, 0.0,
  0.0, 0.0, 0.0, 0.0, 0.0, 0.0
};

void get_exp(float *result), level2(float *result);
void level3(float *result), level4(float *result);
void level5(float *result), level1(float *result);
void level6(float *result), primitive(float *result);
void get_token(void), putback(void);
void unary(char o, float *r);
void arith(char o, float *r, float *h);
void serror(int error);


float find_var(char *s);
int isdelim(char c);


/* Entry point into parser. */
void get_exp(float *result)
{
  get_token();
  if(!*token) {
    serror(2);
    return;
  }
  level1(result);
}

/* Process an assignment statement. */
void level1(float *result)
{
  int slot, ttok_type;
  char temp_token[80];

  if(tok_type==VARIABLE) {
    /* save old token */
    strcpy(temp_token, token);
    ttok_type = tok_type;

    /* compute the index of the variable */
    slot = toupper(*token)-'A';
```

```
    get_token();
    if(*token != '=') {
      putback();  /* return current token */
      /* restore old token - not assignment */
      strcpy(token, temp_token);
      tok_type = ttok_type;
    }
    else {
      get_token();  /* get next part of exp */
      level2(result);
      vars[slot] = *result;
      return;
    }
  }
  level2(result);
}

/*  Add or subtract two terms. */
void level2(float *result)
{
  register char  op;
  float hold;

  level3(result);
  while((op = *token) == '+' || op == '-') {
    get_token();
    level3(&hold);
    arith(op, result, &hold);
  }
}

/* Multiply or divide two factors. */
void level3(float *result)
{
  register char  op;
  float hold;

  level4(result);
  while((op = *token) == '*' || op == '/' || op == '%') {
    get_token();
    level4(&hold);
    arith(op, result, &hold);
  }
}

/* Process an integer exponent. */
void level4(float *result)
{
  float hold;

  level5(result);
  if(*token== '^') {
```

```
    get_token();
    level4(&hold);
    arith('^', result, &hold);
  }
}

/* Process a unary + or -. */
void level5(float *result)
{
  register char  op;

  op = 0;
  if((tok_type==DELIMITER) && *token=='+' || *token=='-') {
    op = *token;
    get_token();
  }
  level6(result);
  if(op)
    unary(op, result);
}

/* Process a parenthesized expression. */
void level6(float *result)
{
  if((*token == '(') && (tok_type == DELIMITER)) {
    get_token();
    level1(result);
    if(*token != ')')
      serror(1);
    get_token();
  }
  else
    primitive(result);
}

/* Find value of number or variable. */
void primitive(float *result)
{

  switch(tok_type) {
    case VARIABLE:
      *result = find_var(token);
      get_token();
      return;
    case NUMBER:
      *result = atof(token);
      get_token();
      return;
    default:
      serror(0);
  }
}
```

```
/* Perform the specified arithmetic. */
void arith(char o, float *r, float *h)
{
  register int t, ex;

  switch(o) {
    case '-':
      *r = *r-*h;
      break;
    case '+':
      *r = *r+*h;
      break;
    case '*':
      *r = *r * *h;
      break;
    case '/':
      *r = (*r)/(*h);
      break;
    case '%':
      t = (*r)/(*h);
      *r = *r-(t*(*h));
      break;
    case '^':
      ex = *r;
      if(*h==0) {
        *r = 1;
        break;
      }
      for(t=*h-1; t>0; --t) *r = (*r) * ex;
      break;
  }
}

/* Evaluate a unary operator. */
void unary(char o, float *r)
{
  if(o=='-') *r = -(*r);
}

/* Return a token to its resting place. */
void putback(void)
{

  char *t;

  t = token;
  for(; *t; t++) prog--;
}

/* Find the value of a variable. */
float find_var(char *s)
{
  if(!isalpha(*s)){
```

```
      serror(1);
      return 0;
   }
   return vars[toupper(*token)-'A'];
}

/* Display an error message. */
void serror(int error)
{
   static char *e[]= {
       "syntax error",
       "unbalanced parentheses",
       "no expression present"
   };
   printf("%s\n", e[error]);
}

/* Get a token. */
void get_token(void)
{

   register char *temp;

   tok_type = 0;
   temp = token;

   while(isspace(*prog)) ++prog;    /* skip over white space */

   if(strchr("+-*/%^=()", *prog)){
     tok_type = DELIMITER;
     *temp++ = *prog++;
     /* advance to next position */
   }
   else if(isalpha(*prog)) {
     while(!isdelim(*prog)) *temp++ = *prog++;
     tok_type = VARIABLE;
   }
   else if(isdigit(*prog)) {
     while(!isdelim(*prog)) *temp++ = *prog++;
     tok_type = NUMBER;
   }

   *temp = '\0';

}

/* Return true if c is a delimiter. */
int isdelim (char c)
{
   if(strchr(" +-/*%^=()", c) || c==9 || c=='\r' || c==0)
     return 1;
   return 0;
}
```

You can still use the same simple **main( )** function that you did for the simple parser. With the enhanced parser, you can now enter expressions like

$$A = 10 \ / \ 4$$
$$A - B$$
$$C = A * (F - 21)$$

SYNTAX CHECKING IN A RECURSIVE DESCENT PARSER

In expression parsing, a syntax error is simply a situation in which the input expression does not conform to the strict rules required by the parser. Most of the time this is caused by human error, usually typing mistakes. For example, the following expressions will not be parsed correctly by the parsers in this chapter:

$$10 * * 8$$
$$(10 - 5) * 9)$$
$$/8$$

The first has two operators in a row; the second has unbalanced parentheses; and the last has a division sign starting the expression. The parsers in this chapter do not allow any of these conditions. Because syntax errors can confuse the parser and cause it to give erroneous results, it is important, indeed necessary, to guard against them.

As you have been studying the code to the parsers, you have probably noticed that the function **serror( )** is called under certain situations. Unlike many other parsers, the recursive descent method makes syntax checking very easy because, for the most part, it occurs in either **primitive( )**, **find_var( )**, or **level6( )**, where parentheses are checked. The only problem with the syntax checking as it now stands is that the entire parser is not aborted when a syntax error occurs. This can lead to the generation of multiple error messages.

The best way to implement the routine **serror( )** is to have it execute a **longjmp( )** to a safe place. The **longjmp( )** function works in conjunction with **setjmp( )**, and these functions are part of Turbo C's library. These two functions allow the program to branch to a different function. Therefore, in **serror( )** you would execute a **longjmp( )** to some safe point in your program outside the parser.

The prototypes for **setjmp( )** and **longjmp( )** are in **setjmp.h**, which also defines a special type called *jmp—buf*. The prototypes are

> void longjmp(*jmp—buf buffer*, int *value*)
> int setjmp(*jmp—buf buffer*)

The **setjmp( )** function saves the current state of the computer into *buffer* each time it is called. If **longjmp( )** is executed, it restores the computer to the state that **setjmp( )** saved, thus resetting the machine to an earlier point. This lets your program "warp" through time and memory space. The *value* parameter of **longjmp( )** becomes the return value of **setjmp( )**, and it must be nonzero. (The **setjmp( )** function returns 0 when it is executed, not when **longjmp( )** "returns" to it.) You can discard the return value if it is not important to your application. For further discussion of these two interesting functions, refer to the *Turbo C Reference Guide*.

Using these functions you need to make the following changes in **main( )** and **serror( )**:

```
/* define a jump buffer */
jmp_buf jb;

main()   /* Parser driver program */
{
  float answer;
  char *p;

  p = malloc(100);
  if(!p) {
    printf("allocation failure\n");
    exit(1);
  }
```

```
   /* Process expressions until a blank line
      is entered.
   */
   do {
     setjmp(jb);  /* save the state of the machine */
     prog = p;
     printf("enter expression: ");
     gets(prog);
     if(!*prog) break;
     get_exp(&answer);
     printf("answer is: %.2f\n", answer);
   } while(*p);
   return 0;
}


/* Display an error message. */
void serror(int error)
{
   static char *e[]= {
      "syntax error",
      "unbalanced parentheses",
      "no expression present"
   };
   printf("%s\n", e[error]);
   longjmp(jb, 1);  /* warp out of error state */
}
```

If you do not use the **setjmp( )** and **longjmp( )** functions, your parser will issue multiple syntax error messages. This could be annoying in some situations but a blessing in others, because in some cases multiple errors will be caught in one pass.

11

CONVERTING TURBO PASCAL TO TURBO C

You might be wondering why anyone would want to convert Turbo Pascal programs into Turbo C. The reason is really very simple: There are a lot of great Turbo Pascal programs already written. Also, a lot of long-time Turbo Pascal users are changing to Turbo C, and they want to bring their existing code along. Whatever the reason, the task of translating Turbo Pascal programs into Turbo C is fairly easy once you know a few tricks. And, as you'll see later in this chapter, it is possible to use a simple computer program to assist you in your efforts.

The Turbo C user manual contains an excellent chapter that helps Turbo Pascal users move to Turbo C by showing many of the specific differences between the languages. If you haven't read this section, you might want to take a look at it before continuing because the following discussion concentrates on the actual translation process—the "how to" of translation, so to speak.

STRUCTURED BUT DIFFERENT

Turbo Pascal and Turbo C have many similarities, especially in their control structures and use of stand-alone subroutines with local variables. This similarity makes it possible to do many one-to-one translations. Often you can simply substitute the equivalent Turbo C keyword or function name for the one in Turbo Pascal.

Even though Turbo Pascal and Turbo C are similar, you should keep in mind two major differences between them:

1. Turbo Pascal is much more restrictive and, in some ways, limited than Turbo C. For example, Turbo Pascal makes it difficult to write system-level programs because its strong type checking does not easily allow the various type conversions usually needed.

2. More important, Turbo Pascal is formally block structured and C is not. The term *block structured* refers to a language's ability to create logically connected units of code that can be referenced as one unit. It also means that procedures can have other procedures—known only to the outer procedure—nested inside them. Although C is commonly regarded as block structured because it facilitates the creation of code blocks, it does not allow functions to be defined inside other functions. For example, the following Turbo Pascal code is valid:

```
procedure A;
  var x:integer;

  procedure B;
  begin
    writeln('inside proc b');
  end;

begin
  writeln('starting A');
  B;
end;
```

As you can see, procedure B is defined inside procedure A. This means that procedure B is known only to procedure A and can be used only by procedure A. Another procedure B could be defined outside of procedure A without conflict. The same code translated into C would have to have two functions. They would be

```
void A(void)
{
  printf("starting A\n");
  B();
}

void B(void)
{
  printf("inside function B\n");
}
```

Also, because **B( )** is no longer shielded by **A( )**, you would have to make sure that there were no other **B( )** functions anywhere else in the program.

Another difference between Turbo Pascal and C is that all Turbo Pascal variables, functions, and procedures must be declared before they are used. This means that in Turbo Pascal, forward references are not allowed without the **forward** statement. In C all variables must be declared before they are used, but functions can be referenced before they are declared. For example, the procedure **sum** must be declared as **forward** in this Turbo Pascal program:

```
program sample;

procedure sum(a, b: integer); forward;

procedure add;
var
  i, j: integer;
begin
  writeln('enter two numbers');
  readln(i); readln(j);
  sum(i,j);
end;
```

```
procedure sum(a, b: integer);
begin
  writeln(a+b);
end;

begin
  add;
end.
```

Using the defaults applied by the compiler, the program will look like this in Turbo C:

```
main()
{
  add();
}


add()
{
  int i, j;

  printf("enter two numbers\n");
  scanf("%d%d", &i, &j);
  sum(i, j);
}

sum(int a, int b)
{
  printf("%d", a+b);
}
```

It is important to remember that in C you have to declare a function before calling it when it returns a type other than integer. Also, the use of function prototypes, which cause the compiler to check the types of the arguments to a function against the types of the parameters, is strongly recommended. The key point, however, is that the definition of a forward reference is optional in Turbo C, but required by Turbo Pascal.

AN IDENTIFIER COMPARISON BETWEEN TURBO PASCAL AND TURBO C

Let's look at how some common Turbo Pascal statements compare to Turbo C statements. Table 11-1 compares Turbo Pascal keywords and Turbo C keywords and operators. As you can see, many of the Turbo Pascal keywords have no Turbo C equivalent because Turbo Pascal uses keywords and Turbo C uses operators to accomplish the same thing. And sometimes Turbo Pascal is simply "wordier" than Turbo C. (The Turbo C user manual contains a complete cross-reference of all Turbo Pascal/Turbo C indentifiers.)

Table 11-1.   Turbo Pascal Keywords Compared to Turbo C Keywords

Turbo Pascal	Turbo C
and	&&
array	
begin	{
case	switch
const	const
div	/ (using integers)
do	
downto	
else	else
end	}
file	
forward	extern (on occasion)
for	for
function	
goto	goto

Table 11-1. Turbo Pascal Keywords Compared to Turbo C Keywords
(*continued*)

Turbo Pascal	Turbo C
if	if
in	
label	
mod	%
nil	(sometimes \0)
not	!
of	
or	‖
packed	
procedure	
program	
record	struct
repeat	do
set	
then	
type	
to	
until	while (as in do-while)
var	
while	while
with	

In addition to the keywords, Turbo Pascal has several built-in *standard identifiers* that can be used directly in a program. These identifiers may be functions, such as **writeln**, or global variables, such as *MaxInt*, that are used to hold information about the state of the system. Turbo Pascal uses standard identifiers, such as **real**, **integer**, **boolean**, and **char**, to specify data types. Table 11-2 shows several of the more common standard Turbo Pascal identifiers with their C equivalents. In addition to those shown, a number of Turbo Pascal's built-in functions have Turbo C equivalents that are found in the library.

In addition to the keywords, built-in functions, and variables, Turbo Pascal differs from Turbo C in its operators. Table 11-3 shows the Turbo Pascal operators and their Turbo C equivalents.

Table 11-2.   Selected Turbo Pascal Standard Identifiers with Their Turbo C Equivalents

Turbo Pascal	Turbo C
boolean	char or integer
byte	char
char	char
EOF	EOF (in stdio library)
false	0
flush	fflush( ) (in stdio library)
integer	integer
read	scanf( ) and others
real	float
true	Any nonzero value
write	printf( )

Table 11-3.   Turbo Pascal and Turbo C Operators

Turbo Pascal	Turbo C	Meaning
+	+	Addition
−	−	Subtraction
*	*	Multiplication
/	/	Division
div	/	Integer division
mod	%	Modulus
^		Exponentiation (no equivalent operator in C)
:=	=	Assignment
=	==	Equals as a condition
<	<	Less than
>	>	Greater than
>=	>=	Greater than or equals
<=	<=	Less than or equals
<>	!=	Not equal

CONVERTING TURBO PASCAL LOOPS INTO C LOOPS

Because program control loops are fundamental to most programs, let's compare Turbo Pascal's loops with Turbo C's loops. Turbo Pascal has three built-in loops: **for**, **while**, and **repeat-until**. Turbo C has corresponding loops for each of these.

The Turbo Pascal **for** has the general form

for *<initial value>* to *<target value>* do statement;

The Turbo Pascal **for** is much more limited than the Turbo C **for** because it does not allow increments other than 1 (or -1 if the **downto** is used), and the loop condition is rigidly tied to the counting mechanism, unlike C's more flexible design. However, these differences are minor when translating from Turbo Pascal into C because the Turbo Pascal **for** is simply a subset of Turbo C's. For example,

```
for x:=10 to 100 do writeln(x);
```

can be translated into C as

```
for(x=10; x<=100; ++x) printf("%d\n",x);
```

The Turbo Pascal **while** and the Turbo C **while** are virtually the same. However, the Turbo Pascal **repeat-until** and the Turbo C **do-while** require different keywords, and the loop test condition must be "reversed" because the Turbo Pascal **until** implies that a loop runs *until* something becomes true, whereas the Turbo C **do-while** loops *while* the loop condition *is* true. A sample translation of both these types of loops is shown here:

```
Turbo Pascal                      Turbo C

while x<5 do                      while(x<5)
begin                             {
   writeln(x);                       printf("%d\n", x);
   read(x);                          scanf("%d", &x);
end;                              }

repeat                            do {
   read(x);                          scanf("%d", &x);
   writeln(x);                       printf("%d\n", x);
until x>5;                        } while(x<=5);
```

Remember to watch out for the **repeat-until** to **do-while** translation. You must reverse the sense of the test condition.

THE case AND if STATEMENTS

For the most part you can directly translate the Pascal **case** statement into the C **switch** statement. For example, these two fragments are functionally equivalent:

```
Turbo Pascal                      Turbo C

case choice of                    switch(choice) {
  'E': enter;                        case 'E': enter();
                                        break;
  'D': display;                      case 'D': display();
                                        break;
  'Q': quit;                         case 'Q': quit();
end;                              }
```

The only time you will have problems is when the **case** statement uses a range. The C **switch** statement cannot accept a range. For example, the following **case** statement cannot be directly translated into a C **switch** statement:

```
case time of
  0..6: sleep;
  7..8: getready;
  9..17: work;
  18..20: rest;
  21..24: sleep;
end;
```

To translate this sort of statement requires the creation of a number of C **case** statements that resolve to a common statement sequence. That is, the first range, 0-6, would be translated as

```
switch (time) {
  case 0:
  case 1:
  case 2:
  case 3:
  case 4:
  case 5:
  case 6:
   sleep();
   break;
```

To translate Turbo Pascal **if** statements into Turbo C **if** statements is straightforward and no exceptions will occur.

RECORDS VERSUS STRUCTURES

Aside from variant records you should have no trouble translating a Turbo Pascal record into a Turbo C structure. To translate a variant record into a structure requires that you first create a **union** to contain the variant part of the record and make this **union** an element of the structure. For example, the variant **record**

```
type
  PayType = (salaried, hourly, LaidOff);

  employee = record
    name: string[40];
    age: integer;
    case PayMethod: PayType of
      salaried: (MonthyWage: real);
      hourly: (HourlyRate: real);
      LaidOff: (NoWage: boolean);
  end;
```

would be translated into Turbo C as

```
union PayMethod {
  float MonthyWage, HourlyWage;
  char NoWage;
};

enum PayType {Hourly, Monthy, InActive};

struct employee {
  char name[40];
  int age;
  enum PayType method;
  union PayMethod Pay;
}
```

Any program that uses this structure will have to set the **method** field manually in accordance with what is actually in the **union pay**.

Using variant records is not considered good programming practice by many professional programmers because of the high likelihood for error, and it is best to avoid them.

PROTOTYPING

Turbo Pascal automatically verifies that the arguments to functions or procedures are of the correct type and number. To enable Turbo C to provide a similar feature you must include full prototypes for all the functions used by your program. This includes the use of the standard library header files and prototypes for the functions you create. Although prototyping is not required for all functions, its use is highly recommended.

A SAMPLE TRANSLATION

To give you the flavor of the translation process, let's convert the following simple Turbo Pascal program into Turbo C:

```
program test (input,output);
var qwerty: real;

procedure func2 (x: integer);
begin
```

```
    writeln(x*2);
end;

function func1 (w: real): real;
begin
    func1 := w/3.1415;
    qwerty := 23.34
end;

begin
    qwerty := 0;
    writeln(qwerty);
    writeln('hello there');
    func2(25);
    writeln(func1(10));
    writeln(qwerty:2:4);
end.
```

The Turbo Pascal program has one function and one procedure declared. Since functions and procedures are the same in C, do not worry about the difference, except, of course, to return the value properly. Therefore, **func2( )** becomes

```
void func2(int x)
{
   printf("%d", x*2);
}
```

and **func1( )** becomes

```
float func1(float w)
{
   qwerty = 23.34;
   return w/3.1415;
}
```

Notice that because **func1( )** is returning a **float** you must explicitly declare it by placing the type declaration **float** in front of **func1( )**.

Next, the **program** code (which starts with the first **begin** not

inside another function or procedure) must be converted into the
main( ) function. It becomes

```
main()
{
  qwerty = 0;
  printf("%f", qwerty);
  printf("hello there\n");
  func2(25);
  printf("%f\n", func1(10));
  printf("%2.4f\n", qwerty):
}
```

The last thing needed is to declare the global variable *qwerty* as a
float. Doing this and putting the pieces together, the program
translated into Turbo C is shown here:

```
#include <stdio.h>

float qwerty;
void func2(int x);
float func1(float w);

main()
{
  qwerty = 0;
  printf("%f", qwerty);
  printf("hello there\n");
  func2(25);
  printf("%f\n", func1(10));
  printf("%2.4f\n", qwerty);
}

void func2(int x)
{
  printf("%d", x*2);
}

float func1(float w)
{
  qwerty = 23.34;
  return w/3.1415;
}
```

USING THE COMPUTER TO HELP CONVERT TURBO PASCAL TO C

It is possible to construct a computer program that will accept source code in one language and output it in another. The best way to do this is actually to implement a complete language parser for the source language, which outputs the destination language in source form rather than generating code. Occasionally you find advertisements for such products in computer magazines, and their prices reflect the complexity of the task. However, a very simple program can help you in your conversion efforts by performing some of the simpler translations. This can be thought of as a "computer assist," and it can really make conversion jobs a lot easier.

The basic idea behind a computer assist translator is that it accepts as input a program in the source language and performs the one-to-one conversions into the destination language automatically, leaving the harder conversions up to you. For example, to assign **count** the value of 10 in Turbo Pascal, you would write

```
count:=10;
```

The statement is the same in Turbo C, except that there is no colon. Therefore, the computer assist program can change the ":=" assignment statement in Turbo Pascal to the "=" for use with Turbo C. But the ways Turbo Pascal and C access disk files are very different, and there is no easy way to perform such a conversion automatically. The translations that cannot be done easily are left to you.

The first thing that is needed for the translator is a function that returns a token at a time from the input file. The function **get—token( )** developed in Chapter 10 can be modified for this use and is shown next:

```
/* Read a token from the input stream. */
void get_token(void)
{

  register char *temp;

  tok_type = 0; tok = 0;
  temp = token;

  if(*prog=='\n') {
    *temp++ = '\r';
    *temp++ = '\n';
    *temp = '\0';
    prog++;
    tok_type = DELIM;
    return;
  }

  if(*prog=='\0') {
    *temp = '\0';
    tok_type = DELIM;
    return;
  }
  while(isspace(*prog)) ++prog;  /* skip over white space */

  /* relational equals */
  if(*prog=='=') {
    prog++;
    strcpy(token, "==");
    tok_type = OP;
    return;
  }

  /* assignment */
  if(*prog==':') {
    prog++;
    if(*prog=='=')
    {
      *temp++ = '=';
      prog++;
    }
    else *temp++ = ':';

    *temp = '\0';
    tok_type = OP;
    return;
  }
```

```
  /* strings */
  if(strchr("'", *prog)) {
    *temp++ = '"';  prog++;
    while(!strchr("'", *prog)) *temp++ = *prog++;
    *temp = '"'; temp++; *temp = '\0'; prog++;
    tok_type = STRING;
    return;
  }

  /* other operators  */
  if(strchr("+-*;.,/^%()", *prog)){
    *temp = *prog;
    prog++; /* advance to next position */
    if(*temp=='.') *temp = ' ';
    temp++;
    *temp = '\0';
    tok_type = OP;
    return;
  }

  /* variables */
  if(isalpha(*prog)) {
    while(isalpha(*prog) || isdigit(*prog)) *temp++ = *prog++;
    *temp = '\0';
    tok_type = IDENTIFIER;
    return;
  }

  /* numbers */
  if(isdigit(*prog)) {
    while(!isdelim(*prog)) *temp++ = *prog++;
    tok_type = NUMBER;
    *temp = '\0';
    return;
  }
  prog++;  /* unknown character */
}
```

The Turbo Pascal assignment ":=" is converted into Turbo C "="
and the "=" is converted into its C equivalent "==" inside **get—
token( )**. This makes it a little easier to code other parts of the
program.

The second important routine is the one that translates Turbo
Pascal keywords and some functions into their C counterparts.
The function **translate( )** shown here uses the two-dimensional
array *trans* to look up Turbo Pascal identifiers and return their
Turbo C counterparts.

```
char *trans[][2] = {
  "and", "&&",
  "begin", "{",
  "case", "switch",
  "div", "/",
  "do", "do",
  "else", "else",
  "end", "}",
  "forward", "extern",
  "for", "for",
  "function", "\n",
  "goto", "goto",
  "if", "if",
  "then", " ",
  "mod", "%",
  "nil", "'\0'",
  "not", "!",
  "procedure", "\n",
  "record", "struct",
  "repeat", "do",
  "until", " while",
  'while', "while",
  "writeln", "printf",
  "read", "scanf",
  "readln", "scanf",
  "write", "printf",
  "real", "float",
  "integer", "int",
  "char", "char",
  "",""
};

/* Translate Turbo Pascal indentifiers into Turbo C. */
void translate(char *s)
{
  register int i;

  for(i=0; *trans[i][0]; i++)
    if(!strcmp(s, trans[i][0])) {
      strcpy(s, trans[i][1]);
      return;
    }
}
```

You can easily add new identifiers to the list to expand what the program can translate. An improved version of this function would require a sorted list of identifiers in *trans* and use a binary search to find the proper entry. You might want to try implementing this improvement yourself. Notice that some Turbo Pascal words, such as **program**, have no equivalent in C; in this case, a newline is substituted. A null string is not used because it is reserved to indicate the end of the file.

The entire translation program is shown here:

```
/* Computer assisted Turbo Pascal to C converter. */

#include <stdio.h>
#include <ctype.h>
#include <string.h>
#include <stdlib.h>
#define OP          1
#define IDENTIFIER  2
#define VAR         3
#define NUMBER      4
#define DELIM       5
#define STRING      6

char token[80];
int tok_type;
int tok;

char s[10000];  /* holds source file */
char *prog;

char *trans[][2] = {
  "and", "&&",
  "begin", "{",
  "case", "switch",
  "div", "/",
  "do", "do",
  "else", "else",
  "end", "}",
  "forward", "extern",
  "for", "for",
  "function", "\n",
  "goto", "goto",
* "if", "if",
  "then", " ",
  "mod", "%",
  "nil", "'\0'",
  "not", "!",
  "procedure", "\n",
  "record", "struct",
  "repeat", "do",
  "until", " while",
  "while", "while",
  "writeln", "printf",
  "read", "scanf",
```

```
    "readln", "scanf",
    "write", "printf",
    "real", "float",
    "integer", "int",
    "char", "char",
    "",""
};

void get_token(void);
int isdelim(char c);
void translate(char *s);

main(int argc, char *argv[])
{
  FILE *fp1, *fp2;
  char *p;
  int indent=0, i;

  prog = s;

  if(argc!=3) {
    printf("usage: input output");
    exit(1);
  }

  if((fp1=fopen(argv[1], "r"))==NULL) {
    printf("cannot open input file\n");
    exit(1);
  }

  if((fp2=fopen(argv[2], "w"))==NULL) {
    printf("cannot open output file\n");
    exit(1);
  }

  while((*prog=getc(fp1))!=EOF)
    prog++; /* read in source */

  *prog = '\0';
  prog = s;

  for(;;) {
    get_token();
    if(!*token) break;  /* end of input file */
    p = token;
    /* if token is an indentifier then translate it */
    if(tok_type==IDENTIFIER) translate(token);

    while(*p) putc(*p++, fp2); /* write it */
```

```
   /* put a space between tokens */
   if(*token!='\r') putc(' ', fp2);

   /* indent code to proper level */
   if(*token=='\r') {
     for(i=0; i<indent; i++) {
       putc(' ', fp2);
       putc(' ', fp2);
     }
   }

   if(*token=='}') indent--;
   if(*token=='{') indent++;
 }
 fclose(fp1); fclose(fp2);
 return 0;
}

/* Read a token from the input stream. */
void get_token(void)
{
 register char *temp;

 tok_type = 0; tok = 0;
 temp = token;

 if(*prog=='\n') {
   *temp++ = '\r';
   *temp++ = '\n';
   *temp = '\0';
   prog++;
   tok_type = DELIM;
   return;
 }

 if(*prog=='\0') {
   *temp = '\0';
   tok_type = DELIM;
   return;
 }
 while(isspace(*prog)) ++prog;  /* skip over white space */

 /* relational equals */
 if(*prog=='=') {
   prog++;
   strcpy(token, "==");
   tok_type = OP;
   return;
 }

 /* assignment */
 if(*prog==':') {
   prog++;
   if(*prog=='=')
   {
```

```
      *temp++ = '=';
      prog++;
    }
    else *temp++ = ':';

    *temp = '\0';
    tok_type = OP;
    return;
  }

  /* strings */
  if(strchr("'", *prog)) {
    *temp++ = '"';  prog++;
    while(!strchr("'", *prog)) *temp++ = *prog++;
    *temp = '"'; temp++; *temp = '\0'; prog++;
    tok_type = STRING;
    return;
  }

  /* other operators  */
  if(strchr("+-*;.,/^%()", *prog)){
    *temp = *prog;
    prog++; /* advance to next position */
    if(*temp=='.') *temp = ' ';
    temp++;
    *temp = '\0';
    tok_type = OP;
    return;
  }

  /* variables */
  if(isalpha(*prog)) {
    while(isalpha(*prog) || isdigit(*prog)) *temp++ = *prog++;
    *temp = '\0';
    tok_type = IDENTIFIER;
    return;
  }

  /* numbers */
  if(isdigit(*prog)) {
    while(!isdelim(*prog)) *temp++ = *prog++;
    tok_type = NUMBER;
    *temp = '\0';
    return;
  }
  prog++;  /* unknown character */
}

/* Return 1 if character is a delimiter; 0 otherwise. */
int isdelim(char c)
{
  if(strchr(" ;,+-/*^%()", c) || c==9 || c=='\r' || c==0)
    return 1;
  return 0;
}
```

```
/* Translate Turbo Pascal indentifiers into Turbo C. */
void translate(char *s)
{
  register int i;

  for(i=0; *trans[i][0]; i++)
    if(!strcmp(s, trans[i][0])) {
      strcpy(s, trans[i][1]);
      return;
    }
}
```

In essence, the Turbo Pascal to Turbo C conversion assist program reads in the entire source code of the Turbo Pascal program, takes a token at a time from it, performs any translations it can, and writes out a Turbo C version. Except for a few operator changes, the standard function **strcmp( )** detects translatable tokens, and **strcpy( )** converts them to the proper Turbo C token. The program as written is case sensitive and expects the Turbo Pascal identifiers to be lowercase. You may want to alter this, depending on how the Turbo Pascal code is written. The translation program automatically indents the translated code by two spaces for each new level.

To see how such a simple program could make life easier, consider this Turbo Pascal program:

```
program test (input,output);
procedure f1(x: integer);
begin
    writeln(x*2);
end;

function f2 (w: real): real;
begin
    if w=100 then writeln('w is 100 inside f2');
    f2:= w/3.1415;
end;

begin
    writeln('hello there');
    f1(25);
    writeln(f2(10));
end.
```

After running it through the translator program, the pseudo-C output is

```
test ( input , output ) ;

f1 ( x : int ) ;
{
  printf ( x * 2 ) ;
  } ;

f2 ( w : float ) : float ;
{
  if w == 100 printf ( " w is 100 inside f2 " ) ;
  f2 = w / 3.1415;
  } ;

{
  printf ( " hello there " ) ;
  f1 ( 25 ) ;
  printf ( f2 ( 10 ) ) ;
  }
```

As you can see, it is not C code, but much typing has been saved and all you need to do is edit it a line at a time, correcting the differences.

FINAL THOUGHTS ON TRANSLATING

Although translating programs can be the most tedious of programming tasks, it is also one of the most common. One of the best overall approaches is first to learn the program you are translating and understand how it works. Then, it will be easier and more interesting to recode because you will know whether your new version is working correctly and the job will no longer be simply a process of substituting one symbol for another.

12

EFFICIENCY, PORTING, AND DEBUGGING

The mark of a professional programmer is the ability to write programs that make efficient use of system resources, are bug free, and are transportable to a new computer. In these areas computer science becomes an art because so few formal techniques are available to ensure success. This chapter presents some of the methods by which you can achieve efficiency and portability. It concludes with an example of debugging recursive routines by using Turbo C's source-level debugger.

EFFICIENCY

When used in connection with a computer program, the term *efficiency* can refer to the speed of execution, the use of system resources, or both. System resources include such things as RAM, disk space, and printer paper—basically anything that can be allocated and used up. Whether a program is efficient is sometimes a subjective judgment that can change from situation to situation. For example, consider a sorting program that uses 128K of RAM, requires two megabytes of disk space, and has an average run time of seven hours. If this program is sorting only 100 addresses in a mailing database, it is not very efficient. If it is sorting the New York telephone directory, however, it is probably quite efficient.

Another point to consider when trying to make your programs efficient is that optimizing one aspect of a program often degrades another. For example, making a program faster also often means making it bigger when in-line code is used to eliminate the overhead of a function call. By the same token, making a program smaller by replacing in-line code with function calls makes it slower. In the same vein, making more efficient use of disk space means compacting the data, which often makes disk accesses slower. In fact this problem even affects Turbo C's code generator. This is why Turbo C lets you decide whether it will optimize for speed or for memory. These and other types of efficiency trade-offs can be very frustrating, especially to the non-programmer end user who cannot see why one thing should affect the other.

In light of these problems, you might be wondering how one can discuss efficiency at all. The answer lies in the fact that some programming practices are always efficient, or at least more efficient than others, and a few techniques make programs both faster and smaller.

The Increment and Decrement Operators

Discussions on the efficient use of C almost always start with a consideration of the increment and decrement operators. In case you have forgotten, the increment operator, ++, increases its argument by one, and the decrement operator, −−, decreases it by one. In essence the increment operator replaces assignment statements like

```
x = x + 1;
```

while the decrement operator replaces assignment statements like

```
x = x - 1;
```

Aside from the obvious advantage of reducing the number of keystrokes needed, because of the way object code is generated by the compiler, the increment and decrement operators have the glorious advantage of both executing faster and needing less RAM than their statement counterparts. Often (for most common microcomputers, for example) it is possible to increment or decrement a word of memory by using a one-step load and store instruction, such as the 8086 INC instruction. For Turbo C to take advantage of this requires that you use the ++ or -- operator. If you don't, the program uses unneeded load and store instructions. For example, the program

```
main()
{
  int t=0;

  t++;

  t = t+1;
}
```

produces the following assembly language code when compiled with the -S (generate assembly listing) option. (The comments beginning with asterisks were added by the author.)

```
        ifndef   ??version
?debug  macro
        endm
        endif
        ?debug   S "test.c"
_TEXT   segment  byte public 'CODE'
DGROUP  group    _DATA,_BSS
        assume   cs:_TEXT,ds:DGROUP,ss:DGROUP
_TEXT   ends
_DATA   segment  word public 'DATA'
d@      label    byte
d@w     label    word
_DATA   ends
_BSS    segment  word public 'BSS'
b@      label    byte
b@w     label    word
        ?debug   C E9CDBD35110479312E63
_BSS    ends
_TEXT   segment  byte public 'CODE'
;       ?debug   L 2
_main   proc     near
        push     si
```

```
;         ?debug  L 4
          xor     si,si
;         ?debug  L 6
; *****  This is the the t++ statement
          inc     si
;         ?debug  L 8
; *****  This is the t = t + 1 statement.  Notice that
; *****  three instructions are used: one to load t into a
; *****  register, one to increment it, and one to store it.
          mov     ax,si
          inc     ax
          mov     si,ax
@1:
;         ?debug  L 9
          pop     si
          ret
_main     endp
_TEXT     ends
          ?debug  C E9
_DATA     segment word public 'DATA'
s@        label   byte
_DATA     ends
_TEXT     segment byte public 'CODE'
_TEXT     ends
          public  _main
          end
```

As you can see, both load and store instructions are absent from
the increment statement, which means that the code will execute
more quickly and be smaller.

Using Register Variables

You should use **register** variables for loop control whenever possible for two reasons:

1. Because the variable is held in an internal register of the CPU,
   its access time is very short—much shorter than if it were
   held in memory.
2. The speed with which the critical loops of a program execute
   sets the pace for the overall speed of the program.

   To see how the code differs between a **register** variable and a
regular memory variable, this program was compiled to an assembly language:

```
int j;

main()
{
  register int i;

  for(i=0; i<100 ;i++) ;

  for(j=0; j<100; j++) ;

}
```

The assembly code file produced is shown here. (The comments
beginning with asterisks were added by the author.)

```
        ifndef  ??version
?debug  macro
        endm
        endif
        ?debug  S "test.c"
_TEXT   segment byte public 'CODE'
DGROUP  group   _DATA,_BSS
        assume  cs:_TEXT,ds:DGROUP,ss:DGROUP
_TEXT   ends
_DATA   segment word public 'DATA'
d@      label   byte
d@w     label   word
_DATA   ends
_BSS    segment word public 'BSS'
b@      label   byte
b@w     label   word
        ?debug  C E981BE35110479322E63
_BSS    ends
_TEXT   segment byte public 'CODE'
;       ?debug  L 4
_main   proc    near
        push    si
;       ?debug  L 8
; ***** The next line initializes i, the register variable
; ***** using only a single instruction.
        xor     si,si
        jmp     short @5
@4:
@3:
; ***** This instruction increments the register variable.
        inc     si
@5:
        cmp     si,100
        jl      @4
@2:
;       ?debug  L 10
; ***** The next two instructions initialize the memory
; ***** variable j.  Notice that this requires a memory
```

```
;  *****  access.
        mov      word ptr DGROUP:_j,0
        jmp      short @9
@8:
@7:
;  *****  Here, a memory access is required to increment j.
        inc      word ptr DGROUP:_j
@9:
;  *****  Another memory access is needed to test j's value.
        cmp      word ptr DGROUP:_j,100
        jl       @8
@6:
@1:
;                ?debug   L 12
        pop      si
        ret
_main   endp
_TEXT   ends
_BSS    segment word public 'BSS'
_j      label    word
        db       2 dup (?)
_BSS    ends
        ?debug   C E9
_DATA   segment word public 'DATA'
s@      label    byte
_DATA   ends
_TEXT   segment byte public 'CODE'
_TEXT   ends
        public   _main
        public   _j
        end
```

To get an idea of the time differences, assume that an 8088 processor executes this program. The register-controlled loop uses the instruction **inc si** to increment the control variable. This requires only two system clock ticks. On the other hand, the memory-controlled loop must use **inc word ptr dgroup:_j**, which requires 29 clock ticks—an almost 15-to-1 increase!

Turbo C automatically makes the first two integer variables in a function into **register** types if no other **register** variables are present. This process is called compiler optimization and is used to increase the overall speed of execution.

Because you can have only two **register** variables, it is important that you choose the correct loops for their use. For example, in the following fragment you would use **register** variables for the two inner loops but not for the outer loop:

```
for(i=0; i<100; i++) {
  .
  .
  .
  for(j=0; j<1000; j++) {
    .
    .
    .
  }
  for(k=0; k<10; k++) ...;
}
```

You would choose the inner loops because they will both be executed 100 times. This means that j will be accessed 100,000 times and k 1000 times, while i is accessed only 100 times.

Pointers Versus Array Indexing

Another optimization that you can do to produce smaller and faster code is to substitute pointer arithmetic for array indexing. The use of pointers always makes your code run faster and take up less space. Take a look at the following two code fragments, which do the same thing:

```
array indexing          pointer arithmetic

                        p = array;
for(;;) {               for(;;) {
  a=array[t++];           a=*(p++);
  .                       .
  .                       .
  .                       .
}                       }
```

The advantage of the pointer method is that once p has been loaded with the address of *array*, only an increment must be performed each time the loop repeats. The array index version must always compute the array index based on the value of t—a more complex task. The disparity in execution speeds between array indexing and pointer arithmetic gets wider when multiple indexes are used. Each index requires its own sequence of instructions, while the pointer arithmetic equivalent can use simple addition.

Remember that you should use array indexes when the index is derived through a very complex formula and the use of pointer arithmetic would obscure the meaning of the program. It is usually better to degrade performance slightly rather than sacrifice clarity.

Use of Functions

You should remember at all times that stand-alone functions used with local variables help form the basis of structured programming. Functions are the building blocks of C programs and are one of C's strongest assets. Do not let anything that is discussed in this section be construed otherwise. However, you should know a few things about C functions and the effects they have on the size and speed of your code.

First and foremost, Turbo C is a stack-oriented language. This means that all local variables and parameters use the stack for temporary storage. When a function is called, the return address of the calling routine is also placed on the stack. This enables the subroutine to return to the location from which it was called. When a function returns, this address, as well as all local variables and parameters, has to be removed from the stack. The process of pushing this information is generally known as the *calling sequence* and the popping process is called the *returning sequence*. Simply put, these sequences take time, sometimes quite a bit of time.

To understand how a function call can slow down your program, look at the two code fragments shown here:

```
version 1                  version 2

for(x=1; x<100; ++x) {     for(x=1; x<100; ++x) {
  t = compute(x);            t = abs(sin(q)/100/3.1416);
}                          }
```

```
float compute(int q)
{
   return abs(sin(q)/100/3.1416);
}
```

Although each loop performs the same function, version 2 will be much faster because the overhead of the calling and returning sequence has been eliminated by using in-line code.

Let's look at another example. When this program is compiled using the -S option it produces the following assembly code listing:

```
main()
{
   int x;

   x = max(10,20);
}

max(int a, b)
{
   return a>b ? a : b;
}
```

The assembly code produced by this program is shown here. The calling and return sequences are indicated by comments beginning with asterisks (added by the author). As you can see, they require a sizable amount of the code in the program.

```
         ifndef  ??version
?debug   macro
         endm
         endif
         ?debug  S "test.c"
_TEXT    segment byte public 'CODE'
DGROUP   group   _DATA,_BSS
         assume  cs:_TEXT,ds:DGROUP,ss:DGROUP
_TEXT    ends
_DATA    segment word public 'DATA'
da       label   byte
daw      label   word
_DATA    ends
_BSS     segment word public 'BSS'
ba       label   byte
baw      label   word
         ?debug  C E9FBBE35110479332E63
_BSS     ends
_TEXT    segment byte public 'CODE'
;        ?debug  L 2
_main    proc    near
         push    bp
```

```
        mov     bp,sp
        sub     sp,2
;       ?debug  L 6
; ***** Beginning of calling sequence.
        mov     ax,20
        push    ax
        mov     ax,10
        push    ax
; *************************************************
        call    near ptr _max
; ***** The next lines are the end of the function's
; ***** return sequence.
        pop     cx
        pop     cx
        mov     word ptr [bp-2],ax
@1:
;       ?debug  L 7
        mov     sp,bp
        pop     bp
; *************************************************
        ret
_main   endp
;       ?debug  L 9
_max    proc    near
; ***** More of the calling sequence.
        push    bp
        mov     bp,sp
; *************************************************
;       ?debug  L 11
        mov     ax,word ptr [bp+4]
        cmp     ax,word ptr [bp+6]
        jle     @4
        mov     ax,word ptr [bp+4]
        jmp     short @3
@4:
        mov     ax,word ptr [bp+6]
@3:
        jmp     short @2
@2:
;       ?debug  L 12
; ***** Beginning of the return sequence.
        pop     bp
        ret
; *************************************************
_max    endp
_TEXT   ends
        ?debug  C E9
_DATA   segment word public 'DATA'
s@      label   byte
_DATA   ends
_TEXT   segment byte public 'CODE'
_TEXT   ends
        public  _max
        public  _main
        end
```

You may be thinking now that you should write programs that have just a few very large functions so that they will run quickly. Well, in the vast majority of cases the slight time differential will not be meaningful, and the loss of structure will be acute. But there is another problem. Replacing functions that are used by several routines with in-line code will make your program very large because the same code is duplicated several times. Remember that subroutines were invented largely as a way to make efficient use of memory. In fact, this is the reason that making a program faster generally means making it bigger, while making it smaller means making it slower.

In the final analysis, it makes sense to use in-line code instead of a function call only when speed is the overriding priority. Otherwise, the liberal use of functions is definitely recommended.

PORTING PROGRAMS

It is very common for a program written on one machine to be transported to another computer with a different processor, operating system, or both. This process is called *porting* and can be very easy or extremely hard, depending on how the program was originally written. A program that can be easily ported is called *portable*. When a program is not easily portable, it is usually because it contains numerous *machine dependencies*, which means that it has code fragments that work only with one specific operating system or processor. Turbo C has been designed to allow the creation of portable code because it supports the proposed ANSI C standard. However, writing portable code still requires care and attention to detail. In this section we will examine a few specific problem areas and offer some solutions.

Using #define

Perhaps the simplest way to make programs portable is to make every system- or processor-dependent "magic number" a #**define** macro substitution directive. These magic numbers will include things like buffer sizes for disk accesses, special screen and keyboard commands, and memory allocation information—that is, anything that has even the slightest possibility of changing when the program is ported. These defines will not only make all magic numbers obvious to the person doing the porting but also simplify the editing job because their values will have to be changed only once instead of several times throughout the program.

For example, here are two functions that use **fread( )** and **fwrite( )** to read and write information from a disk file:

```
f1()
{
    .
    .
    .
    fwrite(buf, 128, 1, fp);
}

f2()
{
    .
    .
    .
    fread(buf, 128, 1, fp);
}
```

The problem here is that the buffer size, 128, is hard-coded into both the **fwrite( )** and the **fread( )** statements. This might be fine for one operating system but less than optimal for another. A better way to code this function is shown here:

```
#define buf_size 128

f1()
{
    .
    .
    .
    fwrite(buf, buf_size, 1, fp);
}

f2()
{
    .
    .
    .
    fread(buf, buf_size, 1, fp);
}
```

In this case only the **#define** has to be changed, and all references to *buf—size* are automatically corrected. This not only makes it easier to change but also avoids many editing errors. You should remember that there will probably be many references to *buf—size* in a real program so the gain in portability is often quite great.

Differences in Data Sizes

As you may know, the size of a word in a 16-bit processor is 16 bits; in a 32-bit processor it is 32 bits. Because the size of a word tends to be the size of an integer, if you wish to write portable code you must never make assumptions about the size of a data type. Therefore, you should use **sizeof( )** whenever your program needs to know how many bytes long something is. For example, this fragment writes an integer to a disk file and will work on any computer:

```
void write_int(int i)
{
  fwrite(&i, sizeof(int), 1, stream);
}
```

Sometimes, however, it is not possible to create portable code even with **sizeof**. For example, the following code, which swaps the bytes in an integer, will work on an 8088-based computer but fail on a 68000. This function cannot be made portable because it is based on the fact that in the 8088 integers are two bytes long. In the 68000 integers are generally four bytes long.

```
void swap_bytes(int *x)
{
  union sb {
    int t;
    unsigned char c[2];
  } swap;

  unsigned char temp;

  swap.t = *x;
  temp = swap.c[1];
```

```
    swap.c[1] = swap.c[0];
    swap.c[0] = temp;
    *x = swap.t;
}
```

DEBUGGING RECURSIVE FUNCTIONS
WITH THE DEBUGGER

Turbo C's debugger is so easy to use that coverage of it in an advanced book may seem somewhat unusual. However, this final section will explore one of its more interesting uses: debugging recursive functions.

Note: This section assumes that you are using Turbo C's integrated program development environment.

Recursive functions are among the hardest functions to debug because often the function calls itself several times in the process of executing, which makes it very difficult to know exactly what is happening inside the function at any given time. However, by using Turbo C's debugger you can track each recursive call. To see how this is done, let's develop a simple recursive function called **factr( )**, which computes the factorial of its argument.

Let's begin with a version of **factr( )** that contains an intentional error, as shown here:

```
/* This program contains an error - do not
   execute it.
*/

#include <stdio.h>

int factr(int i);

main()
{
  printf("%d", factr(4));
}

factr(int i)
{
  return factr(i-1);
}
```

Enter this program. If you tried to run the program in its present form, it would eventually crash your system. Let's see why.

To begin to find the trouble, single step the program by pressing the F7 key several times. After the **factr( )** function has called itself more than four times, press ALT-D to activate the Debug menu and select the **Call stack** option. This displays the calls made to functions in the program. It will look something like this:

factr(−2)
factr(−1)
factr(0)
factr(1)
factr(2)
factr(3)
factr(4)
main( )

As you can see, **factr( )** looks like it will continue to call itself without end. This prompts us to reexamine the code to **factr( )**. It is obvious that there is no terminating condition that stops the recursive calls. To solve this problem, change **factr( )** so that it looks like this:

```
factr(int i)
{
  if(i==0) return 0;
  return i*factr(i-1);
}
```

Now single step the program to its conclusion. It now ends correctly, but gives the wrong answer. It outputs 0, but the answer should be 24. To find the cause of this trouble, you need to be able to watch the value returned by **factr( )**. It is not possible to watch this value directly by using the debugger, so change the function to look like this:

```
factr(int i)
{
  int j;
```

```
   if(i==0) return 0;
   j = i*factr(i-1);
   return j;
}
```

Now activate the **Break/Watch** option, select **Add watch**, and watch *j*. Execute the program by single stepping. When the recursive calls begin returning, you will see that the value assigned to *j* is always 0. By using this information you can easily see that the condition

```
if(i==0) return 0;
```

is wrong. The statement should read

```
if(i==1) return 1;
```

Hence the corrected **factr( )** function looks like this:

```
factr(int i)
{
   if(i==1) return 1;
   return i*factr(i-1);
}
```

The skillful use of Turbo C's debugger can greatly simplify the debugging process. However, it should never be substituted for a good initial design.

DEBUGGING THEORY IN GENERAL

Everyone has a different approach to programming and debugging. However, over time certain techniques have proven to be better than others. In the case of debugging, incremental testing is considered to be the most cost- (and time-) effective method even though it can appear to slow the development process at first. To understand what incremental testing is, you must first see what it is not.

In the early days of computers, programmers were taught to prepare their programs in advance, submit them for execution, and then interpret results. This is called batch programming. It was necessary when computers were scarce, but it is seldom used today because many computers support an interactive programming environment. Batch programming is one of those things that helped give computers a bad image in the early 1960s because it required programmers to spend an enormous amount of time and mental energy developing a program. It was indeed a painful experience. Because all testing also had to be done in batch mode, it was very difficult to try all the possible conditions in which a program could fail. This lack of thorough testing led to the pervasive "computer error" problems so common in many early computer installations.

Today, batch programming is virtually extinct because it cannot support an interactive *incremental testing* environment. Incremental testing is the process of always having a working program. That is, an operational unit is established very early in the development process. An *operational unit* is simply a piece of working code. As new code is added to this unit, it is tested and debugged. In this way the programmer can find errors easily because the errors will most likely occur in the newly added code or in the way that it interacts with the operational unit.

Debugging time can be computed according to the formula

$$DebugTime = (NumOfLines + x)^2$$

where *NumOfLines* is the total number of lines of code that a bug could be in and x is a programmer-dependent constant. As you can see, debugging time is a squared quantity. With incremental testing it is possible to restrict the number of lines of code to only those that are newly added, that is, not part of the operational unit. This situation is shown in Figure 12-1.

Incremental testing theory is generally based on probability and areas. Because area is a squared dimension, as your program grows you must search an N-squared area for bugs. As a programmer you want to deal with the smallest possible area while debugging. Through incremental testing you can subtract the

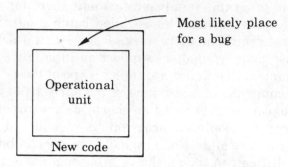

Figure 12-1. The most likely location of a bug in an incremental testing situation

area already tested from the total area, thereby reducing the region where a bug may be found.

In large projects several modules will have only mild interaction. In these cases you can establish several operational units to allow concurrent development.

Incremental testing is important for two reasons:

1. It greatly reduces debugging time because errors are easier to find.

2. It speeds up the development process because design errors can be caught early in the project, before all the code is written. (This should never, of course, take the place of a good design!)

Incremental testing is simply the process of always having working code. As soon as it is possible to run a piece of your program, you should do so, testing that section completely. As you add to the program, continue to test the new sections and the way they connect to the known operational code. In this way you will be concentrating any possible bugs in a small area of code.

A

TURBO C's MEMORY MODELS

One of Turbo C's most confusing aspects is not its fault! You can compile a C program using any of the six different memory models defined by the 8086 family of processors. (On other types of processors Turbo C may not have this ability.) Each model organizes the memory of the computer differently and governs the size of the code, the data, or both. Because the model used has a profound effect on the way a program accesses the system resources—especially memory—this appendix begins with an overview of the various memory models and then develops a program that lets you inspect and change any part of the RAM in your system.

This appendix is specifically for Turbo C on the 8086 family of processors. Furthermore, the discussion of the Turbo C memory models assumes that you loosely understand how the 8086 CPU operates. If you don't, you will still understand the difference between the various memory models in a practical sense even if you don't understand the underlying principles.

THE 8086 FAMILY
OF PROCESSORS

Before you can understand the way the various memory models work, you need to understand how the 8086 family of processors addresses memory. (For the rest of this appendix, the CPU will be referred to as the 8086, but the information applies to all processors in this family, including the 8088, 80186, 80286, and 80386.)

The 8086 contains 14 registers into which information is placed for processing or program control. The registers fall into the following categories:

- General-purpose registers
- Base pointer and index registers
- Segment registers
- Special-purpose registers

All the registers in the 8086 are 16 bits (2 bytes) wide.

The *general-purpose registers* are the "workhorse" registers of the 8086. Values are placed in these registers for processing, including arithmetic operations, such as adding or multiplying; comparisons, such as equality, less than, and greater than; and branch (jump) instructions. Each of the general-purpose registers can be accessed in two ways, either as a 16-bit register or as two 8-bit registers.

The *base pointer and index registers* are used to provide support for such things as relative addressing, the stack pointer, and block move instructions.

The *segment registers* are used to support the 8086's segmented memory scheme. The CS register holds the current code segment, the DS holds the current data segment, the ES holds the extra segment, and the SS holds the stack segment.

The *special-purpose registers* are the flag register, which holds the state of the 8086, and the instruction pointer, which points to the next instruction for the 8086 to execute.

Figure A-1 shows the layout of the 8086 registers.

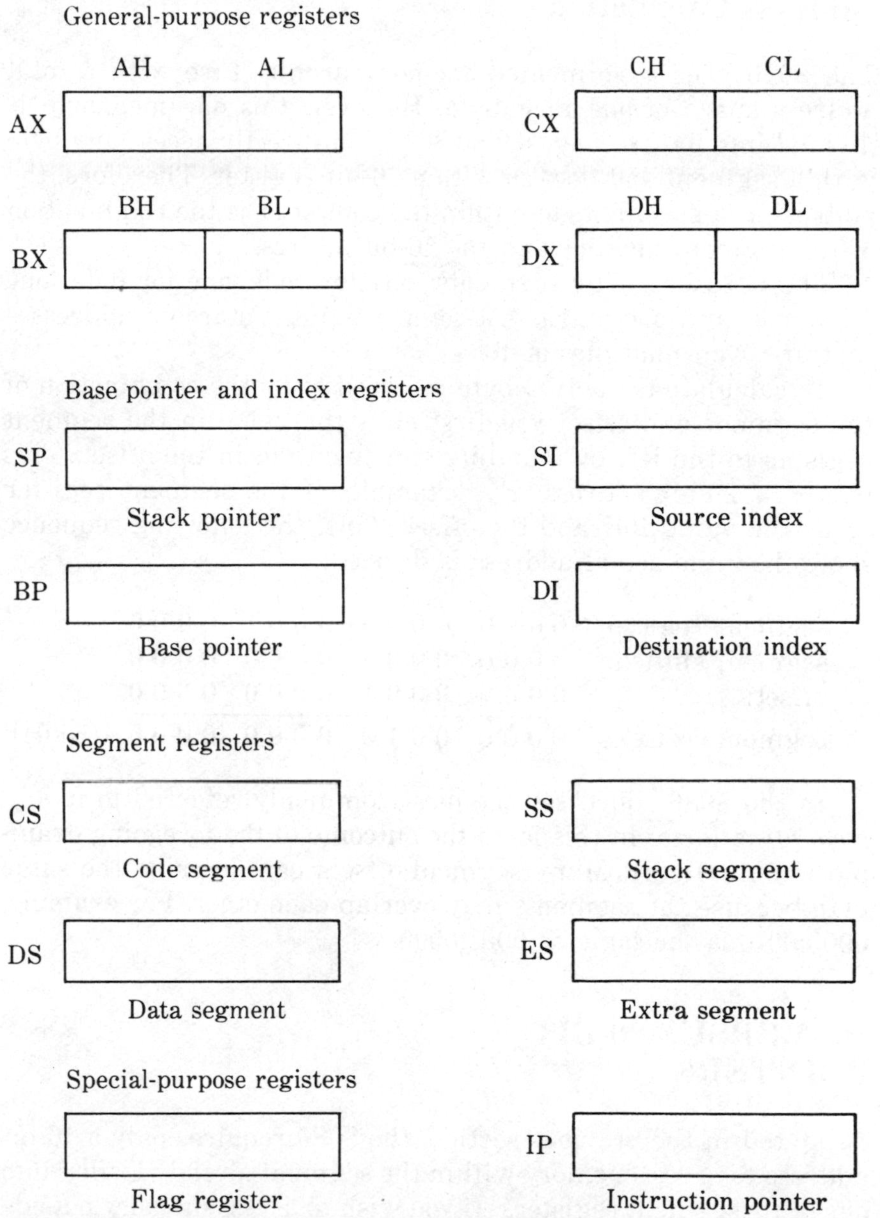

General-purpose registers

AH　　AL　　　　　　　　CH　　CL

AX ☐☐　　　　　CX ☐☐

BH　　BL　　　　　　　　DH　　DL

BX ☐☐　　　　　DX ☐☐

Base pointer and index registers

SP ☐　　　　　SI ☐

Stack pointer　　　　　　Source index

BP ☐　　　　　DI ☐

Base pointer　　　　　　Destination index

Segment registers

CS ☐　　　　　SS ☐

Code segment　　　　　Stack segment

DS ☐　　　　　ES ☐

Data segment　　　　　Extra segment

Special-purpose registers

☐　　　　IP ☐

Flag register　　　　Instruction pointer

Figure A-1. The 8086 CPU registers

Address Calculation

The 8086 uses a segmented memory architecture with a total address space of one megabyte. However, this one megabyte is divided into 64K *segments*. The 8086 can directly access any byte with a segment and does so with a 16-bit register. Therefore, the address of a specific byte within the computer is the combination of the segment number and the 16-bit address.

The 8086 uses four segments: one for code, one for data, one for stack, and one extra. All segments must start on addresses that are even multiples of 16.

To calculate the actual byte referred to by the combination of the segment and offset you first shift the value in the segment register to the left by four bits and then add in the offset. This makes a 20-bit address. For example, if the segment register holds the value 10H and the offset 100H, the following sequence shows how the actual address is derived:

```
segment register:  0 0 0 0  0 0 0 0  0 0 0 1  0 0 0 0
segment shifted:   0 0 0 0  0 0 0 1  0 0 0 0  0 0 0 0
offset:            0 0 0 0  0 0 0 1  0 0 0 0  0 0 0 0
                   ─────────────────────────────────
segment+offset:    0 0 0 0  0 0 1 0  0 0 0 0  0 0 0 0   (200H)
```

In the 8086 addresses are most commonly referred to in *segment:offset* form. In this form the outcome of the foregoing example is 0010:0100H. Many segment:offsets can describe the same byte because the segments may overlap each other. For example, 0000:0010 is the same as 0001:0000.

16- VERSUS 20-BIT POINTERS

As stated in the previous section, the 8086 requires only a 16-bit address to access memory within the segment already loaded into one of its segment registers. If you wish to access memory outside that segment, however, both the segment register and the offset must be loaded with the proper values. This requires a 20-bit address. Since all registers in the 8086 are 16 bits long, however, the 20-bit address requires two registers, or 32 bits, to hold it. (This is why you will sometimes see the phrase "32-bit address" used in place of the more correct "20-bit address.") The difference between accessing memory within a segment and outside a current segment is that it takes twice as long to load two 16-bit registers as it does to load one. Hence your programs run much slower.

MEMORY MODELS

Turbo C for the 8086 family of processors can compile your program six different ways, and each way organizes the computer's memory differently. The six models are called tiny, small, medium, compact, large, and huge. Let's look at how these differ.

Tiny Model

The tiny model compiles a C program so that all the segment registers are set to the same value and all addressing is done using 16 bits. This means that the code, data, and stack must all be within the same 64K segment. This method of compilation produces the smallest, fastest code. Programs compiled using this version can be converted into .COM files using the DOS command **EXE2BIN**.

Small Model

The small model is Turbo C's default mode of compilation and is useful for a wide variety of tasks. Although all addressing is done by using only the 16-bit offset, the code segment is separate from the data, stack, and extra segments, which are in their own segment. This means that the total size of a program compiled this way is 128K, split between code and data. The addressing time is the same for the tiny model, but the program can be twice as big. Most programs that you write will be in this model.

Medium Model

The medium model is for large programs in which the code exceeds the one-segment restriction of the small model. Here the code can use multiple segments and requires 32-bit pointers, but the code, data, and extra segments are in their own segment and use 16-bit addresses. This model is good for large programs that use little data.

Compact Model

The complement of the medium model is the compact model. In this model, program code is restricted to one segment but data can occupy several segments. This means that all accesses to data require 32-bit addressing, but the code uses 16-bit addressing. The compact model is good for programs that require large amounts of data but little code.

Large Model

The large model allows both code and data to use multiple segments. However, static data is limited to 64K. This model is used when your code and data requirements are both large. It runs much more slowly than the other models discussed so far.

Huge Model

The huge model is the same as the large model with the exception that static data can exceed 64K. This degrades run-time speed even further.

Selecting a Model

Generally, you should use the small model unless there is a reason to do otherwise. Select the medium model if you have a lot of program but not much data. Use the compact model if you have a lot of data and not much program. If you have a large amount of both code and data, use the large model unless your total static data is greater than 64K, in which case you will need to use the huge model. Remember that both large and huge models are substantially slower than the others.

OVERRIDING A MEMORY MODEL

During the foregoing discussion you may have been thinking how unfortunate it is that even a single reference to data in another segment requires you to use the compact rather than the small model, thus slowing the execution of the entire program even though only an isolated part of it actually needs a 20-bit pointer. In general, this sort of situation can present itself in a variety of ways. The solution to this type of problem is the *segment override* type modifiers added by Turbo C. They are

    far   near   huge

    _cs   _ds   _es   _ss

These modifiers can be applied only to pointers or functions. When they are applied to pointers they affect the way data is accessed. When applied to functions they affect the way the program calls and returns from the function.

These modifiers follow the base type and precede the variable name. For example, this code declares a **far** pointer called **f_pointer:**

```
char far *f_pointer;
```

far

The most common model override is the **far** pointer because it is very common to want to access some region of memory that is (or may be) outside the data segment. If the program is compiled for one of the large data models, however, all access to data becomes very slow. The solution to this problem is explicitly to declare **far** pointers to the memory outside the current data segment. In this way, only the references to objects actually far away will incur the additional overhead.

The use of **far** functions is less common and is generally restricted to specialized programming situations in which a function may lie outside the current code segment (in ROM, for example). In these cases, the use of **far** ensures that the proper calling and returning sequences are used.

One very important thing about **far** pointers as implemented in Turbo C is that pointer arithmetic affects only the offset. This means that when a **far** pointer with the value 0000:FFFF is incremented, its new value will be 0000:0000 not 0001:FFFD. Therefore, even though the pointer can access objects that are not in its own data segment, it cannot access objects larger than 64K.

In Turbo C two **far** pointers should not be used in a relational expression because only their offsets will be checked. As stated earlier, you can have two different pointers actually contain the same physical address but have different segments and offsets. If you need to compare 32-bit pointers you must use **huge** pointers.

near

A **near** pointer is a 16-bit offset that uses the value of the appropriate segment to determine the actual memory location. The **near** modifier forces Turbo C to treat the pointer as a 16-bit offset to the segment contained in DS. You use a **near** pointer when you have compiled a program using either the medium, large, or huge memory model.

Using **near** on a function causes that function to be treated as if it were compiled using the small code model. When a function is compiled with either the tiny, small, or compact models, all calls to the function place a 16-bit return address on the stack. If a function is compiled with a large code model a 32-bit address is pushed on the stack. Thus, in programs that are compiled for the large code model a highly recursive function should be declared as **near** to conserve stack space and speed execution time.

huge

The **huge** pointer is like the **far** pointer with two additions:

1. Its segment is normalized so that comparisons between **huge** pointers are meaningful.

2. A **huge** pointer can be incremented any number of times; it does not suffer from the "wraparound" problem that afflicts **far** pointers.

_cs, _ds, _es, _ss

The _cs, _ds, _es, and _ss modifiers tell Turbo C which segment register to use when evaluating a pointer. For example, this fragment instructs Turbo C to use the extra segment when using **ptr**:

```
int _es *ptr;
```

You will rarely need to use these segment register overrides.

B

A REVIEW OF
TURBO C

This appendix is meant to help the inexperienced Turbo C programmer by clarifying the aspects of the language that are unclear. It is a reference guide and not a tutorial.

THE ORIGINS OF C

C was invented and first implemented by Dennis Ritchie on a DEC PDP-11 using the UNIX operating system. C is the result of a development process that started with an older language called BCPL, which is still in use primarily in Europe. Martin Richards developed BCPL, which influenced a language called B, invented by Ken Thompson, and led to the development of C.

For many years the de facto standard for C was the one supplied with UNIX version 5 operating system and described in *The C Programming Language* by Brian Kernighan and Dennis Ritchie (Prentice-Hall, 1978). As microcomputers grew in popularity, a large number of C implementations were created. In what could almost be called a miracle, most of these implementations were highly compatible on the source code level. However, because no standard existed, there were discrepancies. To alter this situation, a committee established in the summer of 1983 began work on the creation of an ANSI standard that would define the C language once and for all. As of this writing, the proposed standard is nearly complete and its adoption by ANSI is expected soon. (As you know, Turbo C implements the proposed ANSI C standard.)

C AS A STRUCTURED LANGUAGE

C is commonly considered to be a structured language, with some similarities to Algol and Pascal. Although the term *block-structured language* does not strictly apply to C in an academic sense, it is informally part of that language group. The distinguishing feature of a block-structured language is compartmentalization of code and data. This is the ability of a language to section off and hide from the rest of the program all information and instructions necessary to perform a specific task. Compartmentalization is generally achieved by subroutines with local (temporary) variables. In this way, it is possible to write subroutines so that the events that occur within them cause no side effects in other parts of the program. Excessive use of global variables (variables known throughout the entire program) may allow bugs to creep into a program by allowing unwanted side effects. All subroutines in C are discrete functions.

Functions are the building blocks of C in which all program activity occurs. They allow specific tasks in a program to be defined and coded separately. After debugging a function that uses only local variables, you can rely on it to work properly in various situations without creating side effects in other parts of the program. All variables declared in that function will be known only to that function.

Using blocks of code in C also creates program structure. A *block* is a logically connected group of program statements that can be treated as a unit. It is created by placing lines of code between opening and closing curly braces. In the following example,

```
if(x<10) {
   printf("Invalid input - retry");
   done = 0;
}
```

the two statements between curly braces after the **if** are both executed if x is less than 10. These two statements and the braces represent a block of code. They are linked together; one cannot execute without the other also executing. Every statement in C can be either a single statement or a block of statements. The use of code blocks creates readable programs with easy-to-follow logic.

C is a programmer's language. Unlike most high-level computer languages, C imposes few restrictions on what you can do with it. By using C, a programmer can avoid writing assembly code in all but the most demanding situations. In fact, one reason that C was invented was to provide an alternative to assembly language programming.

Assembly language uses a symbolic representation of the actual binary code that the computer directly executes. Each assembly language operation maps into a single task for the computer to perform. Although assembly language gives programmers the potential to accomplish tasks with maximum flexibility and efficiency, it is notoriously difficult to work with when developing and debugging a program. Furthermore, since assembly language is unstructured by nature, the final program tends to be "spaghetti code," a tangled mess of jumps, calls, and indexes. This makes assembly language programs difficult to read, enhance, and maintain.

C was initially used for systems programming. A *systems program* is part of a large class of programs that form a portion of the operating system of the computer or its support utilities. For example, the following are commonly called systems programs:

- Operating systems
- Interpreters
- Editors
- Assemblers
- Compilers
- Data base managers

As C grew in popularity, many programmers began to use it to program all tasks because of its portability and efficiency. Because there are C compilers for virtually all computers, you can take code written for one machine and compile and run it with few or no changes on another. This portability saves both time and money. C compilers also tend to produce very tight, fast object code—faster and smaller than most BASIC compilers, for example. Since the advent of the fast and efficient Turbo C, it is difficult to justify using any other language.

Perhaps the real reason that C is used in all types of programming tasks is that programmers like it: C has the speed of Assembler, the extensibility of FORTH, and few of the restrictions of Pascal. Each C programmer can create and maintain a unique library of functions that have been tailored to his or her own personality. Because it allows, indeed encourages, separate compilation, large projects are easy to manage.

A REVIEW OF TURBO C

As defined by the proposed ANSI standard, these are the 32 keywords that are combined with the C syntax to form the C language.

Keywords

auto	double	int	struct
break	else	long	switch
case	enum	register	typedef
char	extern	return	union
const	float	short	unsigned
continue	for	signed	void
default	goto	sizeof	volatile
do	if	static	while

Turbo C has added the following keywords to the IBM PC version to allow greater control over the use of memory and other system resources.

_cs	_ds	_es	_ss
cdecl	far	huge	interrupt
near	pascal	asm	

All C keywords are lowercase. Uppercase and lowercase are different in C; that is, **else** is a keyword; ELSE is not.

VARIABLES: TYPES AND DECLARATION

Turbo C has five basic built-in data types, as shown here:

Type	C Keyword Equivalent
Character	char
Integer	int
Floating point	float
Double floating point	double
Valueless	void

However, all of these (with the exception of **void**) can be modified by using the C type modifiers.

signed
unsigned
short
long

Variable names are strings of letters from one to thirty-two characters in length. The underscore may also be used as part of the variable name for clarity (in *first—time*, for example). Remember that uppercase and lowercase are different in C. For example, *test* and *TEST* are two different variables.

All variables must be declared prior to use. The general form of the declaration is

```
type variable—name;
```

For example, to declare an *x* to be a float, *y* to be an integer, and *ch* to be a character, you would type

```
float x;
int y;
char ch;
```

In addition to the built-in types, you can create combinations of the above using **struct** and **union**. You can also create new names for variable types by using **typedef**.

A structure is a collection of variables that are grouped and referenced under one name. The general form of a structure declaration is

```
struct struct—name {
  element 1;
  element 2;
  .
  .
  .
  element N;
} struct variable list;
```

For example, the following structure has two elements: *name*, a character array, and *balance*, a floating-point number:

```
struct client {
  char name[80];
  float balance;
} client_var;
```

To reference individual structure elements, the dot operator is used if the structure is global or declared in the function referencing it. The arrow operator is used with a pointer to a structure.

When two or more variables share the same memory a **union** is defined. The general form for a **union** is

union *union—name* {
   element 1;
   element 2;

   .

   .

   .

   element N;
} union *variable list*;

The elements of a **union** overlay each other. For example,

```
union tom {
  char ch;
  int x;
} t;
```

declares a **union** t that looks like this in memory:

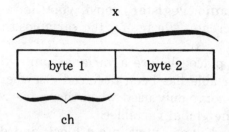

The individual variables that comprise the **union** are referenced by using the dot operator. The arrow operator is used with union pointers.

Another type of variable that can be created is the *enumeration*. An enumeration is essentially a list of objects (or values, depending on how one thinks about it). An enumeration type is simply a specification of the list of objects that belong to the enumeration. When a variable is declared to be of an enumeration type, its values can only be those defined by the enumeration.

To create an enumeration requires the use of the keyword **enum**. For example, the following short program defines an enumeration of cities called **cities**, the variable *c* of type **cities**. Finally, the program will assign *c* the value "Houston."

```
enum cities {Houston, Austin, Amarillo };
enum cities c;

main()
{
   c = Houston;
}
```

The general form of an enumeration type is

enum *name* {*list of values*};

The Storage Class Type Modifiers

The type modifiers **extern**, **auto**, **register**, **const**, **volatile**, and **static** alter the way Turbo C creates storage for the variables that follow.

If the **extern** modifier is placed before a variable name, the compiler knows that that variable has been declared elsewhere. The **extern** modifier is most commonly used when there are two or more files sharing the same global variables.

An **auto** variable is created upon entry into a block and destroyed upon exit. For example, all variables defined inside a function are **auto** by default. The keyword **auto** is seldom used, however, because local variables are **auto** by default.

Traditionally, the **register** modifier can be used only on local integer or character variables, and it causes the compiler to attempt to keep that value in a register of the CPU instead of placing it in memory. However, the ANSI standard stipulates that the **register** modifier can be applied to any type, and it tells the compiler to access the object as fast as possible. This makes all references to that variable extremely fast. Throughout this book, **register** variables are used for loop control. For example, the following function uses a **register** loop control:

```
f1()
{

  register int t;
  for(t=0; t<10000; ++t) {
    .
    .
    .
  }
}
```

Variables of type **const** cannot be changed during execution by your program. For example,

```
const int a;
```

creates an integer called *a* that cannot be modified by your program. It can, however, be used in other types of expressions. A **const** variable receives its value either from an explicit initialization or by some hardware-dependent means.

The modifier **volatile** tells the compiler that a variable's value can be changed in ways not explicitly specified by the program. For example, a global variable's address can be passed to the clock routine of the operating system and used to hold the real time of the system. In this situation the contents of the variable are altered without any explicit assignment statements in the program. This is important because Turbo C automatically optimizes certain expressions by making the assumption that the contents of a variable are unchanging inside that expression to achieve higher performance. The **volatile** modifier prevents such optimizations.

You can also add the modifier **static** to any of the above variables. The **static** modifier instructs Turbo C to keep a local variable in existence during the lifetime of the program instead of creating and destroying it. Remember that the values of local variables are discarded when a function finishes and returns. Using **static** causes their value to be maintained between function calls.

Addressing Type Modifiers

Turbo C has added the following modifiers that can be applied to pointers so that you can explicitly control, and override, the default addressing mode used to compile your program:

```
_cs     _ds    _es    _ss
 far     near   huge
```

The use of these modifiers is covered in Appendix A.

Arrays

You can declare arrays on any of the above data types. For example, to declare an integer array x of 100 elements you would write

```
int x[100];
```

This creates an array that is 100 elements long, with the first element being 0 and the last being 99. For example, the following loop loads the numbers 0 through 99 into array x.

```
for(t=0; t<100; t++) x[t] = t;
```

Multidimensional arrays are declared by placing the additional dimensions inside additional brackets. For example, to declare a 10-by-20 integer array you would write

```
int x[10][20];
```

OPERATORS

Turbo C has a very rich set of operators that can be divided into the following classes: arithmetic, relational and logical, bitwise, pointer, assignment, and miscellaneous.

Arithmetic Operators

C has the following seven arithmetic operators:

Operator	Action
−	Subtraction, unary minus
+	Addition
*	Multiplication
/	Division
%	Modulo division
−−	Decrement
++	Increment

The precedence of these operators is

highest	++ −− −(unary minus)
	* / %
lowest	+ −

Operators on the same precedence level are evaluated left to right.

Relational and Logical Operators

The relational and logical operators are used to produce true/false results and are often used together. In C any nonzero number evaluates TRUE, but a relational or logical expression produces the number 1 for TRUE and 0 for FALSE. The relational operators are

Operator	Meaning
>	Greater than
>=	Greater than or equal
<	Less than
<=	Less than or equal
==	Equal
!=	Not equal

The logical operators are

Operator	Meaning
&&	AND
‖	OR
!	NOT

The precedence of these operators is

highest	!
	> >= < <=
	== !=
	&&
lowest	‖

For example, the following expression evaluates true:

```
(100<200) && 10
```

The Bitwise Operators

Unlike most other programming languages, C provides operators that manipulate the actual bits inside a variable. The bitwise operators can be used only on integers or characters. They are

Operator	Meaning
&	AND
|	OR
^	XOR
~	One's complement
>>	Right shift
<<	Left shift

The truth tables for AND, OR, and XOR are

&	0	1
0	0	0
1	0	1

|	0	1
0	0	1
1	1	1

^	0	1
0	0	1
1	1	0

These rules are applied to each bit in a byte when the bitwise AND, OR, and XOR operations are performed. For example:

```
   0 1 0 0   1 1 0 1
 & 0 0 1 1   1 0 1 1
 ─────────────────────
   0 0 0 0   1 0 0 1
```

```
  0 1 0 0   1 1 0 1
¦ 0 0 1 1   1 0 1 1
  ─────────────────
  0 1 1 1   1 1 1 1


  0 1 0 0   1 1 0 1
^ 0 0 1 1   1 0 1 1
  ─────────────────
  0 1 1 1   0 1 1 0
```

In a program you use the &, ¦, and ^ like any other operators, as
shown here:

```
main()
{
  char x,y,z;

  x = 1; y = 2; z = 4;

  x = x & y;  /* x now equals zero */

  y = x ! z;  /* y now equals 4 */

  z = y ^ 1;  /* y now equals 5 */
}
```

The one's complement operator, ~, will invert all the bits in a
byte. For example, if a character variable, *ch*, has the bit pattern

```
  0 0 1 1   1 0 0 1
```

then

```
ch = ~ch;
```

places the bit pattern

```
  1 1 0 0   0 1 1 0
```

into *ch*.

The right and left shift operators shift all bits in a byte or a
word the specified amount. As bits are shifted, 0's are brought in.

The number on the right side of the shift operator specifies the number of positions to shift. The general form of the shift operators is

variable >> number of bit positions
variable << number of bit positions

Given this bit pattern

0 0 1 1   1 1 0 1

a shift right yields

0 0 0 1   1 1 1 0

while a shift left produces

0 1 1 1   1 0 1 0

A shift right is effectively a division by 2 and a shift left is a multiplication by 2. The following code fragment first multiplies then divides the value in *x by 2:*

```
int x;
x = 10;
x = x<<1;
x = x>>1;
```

Because of the way negative numbers are represented inside the machine, you must be careful if you try to use a shift for multiplication or division, because moving a 1 into the most significant bit position makes the computer think it is a negative number.

Remember that the bitwise operators are used to modify the value of a variable. They differ from the logical and relational operators, whose function is to produce a true or false result.

The precedence of the bitwise operators is

highest   ~

          >> <<

          &

          ^

lowest |

Pointer Operators

Pointer operators are very important in C. Not only do they allow arrays to be passed to functions, but they also allow C functions to modify their calling arguments. The two pointer operators are * and &. It is unfortunate that these operators use the same symbols as the multiplication operator and bitwise AND because they have nothing in common with them.

The & operator returns the address of the variable it precedes. For example, if the integer x is located at memory address 1000,

```
y = &x;
```

places the value 1000 into y. The & can be thought of as "the address of." For example, the previous statement could be read as "place the address of x into y."

The * operator takes the value of the variable it precedes and uses that value as the address of the information in memory. For example,

```
y = &x;

*y = 100;
```

places the value 100 into x. The * can be remembered as "at address." In this example, it could be read, "place the value 100 at address y." The * operator can also be used on the right-hand side of an assignment. For example,

```
y = &x;
*y = 100;
z = *y/10;
```

places the value 10 into *z*.

Pointers of Type void

A pointer of type **void** is said to be a generic pointer; it can be used to point to any type of object. This implies that pointers of any type can be assigned to pointers of type **void** and vice versa. To declare a **void** pointer you use a declaration like this:

```
void *p;
```

The **void** pointer is particularly useful when various types of pointers will be manipulated by a single routine.

Assignment Operators

In C the assignment operator is the single equal sign. However, C allows a very convenient form of "shorthand" for assignments of the general type

variable1 = *variable1 operator expression*;

For example,

$x = x+10$;
$y = y/z$;

Assignments of this type can be shortened to

variable1 operator = *expression*;

or, specifically in the case of the examples above,

x += 10;
y /= z;

You will often see this shorthand notation used in C programs written by experienced C programmers, so you should become used to it.

The ? Operator

The ? operator is a ternary operator that is used to replace **if** statements of the general type

if *expression1* then x=*expression2*
   else x=*expression2*

The general form of the ? operator is

variable = *expression1* ? *expression2* : *expression3*;

If *expression1* is TRUE, the value assigned is that of *expression2;* otherwise it is the value of *expression3*. For example,

x = (y<10) ? 20 : 40;

assigns x the value of 20 if y is less than 10 and 40 if it is not.

This operator allows C to produce very efficient code for this statement (much faster than the similar **if/else** statement).

Miscellaneous Operators

The . (dot) operator and the → (arrow) operator are used to reference individual elements of structures and unions. The dot operator is used when the structure or union is global or when the referencing code is in the same function as the structure or union declaration. The arrow operator is used when only a pointer to a structure or a union is available. For example, given the global structure

```
struct date_time {
  char date[16];
  int time;
} tm;
```

to assign the value "3/12/88" to element *date* of structure **tm**, you would write

```
strcpy(tm.date, "3/12/88");
```

The comma operator is used mostly in the **for** statement. It causes a sequence of operations to be performed. When it is used on the right side of an assignment statement, the value of the entire expression is the value of the last expression of the comma-separated list. For example:

```
y=10;

x = (y=y-5, 25/y);
```

After execution x will have the value 5 because y's original value of 10 is reduced by 5, and that value is divided into 25, yielding 5 as the result.

Although **sizeof** is a keyword, it is also a compile-time operator used to determine the size, in bytes, of a data type, including user-defined structures and unions. For example,

```
int x;

printf("%d", sizeof(x));
```

will print the number 2.

Parentheses are considered operators that do the expected job of increasing the precedence of the operations inside them.

Square brackets perform array indexing.

A *cast* is a special operator that forces one data type to be converted into another. The general form is

  (*type*) *variable*

For example, for the integer *count* to be used in a call to **sqrt( )**, C's standard library square root routine, which requires a floating-point parameter, a cast is used to force *count* to be treated as type **float** in this instance.

```
float y;
int count;

count = 10;

y = sqrt((float)count);
```

Figure B-1 lists the precedence of all C operators. Note that all operators, except the unary operators and ?, associate from left to right. The unary operators, *, &, and −, and the ? operator associate from right to left.

FUNCTIONS

A Turbo C program is a collection of one or more user-defined functions. One of the functions must be called **main( )** because execution will begin at this function. Historically **main( )** is the first function in a program, but it could go anywhere in the program.

The general form of a C function is

  type *function—name*(*parameter list*)
  {
    body of function
  }

Highest () [ ] → .

! ~ ++ −− − (type cast) * & sizeof

* / %

+ −

≪ ≫

< <= > >=

== !=

&

^

|

&&

||

?:

= += −= *= /= %= >>= <<= &= ^= |=

Lowest ,

Figure B-1.   Precedence of C operators

If the function has no parameters, no parameter declaration is needed. The type declaration is optional; if no explicit type declaration is present, the function defaults to integer. Functions terminate and return automatically to the calling procedure when the last brace is encountered. You can force a return before that by using the **return** statement.

All functions, except those declared as **void**, return a value. The type of the return value must match the type declaration of the function. If no explicit type declaration has been made, the return value defaults to integer. If a **return** statement is part of the function, the value of the function is the value in the **return** statement. If no **return** is present, the function returns an indeterminate value. For example,

```
f1()
{
  int x;

  x = 100;
  return(x/10);
}
```

returns the value 10, whereas

```
f2()
 {
   int x;

   x = 100;
   x = x/10;
 }
```

returns an indeterminate value because no **return** statement is used.

Technically, functions that do not return values should be declared as **void** instead of **int**.

Because all functions, except those declared as **void**, have a value, they can be used in any arithmetic statement. For example, beginning C programmers tend to write code like

```
x = sqrt(y);

z = sin(x);
```

whereas an experienced programmer would write

```
z = sin(sqrt(y));
```

Remember that the function must be executed in order to return the value of a function. For example, the following code will read keystrokes from the keyboard until you type a *u:*

```
while((ch=getche())!='u') ;
```

This code works because **getche( )** must be executed to determine its value, which is the character typed at the keyboard.

Function Prototypes

A function prototype is essentially a forward declaration of a function. It informs the compiler about the return type, argument types, and number of arguments of a function. Although optional, this information allows Turbo C to perform a far better job of type checking and error reporting than it can in the absence of a prototype.

The general form of a function prototype is

type *func__name*(*parm__list*);

For example, for this function

```
float compute(float a, int b, char c)
{
   .
   .
   .
}
```

the prototype is

float compute(float a, int b, char c);

Note: Function prototyping was added to C by the ANSI standardization committee. If you are unfamiliar with this important construct, refer to an introductory book on Turbo C. A good discussion of prototypes can be found in *Using Turbo C* by Herbert Schildt (Osborne/McGraw-Hill, 1988).

The Scope and Lifetime of Variables

C has two general classes of variables: global and local. A global variable is available for use by all functions in the program, while a local variable is known and used only by the function in which it was declared. In some C literature global variables are called external variables, and local variables are called dynamic or automatic variables. This appendix uses *local* and *global* because they are the more generally accepted terms.

A global variable must be declared outside all functions, including the **main( )** function. Global variables are generally placed at the top of the file, prior to **main( )**, for ease of reading and because a variable must be declared before it is used. A local variable is declared inside a function's opening brace. For example, the following program declares one global variable, *x*, and two local variables, *x* and *y*.

```
int x;
int f1(void);

main()
{
  int y;

  y = get_value();
  x = 100;
  printf("%d %d", x, x*y);
}

f1(void)
{
  int x;

  scanf("%d", &x);
  return x;
}
```

This program multiplies the number entered from the keyboard by 100. Note that the local variable *x* in **f1( )** has no relationship to the global variable *x*. Local variables that have the same name as global variables always take precedence over the global ones.

Global variables stay in existence during the entire program, while local variables are created on entering and destroyed on exiting the function. This means that local variables do not hold their values between function calls. You can use the **static** modifier, however, to preserve values between calls.

The formal parameters of a function are also local variables and, aside from their job of receiving the value of the calling arguments, behave and can be used like any other local variable.

The main( ) Function

As mentioned earlier all C programs must have a **main( )** function. When execution begins, this is the first function called. You must not have more than one function called **main( )**. When **main( )** terminates, the program is over and control passes back to the operating system.

Two parameters that are allowed in **main( )** are *argc* and *argv*. These two variables hold the number of command-line arguments and a character pointer to them, respectively. Command-line arguments are the information that you type in after the program name when you execute a program. For example, when you compile a Turbo C program with the command-line option, you type something like

TCC MYPROG.C

where MYPROG.C is the name of the program you wish to compile and is a command-line argument.

The parameter *argc* will always be at least 1 because the program name is the first argument as far as C is concerned. The parameter *argv* must be declared as an array of character pointers. The usage is shown below in a short program that prints your name on the screen:

```
main(int argc, char *argv[])
{
    if(argc<2)
      printf("enter your name on the command line.\n");
    else
      printf("hello %s\n",argv[1]);
}
```

Notice that *argv* is declared as a character pointer array of unknown size. The Turbo C compiler automatically determines the size of the array necessary to handle all the command-line arguments.

Command-line arguments give your programs a professional look and feel and allow them to be placed into a batch file for automatic use.

You can return a value from **main( )** to the calling process in two ways:

1. You can use the **return** statement.
2. You can call the **exit( )** function. (The **exit( )** function call causes the immediate termination of your program in addition to returning a value.)

STATEMENT SUMMARY

There follows a brief synopsis of the keywords in Turbo C. The memory model keywords, **far**, **near**, **huge**, **_es**, **_ds**, **_ss**, and **_cs** are discussed in Appendix A.

auto

The **auto** keyword is used to create temporary variables upon entry into a block and destroy them upon exit. For example, in

```
#include <stdio.h>
#include <conio.h>

main()
{
  for(;;) {
    if(getche()=='a') {
      auto int t;
      for(t=0; t<'a'; t++)
        printf("%d ", t);
    }
  }
}
```

the variable t is created only if the user types an a. Outside of the **if** block, t is completely unknown and any reference to it generates a compile-time syntax error.

break

The **break** keyword is used to bypass the normal loop condition and exit from a **do**, **for**, or **while** loop. It is also used to exit from a **switch** statement.

An example of **break** in a loop is shown below:

```
while(x<100) {
  x = get_new_x();
  if(kbhit()) break;   /* key hit on
                             keyboard */
  process(x);
}
```

Here, if a key is pressed, the loop terminates, no matter what the value of x is.

A **break** always terminates the innermost **for**, **do**, **while**, or **switch** statement, regardless of the way they are nested. In a **switch** statement, **break** effectively keeps program execution from "falling through" to the next **case**. (Refer to the **switch** statement for details.)

case

Refer to the **switch** statement.

cdecl

The **cdecl** keyword is specific to Turbo C and is not part of the ANSI standard. It is used to force Turbo C to compile a function so that its parameter passing conforms with the standard C calling convention. It is used only when you are compiling an entire file with the Pascal option and you want a specific function to be compatible with C.

char

The **char** data type is used to declare character variables. For example, to declare *ch* as a character type, you would write

```
char ch;
```

const

The **const** modifier tells the compiler that the variable that follows cannot be modified.

continue

The **continue** keyword is used to bypass portions of code in a loop and force execution of the conditional test. For example, the following **while** loop simply reads characters from the keyboard until you type an *s*.

```
while(ch=getche()) {
  if(ch!='s') continue;  /* read another char */
  process(ch);
}
```

The call to **process( )** does not occur until *ch* contains the character *s*.

default

The **default** keyword is used in the **switch** statement to signal a default block of code to be executed if no matches are found in the **switch**. See "**switch**."

do

The **do** loop is one of three loop constructs available in C. The general form of the **do** loop is

```
do {
    statements block
} while(condition);
```

If only one statement is repeated, the braces are not necessary, but they do add clarity to the statement.

The **do** loop is the only loop in C that always has at least one iteration, because the condition is tested at the bottom of the loop.

The **do** loop is commonly used to read disk files. The following code reads a file until an EOF is encountered:

```
do {
  ch = getc(fp);
  store(ch);
} while(!feof(fp));
```

double

The **double** data type specifier is used to declare double precision floating-point variables. To declare *d* to be of type **double** you would write

```
double d;
```

else

See "**if**."

enum

The **enum** type specifier is used to create enumeration types. An enumeration is simply a list of objects. Hence an enumeration type specifies what that list of objects contains. An enumeration type variable can be assigned only values that are part of the enumeration list. For example, the following code declares an enumeration called *color* and a variable of that type called *c* and performs an assignment and a condition test:

```
#include <stdio.h>

enum color {red, green, yellow};
enum color c;

main()
{
  c = red;
  if(c==red) printf("is red\n");
}
```

extern

The **extern** data type modifier tells the compiler that a variable is declared elsewhere in the program. This is often used in conjuction with separately compiled files that share the same global data and are linked. In essence it notifies the compiler of a variable without redeclaring it.

For example, if *first* were declared in another file as an integer, in subsequent files the following declaration would be used:

```
extern int first;
```

float

The **float** data type specifier is used to declare floating-point variables. To declare *f* to be of type **float** you would write

```
float f;
```

for

The **for** loop allows automatic initialization and incrementation of a counter variable. The general form is

    for(*initialization; condition; increment*) {
      statement block
    }

If the *statement block* is only one statement, the braces are not necessary.

Although **for** allows a number of variables, generally the *initialization* is used to set a counter variable to its starting value. The *condition* is generally a relational statement that checks the counter variable against a termination value, and *increment* increments (or decrements) the counter value.

The code below prints the message "hello" ten times.

```
for(t=0; t<10; t++) printf("hello\n");
```

goto

The **goto** statement causes program execution to "jump" to the label specified. The general form of the **goto** statement is

      goto *label*;
      .
      .
      .
    label:

All *labels* must end in a colon and must not conflict with keywords or function names. Furthermore, a **goto** can branch only within the current function, not from one function to another.

The following example prints the message "right" but not the message "wrong."

```
goto lab1;
  printf("wrong");
lab1:
  printf("right");
```

if

The general form of the **if** statement is

```
if(condition) {
  statement block 1
}
else {
  statement block 2
}
```

If single statements are used, the braces are not needed. The **else** is optional.

The condition may be any expression. If that expression evaluates to any value other than 0, *statement block 1* is executed; otherwise, *statement block 2* is executed.

The following code fragment can be used for keyboard input and to look for a *q*, which signifies "quit."

```
ch = getche();
if(ch=='q') {
  printf("program terminated");
  exit(0);
}
else  proceed();
```

int

The **int** type specifier is used to declare integer variables. For example, to declare **count** as an integer, you would write

```
int count;
```

interrupt

The **interrupt** type specifier is specific to Turbo C and is not part of the ANSI standard. It is used to declare functions that will be used as interrupt service routines.

long

The **long** data type modifier is used to declare double length integer variables. For example, to declare *count* as a **long** integer, you would write

```
long int count;
```

pascal

The **pascal** keyword is specific to Turbo C and is not defined by the ANSI standard. It is used to force Turbo C to compile a function so that its parameter passing convention is compatible with Pascal rather than Turbo C.

register

The **register** modifier is used to request that a variable be stored in the area of fastest retrieval of the host system. It can be used only with local variables. To declare *i* to be a **register** integer, you would write

```
register int i;
```

return

The **return** statement forces a return from a function and can be used to transfer a value back to the calling routine.

For example, the following function returns the product of its two integer arguments:

```
mul(int a, int b)
{
    return(a*b);
}
```

Keep in mind that as soon as a **return** is encountered, the function returns, skipping any other code in the function.

short

The **short** data type modifier is used to declare 1-byte integers. For example, to declare *sh* a **short** integer, you would write

```
short int sh;
```

signed

The **signed** type modifier is used to specify a **signed char** data type.

sizeof

The **sizeof** compile-time operator returns the length of the variable it precedes. For example,

```
printf("%d", sizeof(int));
```

prints a 2 for Turbo C.

The **sizeof** statement's principal use is to help generate portable code when that code depends on the size of the Turbo C built-in data types.

static

The **static** data type modifier tells the compiler to create permanent storage for the local variable that it precedes. This enables the specified variable to maintain its value between function calls. For example, to declare *last_time* as a **static** integer, you would write

```
static int last_time;
```

struct

The **struct** statement is used to create complex or conglomerate variables, called structures, that are made up of one or more elements of the seven basic data types. The general form of a structure is

struct *struct_name* {
  type *element1*;
  type *element2*;

    .

    .

    .

  type *elementN*;
} *structure_variable_name*;

The individual elements are referenced by using the dot or arrow operators.

switch

The **switch** statement is C's multiway branch statement. It is used to route execution one of several different ways. The general form of the statement is

```
switch(variable) {
  case (constant1): statement set 1;
    break;
  case (constant2): statement set 2;
    break;
    .
    .
    .
  case (constant N): statement set N;
    break;
  default: default statements;
}
```

Each *statement set* may be from one to several statements long. The **default** portion is optional.

The **switch** works by checking the *variable* against all the *constants*. As soon as a match is found, that set of statements is executed. If the **break** statement is omitted, execution continues until the end of the **switch**. You can think of the **case**s as labels. Execution continues until a **break** statement is found or the **switch** ends.

The following example can be used to process a menu selection:

```
ch = getche();

switch (ch) {
  case 'e': enter();
      break;
  case 'l': list();
      break;
  case 's': sort();
      break;
  case 'q': exit(0);
  default: printf("unknown command\n");
      printf("try again\n");

}
```

typedef

The **typedef** statement allows you to create a new name for an existing data type. The data type can be either one of the built-in types or a structure or union name. The general form of **typedef** is

typedef *type—specifier new—name*;

For example, to use the word *balance* in place of **float**, you would write

```
typedef float balance;
```

union

The **union** keyword is used to assign two or more variables to the same memory location. The form of the definition and the way an element is referenced are the same as for **struct**. The general form is

```
union union_name {
   type element1;
   type element2;
     .
     .
     .
   type elementN;
} union variable_name;
```

unsigned

The **unsigned** type modifier tells the compiler to eliminate the signed bit of an integer and to use all bits for arithmetic. This doubles the size of the largest integer but restricts it to positive numbers. For example, to declare *big* an unsigned integer, you would write

```
unsigned int big;
```

void

The **void** type specifier is primarily used to declare explicitly functions that return no (meaningful) value. It is also used to create **void** pointers (pointers to **void**), which are generic pointers capable of pointing to any type of object.

volatile

The **volatile** modifier tells the compiler that a variable can have its contents altered in ways not explicitly defined by the program (for example, variables that are changed by hardware, such as real-time clocks, interrupts, or other inputs).

while

The **while** loop has the general form

```
while(condition) {
    statement block
}
```

If a single statement is the object of the **while**, the braces can be omitted.

The **while** tests its *condition* at the top of the loop. If the *condition* is false to begin with, the loop will not execute at all. The *condition* can be any expression.

An example of a **while** is shown below. It reads 100 characters from a disk file and stores them in a character array.

```
t = 0;

while(t<100) {
  s[t] = getc(fp);
  t++;
}
```

THE TURBO C PREPROCESSOR

Turbo C includes several preprocessor commands that are used to give instructions to the compiler.

#define

The **#define** command is part of the C preprocessor. It can be used to perform macro substitutions of one piece of text for another throughout the file in which it is used. The general form of the directive is

#define *name string*

Notice that there is no semicolon in this statement.

If you wish to use TRUE for the value 1 and FALSE for the value 0, you can declare two macro **#define**s:

#define TRUE 1
#define FALSE 0

This causes the compiler to substitute a 1 or a 0 each time TRUE or FALSE is encountered.

#error

The **#error** directive forces the compiler to stop compilation when it is encountered. It is used primarily for debugging. Its general form is

#error *message*

When **#error** is encountered, Turbo C displays the message and the line number.

#include

The **#include** preprocessor directive instructs the compiler to read and compile another source file. The source file to be read in must be enclosed between double quotes. For example,

```
#include "stdio.h"
```

instructs the C compiler to read and compile the header for the disk file library routines.

#if, #ifdef, #ifndef, #else, #elif, #endif

These preprocessor directives are used to selectively compile various portions of a program. These are of the greatest use to commercial software houses that provide and maintain many customized versions of one program. The general idea is that if the expression after an **#if**, **#ifdef**, or **#ifndef** is true, the code that is between one of the preceding and an **#endif** will be compiled; otherwise it will be skipped. The **#endif** marks the end of an **#if** block. The **#else** can be used with any of the above in a manner similar to the **#else** in the C **if** statement.

The general form of **#if** is

#if *constant expression*

If the constant expression is TRUE, the block of code is compiled.

The general form of **#ifdef** is

#ifdef *name*

If the *name* has been defined in a **#define** statement, the block of code following the statement is compiled.

The general form of **#ifndef** is

#ifndef *name*

If *name* is currently undefined by a **#define** statement, the block of code is compiled.

For example, here is the way some of the these preprocessor directives work together:

```
#define ted 10

main()
{
```

```
#ifdef ted
  printf("Hi Ted\n");
#endif
  printf("bye bye\n");
#if 10<9
  printf("Hi George\n");
#endif
}
```

This code prints "Hi Ted" and "bye bye" on the screen, but not "Hi George."

The **#elif** directive is used to create an if-else-if statement. Its general form is

> #elif *constant expression*

The **#elif** can be used with the **#if** but not the **#ifdef** or **#ifndef** directives.

#pragma

The **#pragma** directive is an implementation-defined directive that allows various instructions, defined by the compiler's creator, to be given to the compiler. The general form of the **#pragma** directive is

> #pragma *name*

where *name* is the name of the **#pragma** you want. Turbo C defines three **#pragma** statements: **warn**, **inline**, and **saveregs**.

The **warn** directive causes Turbo C to override warning message options. It takes the form

> #pragma warn *setting*

where *setting* is one of the various warning error options defined in the the *Turbo C Reference Guide*. For most applications you will not need to use this #**pragma**.

The **inline #pragma** has the general form

#pragma *inline*

This tells Turbo C that inline assembly code is contained in the program.

The **saveregs** option forces a function compiled for the huge memory model to save all registers. The #**pragma** must immediately precede the function and it affects only that function. You will need to use it only in rare cases.

PREDEFINED MACRO NAMES

The proposed ANSI standard specifies five built-in predefined macro names. They are

```
__LINE__
__FILE__
__DATE__
__TIME__
__STDC__
```

Turbo C also defines the following built-in macros:

```
__CDECL__
__COMPACT__
__HUGE__
__LARGE__
__MEDIUM__
__MSDOS__
__PASCAL__
__SMALL__
__TINY__
__TURBOC__
```

The __DATE__ macro contains a string of the form *month/day/year* that is the date of the translation of the source file into object code.

The time of the translation of the source code into object code is contained as a string in __TIME__. The form of the string is *hour:minute:second*.

The macro __STDC__ contains the decimal constant 1. This means that only ANSI standard keywords are allowed.

The __CDECL__ macro is defined if the standard C calling convention is used, that is, if the Pascal option is not in use. If this is not the case, the macro is undefined.

Only one of these macros is defined, based on the memory model used during compilation: __TINY__, __SMALL__, __COMPACT__, __MEDIUM__, __LARGE__, OR __HUGE__.

The __MSDOS__ macro is defined with the value 1 under all situations when using the MS-DOS version of Turbo C.

The __PASCAL__ macro is defined only if the Pascal calling conventions are used to compile a program. Otherwise, it is undefined.

Finally, __TURBOC__ contains the version number of Turbo C.

For the most part, these built-in macros are used in fairly complex programming environments when several different versions of a program—perhaps running on different computers—are developed or maintained.

THE TURBO C STANDARD LIBRARY

Unlike most other languages, C does not have built-in functions to perform disk I/O, console I/O, and a number of other useful procedures. These things are accomplished in C by using a set of predefined library functions that are supplied with the compiler. This library is usually called the C Standard Library. Library functions can be used by your program at will. Turbo C automatically links the functions in during the link process.

Turbo C contains a very large number of library functions, and these are fully described in the Turbo C *User Guide. Turbo C: The Complete Reference* by Herbert Schildt (Osborne/McGraw-Hill, 1988) also discusses the library functions in considerable detail.

TRADEMARKS

DEC™	Digital Equipment Corporation
FORTH®	FORTH, Inc.
IBM®	International Business Machines Corporation
Microsoft®	Microsoft Corporation
PCjr™	International Business Machines Corporation
Turbo C®	Borland International, Inc.
Turbo Pascal®	Borland International, Inc.
UNIX®	AT&T
The Wall Street Journal™	Dow Jones & Co., Inc.

INDEX

The manuscript for this book was prepared and
submitted to Osborne/McGraw-Hill in electronic form.
The acquisitions editor for this project was
Jeffrey Pepper, the technical reviewers were
Robert Goosey and James L. Turley, and the project
editor was Fran Haselsteiner.

Text design uses Century Expanded for text body
and display.

Cover art by Bay Graphics Design Associates. Color
separation and cover supplier, Phoenix Color
Corporation. Screens produced with InSet, from InSet
Systems, Inc. Book printed and bound by R.R.
Donnelley & Sons Company, Crawfordsville, Indiana.